The spontaneous standing ovation you received at the conclusion of your speech is an indication of how well you were received. You have spoken four times to three different divisions of IBM in the last five months. WOW! IBM will most certainly use you again and again. We recommend you to audiences everywhere!

—IBM North America Sales Centers

We have had Dan Clark speak for our company over five times to all of our divisions. We've even had Dan speak for an international customer event in Rome, Italy. No one is better than Dan! His amazing ability to take his audience on an emotional roller coaster ride and customize his remarks around our needs is unmatched by any speaker in the industry. We've laughed and cried at every speech.

—Amy Hawkins, Georgia Pacific

Your presentations were singled out as the highlight of the week. In fact, I continue to hear incredibly positive comments from our staffs and the community at large – always ending up with "When will you bring him back?" The feature article on you in our Mayo Magazine was a wonderful tribute to you and your work. I understand it was so well received, we are running your article again in our Alumni Magazine!

—Gerald T. Mahoney, Chair, Heritage Days Planning
Committee, Mayo Clinic

Thank you for your inspiring message to our agents and agency management. Your ability to incorporate specific information regarding our company and its initiatives was invaluable and helped drive your motivational message points home. I have never seen our people so enthused, which was clearly evidenced in the long standing ovation you received!

—State Farm Insurance Company

The most visible creators are those artists whose medium is life it-self. The ones who express the inexpressible without brush, hammer, clay or guitar. They neither paint nor sculpt. Their medium is being. Whatever their presence touches has increased life. They see and don't have to draw. They are the artists of being fully alive.

—J. Stone

Books Available By Dan Clark:

Best or Right: Why Great Is Not Good Enough
Chicken Soup for the College Soul
Dan's Most Popular Stories in Chicken Soup for the Soul
Puppies for Sale and Other Inspirational Tales
Puppies for Sale Illustrated Story
Clark's Children's Classics
Soul Food Volumes I & II (The Collection)
The Funniest Things Happen When You Look for Laughs
The Thrill of Teaching
Wisdom, Rhymes, and Wizardry
Rainbows Follow Rain
Lyrical Poetry
The Privilege of the Platform
Only the Best on Leadership
Only the Best on Customer Service

FORGOTTEN FUNDAMENTALS

The Answers Are in the Box

*How What You Already Know Can Make
You More of Who You Already Are*

ISBN 13: 978-1-59955-027-5

Published by CFI, an imprint of Cedar Fort, Inc., 2373 W. 700 S., Springville, UT, 84663
Distributed by Cedar Fort, Inc. www.cedarfort.com

Cover design by Nicole Williams
Cover design © 2007 by Lyle Mortimer
Edited and typeset by Kimiko M. Hammari

Printed in the United States of America

10 9 8 7 6 5 4 3 2 1

Printed on acid-free paper

FORGOTTEN FUNDAMENTALS

The Answers Are in the Box

*How What You Already Know Can Make
You More of Who You Already Are*

by Dan Clark

CFI
Springville, Utah

DEDICATION

To Kelly—for everything.

To Danny, Nikola, McCall, and Alexandrea for your unconditional love and support.

To S. Wayne and Ruby Clark, Sam, Liz, Debbie, Paul, Kristi Clark, Doc and Barb Sansom, Bob Mendenhall, Normand Gibbons, Zig Ziglar, Jim and Karen Koeninger, Vince Zimmer, Royden and Ali Derrick, Mont Beardall, Phillip Gibson, Mark Tuttle, Gary Mangum, Todd Peterson, Blain Hope, Scott Buie, Mark Monsen, Brent Bowen, Todd Morgan, Brad Morris, Brian Thurgood, Michael Gale, Charles Reid, Robert Peterson, General Hal Hornburg, General Johnny Weida, Steve Cosgrove, Pat Mutch, Mark Kidd, Stephen Munn, and Bob Boothby for helping to create the most significant events in my life and incredibly influencing my physical, mental, spiritual, and emotional growth.

To Sandy Inman, Tom Thorem, Gene Thompson, Din Morris, Grant Martin, Ted Weight, Dale Simons, Chuck Banker, Homer Warner, Bob Whittman, Mike Hale, Bob Raybould, Bill Kimball, Paul Mendenhall, Russ Anderson, Warren Pugh, Doug Miller, Don Pugh, Gerry Howells, Fred Ball, Lila Bjorkland, Dale Zabriski, and Deward Timothy for believing in me when others did not.

To super-smart Paul Clark, Kelly Clark, Ruby Clark, Renee Strom, Keith Harrell, Les Hewitt, Jack Canfield, Mark Victor Hansen, Dave Alexander, Don Gale, Mickey Fisher, Jennifer Lapine, Ernie Wilhoit, and Laura Calchera for helping me build and grow my business.

To the extraordinary typist/editor/friend Sue Purcell and to final typist Heather Nelson; to editors Michael Morris and Kimiko Hammari and to Lyle Mortimer and Lee Nelson for keeping me focused with kindness and caring to finish.

I love and appreciate each of you and would not be where I am if it wasn't for my personal relationship with you. Every day you have reminded me about the forgotten fundamentals, and because of you it's easy to say, "I like me best when I'm with you. I want to see you again."—Dan

TABLE OF CONTENTS

FOREWORD

This book is not a creation, but an observation. Originally, Dan Clark set out to blaze a new trail to success, but on the path he found something more. Before he could turn off the busiest, most popular road to take the road less traveled and purposefully make life hard, Dan realized that our greatest human challenge is not in choosing the path or direction we take, but in choosing to be unique and significant among the masses taking our path. This purposefully makes life simple.

Although Dan set out to write a business leadership/management book, in the process of watching, listening, and interviewing some of the great thinkers of our time, he discovered a complete instruction manual in the art of being fully alive. Just as Dan's platform speeches inspire and change lives, this book will also significantly impact your life.

Dan writes a lot like he speaks, which means this book will make you laugh, cry, think, and feel as it teaches you how to become more of who you already are. Dan talks to you from his head and heart to your head and heart, using his once-in-a-lifetime adventures, extensive research data, and world-famous short stories to connect with each of us at the deepest emotional level. The powerful thing about this book is that while Dan is reminding us about forgotten fundamentals and becoming brilliant at the basics, he is explaining what it takes to run a competitive, profitable, high performance, world-class organization. There is no better person or more qualified expert than Dan Clark to teach us how to find strength from within, overcome obstacles, create opportunities in change, and get better answers because we ask better questions.

If you will abide by the precepts and principles in this book, you will become a better leader, manager, spouse, parent, teacher, coach, and friend. Read on. You will never be the same.

Jack Canfield, co-creator of *Chicken Soup for the Soul*®
and author of *The Success Principles: How to Get From Where You Are to Where You Want to Be*™

MUST-READ INTRODUCTION

Dale Carnegie wrote, "The ideas I stand for are not mine. I borrowed them from Socrates. I swiped them from Chesterfield. . . . I quoted them from science and medicine and put them in this book. If you don't like their rules, whose would you use?"

Obeying rules is a fundamental principle we will discuss throughout this work, and the constant question of "Who says so?" will always permeate the conversation. For this reason, I must immediately come clean on one rule's issue. With all due respect to my high school English teacher, Mrs. Smart, who taught me better, I must break two writing rules. Because my material here is so personal, I have tried to use the same style I would in my speeches, including the elliptical, colloquial, ironic, and sarcastic.

I was also taught that a book without notes is usually not worth reading, since an absence of documentation implies that the contents are merely the author's own opinions unsupported by outside scholarship. Goethe wrote: "If a man writes a book, let him set down only what he knows. I have guesses enough of my own."

I agree and have quoted original sources when I have had them. The rest is my own eyewitness observations, practical perceptions, and real-life experiences resulting in success. This is not a book of ideas, but rather a mental meal, a behavioral bible, a principle-centered prognostication of what works, what doesn't, why, and how we can improve our human performance.

As far as we can determine through historical fact and documentation, there is one Italian who understood more about human potential and the relentless pursuit of peak performance than any other. No, it wasn't Julius Caesar or Constantine. The man I'm thinking of was born in Florence in AD 1475, lived most of his life in Rome, and through his art consolidated the teachings on self and man's relationship with the universe pontificated by Aristotle, Socrates, and Thomas Aquinas into a simple philosophy.

On my first visit to Italy, I had only one 90-minute speaking engagement, yet I stayed with the corporate group for four days to do some sightseeing at the Forum, the Catacombs, Trevi Fountain, Spanish Steps, Vatican City, Sistine Chapel, Circus Maximus, the Baths, and, of course, the Parthenon and Coliseum in Rome. I was wined and dined in palaces and was completely mesmerized by the beautiful people, elegant food, and thousands of years of history.

I mention all of this not as a travelogue but as a backdrop reminder that woven throughout this tapestry of breathtaking brilliance, we find a unique thread, a single strand of unparalleled success that stands out above all the rest. I am speaking of the fifteenth century architect, artist, painter, and sculptor—the one and only Michelangelo. He never painted or sculpted to be the best, but rather pursued perfection until he got it right.

At the age of twenty-three, he sculpted the *Vatican Pieta*, the Virgin Mary holding her son Jesus just after he had been taken down from the cross. At the age of twenty-six, he sculpted the mighty *David*, which is his most famous work. I spent a full day in Florence visiting museums, shops, and cathedrals, but for at least one hour I examined the detail and personality of this amazing statue. At thirty-two, Michelangelo sculpted *Moses*. At age thirty-three, he started his four-year project painting the ceiling of the Sistine Chapel. At sixty-one, he painted *Last Judgment* on the end wall of the Sistine Chapel.

Before his death at the age of eighty-nine, he had left us with countless masterpieces of artistic expression, including designing and constructing the church for the Pope on Vatican Square—

the incomparable St. Peter's Basilica, the largest cathedral in the world, with an architecturally wondrous forty-story dome.

The reason Michelangelo stands out among his peers is not only because of his unmatched talent and amazing body of work but also because of who he was and his philosophy toward art. At five feet tall, with a smashed nose that was broken in a fight when he was seventeen, Michelangelo never felt that he was handsome. With his lack of looks and low self-esteem, he did, however, reveal a personal acknowledgment that God overcompensated for his ugliness by giving him some talent in the arts. It was from this personal, pain-filled perspective that he developed his belief that beauty and success come from the inside out.

Michelangelo never considered himself a painter and never had a great desire to master painting because, as he put it, "painting begins and ends on the surface, and that is all it is." A painting is only the painter's interpretation of a person, place, or inanimate object.

Michelangelo did, however, consider himself a master sculptor. When his commission to sculpt got delayed and he was told by the Pope to paint the ceiling of the Sistine Chapel, in defiance he signed his contract "Michelangelo the Sculptor."

A master at not merely creating a figure from marble but rather, with hammer and chisel, a master at liberating the soul deep within the stone, Michelangelo believed that the figure was already in the piece of stone and only hidden from sight. His job was not to create something from nothing but rather to chip away the layers of marble to free the captive being that was already inside.

His past and present colleagues subscribed to—and his teachers taught—first sketching out the figure on the rock and then measuring the nose to the ear, the top of the head to the jaw, the width of the rib cage, and the length of the limbs to ensure that before they began, the proportions were accurate. Michelangelo, however, simply eyed the uncut block, picked up his tools, and started carving because he believed the full, complete figure in whole and perfect proportion was just waiting to be released.

As each of his works of art was commissioned, Michelangelo would actually travel to the Carrera marble quarry and personally pick out each chunk of stone, believing that only he knew who was alive inside and that only he possessed the keys to unlock the door and introduce the world to his long-lost friend.

Although *David* is magnificent beyond description, the greatest representation of Michelangelo's attitude toward sculpting is seen and felt in his works called *The Captives*. In these four pieces we actually see the intentionally unfinished figures struggling to free themselves of the confines of stone. These four pieces fully reflect Michelangelo's idea of sculpting as a process of freeing form from matter, of extracting an idea already existing in the rock. It requires no imagination to see the captive figures, often referred to as "The Prisoners," emerging from the stone as if it held them imprisoned. When Michelangelo died in his sleep in his studio, these four statues were found by his side as if to say, "This is what I've been doing. This is how it is for everybody. Defining and liberating our true, whole selves is the single purpose of our existence."

"Wow!" you say. "Italy and Michelangelo are wonderful, but what do they have to do with a book on personal development, leadership, and management?" The answer is an unequivocal, absolute everything! Whether we are striving to become a master sculptor or to master the art of living, both require the same thought process and practiced skill of a Michelangelo. We are not trying to create something from nothing. Our single, daily purpose is to "be like Mike" and chisel away our heavy burdens of shallow thinking, absence of mental toughness, low expectations, lack of focus, unbalanced priorities, and blurred vision to reveal and set free the full potential of the complete human being within us. Yes, regardless of our current level of success, each of our greater "best" selves is still stuck deep inside somewhere, and there is no more important work on earth than to sculpt ourselves and our personal and professional relationships into all they were born to be.

Max DePree said, "We cannot become what we need to be by remaining what we are." Thomas Watson Jr. added, "If you stand up and be counted, from time to time you may get yourself knocked down, but remember that a man flattened by an opponent can get up again; a man flattened by conformity stays down for good."

My closest friends have always seen me as a bit of a maverick—always questioning and striving for more, seldom going along just for the sake of going along. Too many times I've seen the blind leading the blind, and they both fall in the ditch. So I'm sure it seems strange that I would write a book with such a conservative title, implying an apparent old-school message of in-the-box obedience.

Not to worry. I do not write and encourage obedience to natural laws and time-tested precepts because we are blind. I emphatically state that we should obey because we see! We see the difference between eyesight and insight. We see that success is not determined by our abilities but rather by our choices. We see that no one can ever exceed his or her potential; we only misjudge our potential!

This book is about seeing the big picture and simplifying it into right and wrong, what works (for centuries), what doesn't, and why. It's about realizing that if the things we believe in and think deeply about are in contradiction with the things we do, then we will never have peace of mind, never experience self-actualization, and never garner the incredible benefits that come through genuine personal happiness. Consequently, this book is foremost about asking the right questions, figuring out exactly what we do believe in, and strengthening our beliefs to the point that we do more than practice what we preach—we preach only what we practice.

It's not breaking news when I proclaim that I am much different now from what I was in high school and college. In fact, I am different today from what I was last week—physically, mentally, spiritually, emotionally, financially, and socially. Why? Because the people I've met, the jokes I've heard, the inspirational stories I've been told, and the thought-provoking books I've read in the past seven days have taken me to a place I could not take myself.

You are the sculptor. The statue you present of yourself to the world is totally up to you. In the pages ahead, I intend for you to chisel away the rough edges in your styles of leadership, management, parenting, teaching, coaching, and living to reveal a deeper, more amazing, authentic you. Henry David Thoreau said, "Aim above morality. Be not simply good; be good for something."

Herein lies the entire premise of this book. When best is possible, good is not good enough. But being best is usually not enough either. Our primary purpose is to go from being great to being best and then transform ourselves into the right person, at the right time, in the right place, for the right reasons. Sounds too easy? It's not easy. It's simple, but most likely hard. Anybody can be great or best. The hard is what makes you right.

Yes, life is simple. We just need some luck and common sense. The much-quoted definition of luck is "where preparation and opportunity intersect." It seems that the harder we work, the luckier we get. The fundamental catalyst to becoming lucky is common sense. Coming in out of the rain, spending less than you earn, being loyal to those who are not present, treating others as they want to be treated, doing unto others as you would have others do unto you, thinking before you talk, and doing your best are all no-brainers. Simple common sense, right? You would think so!

But in our world—where schools are required to get parental consent to administer aspirin to students but cannot inform parents when a student wants to get an abortion, and where a woman won a million-dollar lawsuit after spilling hot coffee on herself—we need people who will stand up and step out of the crowd. We need people who will lead and guide others, showing them how they can become their best selves. In an attempt to strengthen you and inspire you to become one of these vitally important leaders, managers, coaches, teachers, parents, neighbors, and friends, I present to you this book.

I want you to laugh, think, feel, cry, philosophize, psychoanalyze, and realize that for life's most important and provocative questions, the answers are discovered and revealed only when we get emotional, challenge the status quo, focus on the fundamentals, become brilliant in the basics, and follow a formula that eliminates chance and generates desired results. Everything you need to succeed and become the whole human being you were born to be is already inside of you. Galileo said, "We don't teach a person anything. We only help him discover it within himself." As you read, you will quickly discover (as Michelangelo did in the fifteenth century) that the secrets to achieving flawless high performance, to moving from best to right, and to consistently winning and becoming more of who you already are, have been and still are—in the box!

Fundamental 1

THE ANSWERS ARE IN THE BOX

The paradox of our time in history is that we have taller buildings but shorter tempers; wider freeways but narrower viewpoints. We spend more but have less; we buy more but enjoy less. We have bigger houses and smaller families; more conveniences but less time. We have more degrees but less sense; more knowledge but less judgment; more experts yet more problems; more medicine but less wellness. We've learned how to make a living but not a life; we've added years to life not life to years. We've been all the way to the moon and back but have trouble crossing the street to meet a new neighbor. We conquered outer space but not inner space. We've done larger things, but not better things.

—George Carlin

Once when I was a guest on a live television talk show in Stamford, Connecticut, the hostess commented, "So you are an author and speaker, which makes you a perceived expert. Who said your values are the right values? Who gave you the right to impose your core beliefs on any of us? Who put you in charge of legislating morality?"

She blindsided me, but her questions were provocative and welcome. I answered, "You are absolutely right. I do not, nor does anyone, have the right to impose my values on anybody, especially in a public school or at a government agency. It's never about *who* is right, but *what* is right. Let's not talk about *my*

1

values; I never do anyway. What values do you *not* want me to teach? Charity, forgiveness, honesty, love, tolerance, hard work, integrity, service, excellence?" The hostess was baffled and quickly changed her questioning.

Although this interview lasted a mere ten minutes, my off-the-cuff comment stirred within me a blatant realization that some things are true whether we believe them or not; everybody is entitled to their own opinion, but nobody is entitled to the wrong facts. Yes, we have gurus suggesting what's good and how to make it great; and each of us have had personal experiences where we were best at something or right for the occasion. But when will we finally fess up that it's all relevant depending on the comparison? Says who? Powerful people? Compared to what? Profitable companies? What about the principles that cannot be voted on and the specific values that can't be excused or explained away?

For more than a decade, corporate business speakers and organizational trainers have abused their privilege of the platform and perpetuated this success from the outside-in model by exclaiming, "Think outside the lines; you've got to think outside-the-box." But what if the answers are still in the box? Most people attend meetings and read books in search of new answers, when don't you think we should be searching for the right answers? Too many for too long have been force-fed to believe that courses on personal change, corporate growth strategies, and the latest and greatest state-of-the-art solutions have somehow been secretly stashed in the universe awaiting our discovery. Some argue that their problems are in the box, and quote Einstein: "We can't solve problems with the same level of thinking that created them." Others suffer from the paralysis of analysis by overthinking the simple to make it complex, backing up their egos with the overused excuse: "If you keep doing what you did, you'll keep getting what you got," reminding us that insanity is "doing the same thing and expecting a different result." I agree, but I fail to see any conflict with my question.

Can't the outside-the-box thinking naysayers see that there are sports teams with rosters crammed full of the best players in the world who still lose games they shouldn't and never win championships? Can't they see there are companies filled with the best trained employees in the industry who still lose market share and go out of business? And isn't it obvious that their failures usually have little to do with anything outside of their organizations? The same can be said of the solutions required to overcome those failures. Are not passion, creativity, imagination, discipline, commitment, perseverance, and obedience to natural laws all attributes and solutions found inside the box? And with regard to my mentioned TV interview, are not charity, integrity, and the rest of my listed values found inside individuals and organizations? Have we forgotten that crisis does not make or break the man or woman; it just reveals the true character within? And doesn't crisis trigger a higher level of thinking?

I have written this book because you can't get right answers from wrong questions; because there is no right way to do the wrong thing; because the things we hate to hear the most are usually the things we need to hear the most; because change is never a function of skill but rather a function of motivation; because you cannot fix your team, your organization, or yourself with just a keynote speech; because you will never grow unless you do something beyond that which you have already mastered; and because language sparks feelings and feelings alter behavior.

No, this is not a rah-rah rally cry. I am not a motivational speaker who says things like, "We become what we think about." That's not true. If it were true, I would have been a woman by the time I was twelve years old! I am an inspirational speaker who blends facts and feelings, left brain with right brain, cognitive with strong emotion, taking the lead roll in both my presentation and in your application. I am a challenger of the status quo who seeks to simplify the complex and change the lenses through which we see and interpret success.

IN-THE-BOX AUDIT

For example, do you fully comprehend that wealth flows through you, not to you? That in order to get what you want, you must help others get what they want? That fortune and fame don't come with a "scarcity" mentality (it's all about *me*, and there's only enough for *me*), but instead through an "abundance" mentality (there is enough to go around for everybody to succeed)? All of this sounds like in-the-box thinking to me.

Do you realize that in business, although it costs five to six times more to attract a new customer, most marketing efforts continue to be acquisition-oriented rather than retention-oriented? (According to the Bain Company, businesses can actually boost profits almost 100 percent by retaining only 5 percent more of existing customers. A 2 percent increase in retaining current customers has the same effect on profits as cutting costs by 10 percent.)

Do your employees, especially your sales and service professionals, realize that catering to and keeping existing customers is vital to the stability and rapid growth of every business. Current loyal customers always give you referrals, they are definitely less price sensitive (if price becomes the issue, it means the presentation is weak and the relationship is shallow), and they purchase more products and services because you make them feel important by knowing their names and needs.

Have we forgotten that loyalty is bred, not bought, and that employees are loyal when they have a friend at work, participate in company functions, and feel genuinely needed by co-workers and management? And do not all of these inside-the-organization solutions validate Bill Marriott's famous words: "If you take care of the employees, the employees will take care of the customers"? In our schools, is it not true that if you take care of the teachers, the teachers will take care of the students?

Even the restaurant business, which is one of the most competitive businesses in the world, is privy to our in-the-box premise. Success and failure have little to do with other restaurants or the economy. There will always be a wealthy class requesting fine dining and a middle-class seeking value, which means price is never the big issue. There will always be a McDonald's on one corner and a Burger King, a Wendy's, and a KFC or Taco Bell on the other three—not so that they can compete against each other, but so that they can generate traffic and prove themselves. Restaurants succeed or fail based on management, food, service, cleanliness, and environment—all of which are found and tweaked from within. Anyone who thinks answers are found in menus and not chefs, in programs and not people, in *best* intelligence and knowledge instead of *right* perspective and wisdom, needs to think again.

EVERYTHING I NEEDED TO LEARN IN COLLEGE I LEARNED OUTSIDE CLASS

In-the-box right answers present a challenge. Too often the learned discount them because they are simple and ordinary enough for the unlearned to understand. For some reason, we think that unless an answer is complicated, it isn't sophisticated, and if it's obvious, it can't be life-altering or an educational experience worth our while. Apparently they have never met anybody like my big buddy Blain!

He was my first roommate at the university. A big, strong, soft-spoken cowboy. He had a huge smile, was always polite, and did not speak much. When we met, I asked, "What's your name?"

"Blain," he answered.

Five minutes of silence later, I asked, "Where are you from?"

"Idaho."

Five minutes of silence later, I asked, "Do you live in the city or the country?"

"Country."

Five minutes of silence later, I asked, "What is your major?"

"Communications."

Yes, Blain was a man of few words, but when he did speak, he was always deep and profound. In our first seven days together, Blain taught me everything I needed to know to succeed for the rest of my life. For the rest of forever I will always know the answers are definitely in the box.

Day One: We were late checking into our dorm room, so we got last pick of the accommodations. We were told that the only thing left was an older corner room. I complained all the way down the hall, moaning, "I never get a break." Then we opened the door and saw a big, oak-trimmed suite. Blain quietly said, "The early bird gets the worm, but the second mouse always gets the cheese."

Day Two: I had an old car with squeaky brakes. I asked Blain if he knew anything about cars. He said, "I'll see." That afternoon he jacked up my car and took off a wheel. He quickly checked it and put it back on. He then opened the hood and fiddled around for a minute. Dumbfounded, I asked him what he was doing. He simply replied, "I couldn't fix your brakes, so I just made your horn louder!"

Day Three: We had the first class of the day together. It was Introduction to Marketing. The professor said, "Take thirty minutes and write an ad. Use as many words as necessary, but keep it to one page." After a while the professor called on three different people to share. They read full-page, wordy essays. The professor then called on Blain. He quietly read, "For sale: Parachute, only used once, never opened, small stain." We laughed. The professor was intrigued and inquired if he had any other thoughts he would like to share. Blain quietly drawled, "Well, I kinda, sorta got a real-estate marketing idea I also wrote here."

The professor said, "Yes?" as we all held our breath.

Blain read, "Statistics prove that most people have serious accidents within five miles of their home. So call me as your realtor, and I'll help you move!" We all burst into belly-shaking hoots and cheers.

Day Four: The sociology professor ironically didn't seem to care about anything or anyone. He didn't call the roll and only talked for one minute at the beginning of class to tell us what chapters to read. Then he sat down, put his feet up on a table, and read a magazine for the next thirty minutes. I commented to Blain, "How can he teach us when he is not even involved in the class?"

"He can't," Blain replied. "You can't farm from the city." I then asked him if he were the professor, what would he teach? Blain replied, "Ninety percent of success is half mental."

I laughed and asked, "What?"

With a serious face, Blain explained: "Yep. Success is 10 percent inspiration and 90 percent perspiration—10 percent what happens to you and 90 percent what you do with what happens to you. The half mental is attitude and the other half is action."

Day Five: Already, some of the guys in our dorm had started to party during the week with their wild roommates. I commented, "Mike came in here straight, with high moral standards and high athletic and education goals, but John sure is a bad influence on him."

Blain replied, "Yep. I had to write poetry in English class today and wouldn't you know it, it pretty much explains what's goin' on with these fellas: 'On top of old Smokey all covered with snow, I lost my best bird dog by aiming too low.' It's better to shoot for the stars and miss than to aim for a pile of manure and hit!"

I hadn't seen Blain talk this much all at once since I met him, and I definitely didn't want to cut him off. I'm glad I didn't because he then shared this poem:

With garbage and junk our big can is well fed,
This trash we don't want we can burn it instead.
But what about dirt that you've heard or you've said,
Oh what can be done with a garbage can head?

Day Six: It was the weekend, and I asked Blain if he wanted to go to a party. We went. Within fifteen minutes the fraternity boys tried to pressure him with the usual, "C'mon. Chill out. Loosen up. Smoke a little dope, drink a few shots, get down tonight." I asked him if he wanted to leave. Blain answered, "No. But they shouldn't try to teach a pig to sing. It's a waste of your time, and it annoys the pig! Why should I let what others say and do change who I am or what I do?"

Day Seven: I was tired and wanted to sleep in. But Blain was up bright and early. I asked him where he was going all dressed up. He said, "Church."

Sarcastically I poked fun. "Why would you go to church? Your parents aren't here to make you."

Blain put me in my place with his answer: "It's what you do when the coach is not around that makes you a champion. We shouldn't just learn and do things that will help us while we're alive; we should learn and do things that will help us when we're dead! You should come to church with me."

I defiantly demanded, "Give me one good reason why I should."

Blain pretty much summed up the week and the previous in-the-box principles of success he had already taught me when he answered, "It's better to build a fence at the edge of the cliff than to park an ambulance at its base!"

In seven days and in about seven minutes total, I learned patience and some other valuable lessons: never say never, you can only do what you can do, less is more, you must be present to win, choose your influences, be true to your values and yourself, and prevention is always better than rehabilitation. These common sense truths remain right and true regardless of taste, opinion, age, sex, race, belief, language, culture, political party, or country. Right has always been right, or we can't call it right! So, whoever thinks all of our personal growth and corporate advancement opportunities are dictated by our past schoolroom performance or IQ needs to think again!

EMOTIONAL QUOTIENT

Traditionally, IQ (Intelligence Quotient) has been the predominant measuring stick of success in school and a cause for prestigious job placements after graduation. We need to be lifelong learners. Knowledge is power, and being bright *is* the single most attractive quality in anyone. But what about EQ (Emotional Quotient), which links strongly to all of the intangible qualities of success previously mentioned? EQ reassures us of love, spirituality, service, people's capabilities, and the fact that everybody has value. It brings compassion and humanity to work through empathy, vision, and integrity. Are these not all in-the-box answers?

In the early 1990s, Dr. John Mayer, PhD, and Dr. Peter Saloven, PhD, introduced their research data as "emotional intelligence" in the *Journal of Personality Assessment.* Daniel Goleman popularized this breakthrough in his 1995 book *Emotional Intelligence.* According to the research, success requires both IQ *and* the attitudinal, behavioral, and maximizing-potential of EQ, which increases stability and harmony in relationships.

For instance, we have all met brilliant people with academic honors who are socially and interpersonally inept as well as unsuccessful in business. On the other hand, we also know those who are street savvy and whose only degree is from the school of hard knocks, yet they started and are running multimillion-dollar corporations. How to they do it? Which is more important, IQ or EQ? Which is best? Which is right? In which category do you fit, and can you become more of one or the other or both?

In my twenty-five years as a professional speaker, I've noticed that most people abhor meetings out of fear and frustration that the newest fad program will be added to their previously introduced "do more with less" fad program (with emphasis on IQ). Hey, we are already busy enough and don't need another assignment—something new on our plate and someone telling us to change from the outside in. Everybody I've ever met already knows enough to be successful right now, where they are, with what they have.

Success is not about programs, it's about principles. The purpose of a meeting is to remind us about this, get us away from the regular to evaluate what is extraordinary, give us an emotional experience we can't get at home and to take us to a place we cannot take ourselves.

When all is said and done, all anyone really needs to succeed are the in-the-box right answers that have already passed the test of time. We must remember, great isn't always best, and both are only always relevant, depending on the comparison. Only right is always right—yesterday, today, and forever. As we previously stated, everybody is entitled to an opinion, but nobody is entitled to wrong facts.

WRONG FACTS?

Is this an oxymoron? No. Wrong information has often been masqueraded as fact. For example, take Enron's financial records, a company's inflated stock value, revisionist history books, many unregulated websites, and so forth. The National Speakers Association is even guilty of wrong facts when it suggests that a "high-content program" is statistical analysis and research data packaged in PowerPoint. To the contrary, inspirational stories, humorous tales, metaphors, analogies, and eyewitness accounts presented in an emotional way offer higher-content facts with longer-lasting, life-altering messages—something numbers can't offer.

According to Dr. Albert Mehrabian's extensive research published in his communications studies, most of what we remember is emotional. His famous "Rule" states that words account for 7 percent of what we remember, tone of voice accounts for 38 percent, and body language accounts for 55 percent of the message. Ninety-three percent of what goes on in the brain is dedicated to nonverbal communication and emotion. Only 7 percent is dedicated to facts. In Mehrabian's diagram titled "Sources of Impression Formation," Mehrabian displays the major persuasive influences on attitude, behavior, and performance. Emotion clearly sits at the top of all things relating to retention.

Without emotion, we feel no conviction to obey the rule of law, experience no environment conducive to logic, and find no reason to check whether a source of facts is credible or corrupt. Emotion is the root of all sales, customer service, coaching, teaching, and parenting. Every successful ad campaign is based on emotional photos, music, and well-written copy using colorful adjectives and active verbs. Ninety percent of how people react to anything is based on emotion. Consequently, it is the combination of both knowledge and emotion that constitute right answers, and it is only the right answers that apply to every industry and connect us in every aspect of our personal and professional lives.

For example, understanding human potential and productivity is made easier when we connect with the truths about agricultural potential and productivity. From 1948 to 2002, the amount of farmable acreage in America did not increase. It remained the same for more than fifty years. However, the productivity from those same acres increased by three-and-a-half times in the same time period. The right answers were found in the land (in the box) and within the farmer's passion, creativity, imagination, pride, and work ethic (EQ).

DOES CAN'T MEAN WON'T?

A recent experience revealed the in-the-box truth about customer service. I have flown almost five million miles on Delta Airlines, and I absolutely love Delta and the way they treat me. I hold their highest Platinum Medallion status. Consequently, I have been awarded access to their customer service hotline, called Special Member Services, and I have used it often when I needed VIP assistance. The other day my flight into Washington, DC's Reagan National Airport was canceled. When I phoned the special number for emergency help, a polite, professional woman in Cincinnati greeted me by name and asked how she could help me. I explained my crisis and what I needed her to do. She said, "I'm sorry, Mr. Clark, I can't do that."

In the past I would have used my persuasive skills to explain that "can't" means "won't." I knew that her refusal to help me was her choice. Where there's a will there is always a "won't," but there's also a way—she just needed to find it. Not once have I ever been successful at getting a customer service agent to change his or her mind, so I didn't waste any time. Instead, I said "thank you," hung up the telephone, and immediately called back the same special number. A different woman answered, politely and professionally greeted me by name, and asked the same question: "How may I help you?" I explained my crisis and again made the exact same request. She said,

"No problem, Mr. Clark. I can do that." She took care of me quickly and completely.

Both customer service agents had gone through the same training and had access to the same software, computer screens, and solutions. One said no, one said yes. One was one of the *best* but seemed to take her job for granted; one was *right* and seemed to appreciate her employment and take pride in her career. I was in a huge hurry, but I asked this second customer service agent in which call center she was working. With a beautiful, barely noticeable accent, she humbly replied, "India."

Right and true are always right and true—even internationally. Champions and winners in every language and country know we are not paid by the hour, but rather, for the value we bring to that hour. Regardless of the culture, champions know that when our attitudes are right, our abilities will always catch up. Sir Winston Churchill was right in 1940. After the Nazis bombed his beloved England on one of the bleakest days of World War II, he rallied his fellow citizens with a reminder: "It is not enough to say I will do my best. We must do that which is necessary to succeed." Because this is a universal truth, Churchill was right then, and he is still right today!

CHANGE

If right is right yesterday, today, and forever, then why do so many corporate meetings seem to be about change? It has been said that change is the one constant in life, but how, and in what way? Of course there are outside influences that are in a constant state of flux, but if they are negative, why should we let them change our attitudes and actions? The very suggestion from someone that we should change (usually coming from a company manager, spouse, significant other, or coach) implies that they think we were born "flawed," that we came into the world ill-equipped to succeed. But out of the goodness of their hearts they will pay our registration fee for a seminar and give us time off to attend it so we can "put in" what was "left out" at birth.

Are you kidding me? What they are really saying is that we are "boneheads" who are not good enough the way we are, and because we are weak, we are at the mercy of outside influences to alter our attitudes, ethics, and behavior. And if we believe them, before long we start turning into "woe is me, life ain't fair, I'm out of control and have no say in my destiny" victims that people hate to be around. Do you know anybody like this? Someone with a victim mentality looks out the window when it's raining and complains, "What a horrible day." No it's not. When it rains in Los Angeles, the water dissipates the smog and you can actually see what you are paying for! Rain is Mother Nature's way of replenishing our water supplies and making all things grow. Of course too much moisture can at times be negative, but even then, weather is the quickets test of whether we are affected more by outward or inward influences.

For example, I live by Snowbird Ski Resort in the mountains of Utah. When it snows in Utah, we ski. In 2005, it snowed while I was in Charlotte, North Carolina; Atlanta, Georgia; and Dallas, Texas. When it snows in the south, they crash their cars! When it snows in the midwest, they fish! In 2006 I was in Malibu Beach, California, when it snowed for the first time ever. Most residents had never seen snow before. All the crazies were out on the sidewalk with their noses to the ground snorting "lines," thinking it was cocaine from God, saying "Whoa, dude, I believe!"

Allowing ourselves to negatively react strongly to outside influences is a choice we don't have to make. The only thing we are not in charge of is whether or not we are in charge. We should be stronger and proactively change only when, where, and how we decide. And if you think about it, when we do this, it really isn't change at all. It's self-improvement, not because it's expected by others but because it's demanded of ourselves. It's stretching to become more of who we already are; it's finally getting ourselves to the mental and emotional state where we know that to get better answers we must ask better questions, and that instead of asking so many questions of others, we should start asking the toughest questions of ourselves.

CROSSROADS

I hope I have found you full of curiosity and inquiry and at a crossroads in your life, ready to leave the past behind; where you are fully aware that you already possess what is necessary to take it to the ultimate level in life and love, personally and professionally. As I invite you into the following experiences, you will realize that although experience is a tough teacher, it is the right teacher because it tests us first and then offers the lesson.

Always in search of the next high adventure, I participated in a re-enactment of the 1856 western migration of pioneers along the Oregon/Mormon Trail. From July 17–20, 2006, our group of 380 men, women, and teenagers picked up the historic trail on the plains of Wyoming at a place called Martin's Cove. It was here that the Martin Handcart Company sought shelter from a brutal storm in the fall of 1856. They had already pulled their five-hundred-pound handcarts from Omaha, Nebraska, and had worn out their shoes, some walking barefoot. Many wore torn, thin coats, and they had little food. Many died from exposure to the elements and were buried in shallow graves along the way.

With five to eight people assigned to each of our carts, our group left this special place pulling three-hundred-pound handcarts on a forty-one-mile, three-and-a-half-day trek that would take us up difficult soft-sand mountain climbs, back down dusty hills, twice across the Sweetwater River, and along flat plains in 100-degree weather—the hot sun always perched high overhead, and the wind blowing dirt in our faces.

Our first night camping, we were attacked by a sudden fifty-mile-an-hour wind/rainstorm that collapsed our tents and blew everything over. Our first day, some members of our group got heatstroke; others experienced dehydration, requiring I.V.s from our trek medical staff. I suffered from the biggest, most grotesque blisters on my toes and heels that anyone had ever seen! Although difficult beyond our wildest imaginations, all 380 of us made it the forty-one miles and emerged stronger and more in tune with ourselves than ever before.

It is my nature and job to quote my favorite success principles I've learned from others. But from this trek, I now have my own quotes and know for sure that none of us can ever know what our full potential is. We must keep pushing one day at a time, one step at a time, to become better today than we were yesterday. I now know for sure that we will never know how strong we are and how good we can become until we are stretched and tested. I am an eyewitness to the fact that what we have been in the past does not make us who we are today. What we hope to become in the future makes us who we are today.

On a spiritual note, I discovered that those who prayed along the way still got blisters; even the most righteous leaders experienced pain. This was an epiphany for me, realizing that no matter who we are or the depth of our faith, the Almighty chooses not to take away our pain but instead gives us the necessary strength to deal with it. This trek validated that pain is good. You have to stretch before you can strengthen, and all the strengthening occurs in the area past the point of discomfort.

THE ULTIMATE INSPIRATION

Our trek culminated in a five-and-a-half-mile climb over a steep, treacherous, extremely bumpy stretch of the historic Oregon/Mormon Trail called Rocky Ridge, appropriately named because of the countless sharp, jagged, sometimes large and often-slippery rocks that poked out of the rutted ground. Completing this testy climb was rewarded by a fairly flat two-mile stretch that led to our final campsite. Rocky Ridge was one of the highest peaks on the more than 1,300 total miles of the trail and was just more than 7,000 feet in elevation. Consequently, it took us four hours to pull and push our handcarts up and over the mountain and out to Rock Creek Camp.

As we concluded these seven-and-a-half miles, we arrived at a small cemetery where thirteen gravestones honored those who had passed away at this location along the trail. It was here during an evening memorial service that I heard the following story.

Having just experienced an unbelievable personal test of character that tested my will to succeed and my ability to endure to the end, I was moved to tears when I realized that what I had just accomplished was nothing compared to what the pioneers endured in 1856—especially James Kirkwood.

JAMES KIRKWOOD—ELEVEN-YEAR-OLD HERO
(TAKEN FROM A JOURNAL ENTRY OF ONE WHO WAS THERE)

James and his family came from Scotland. They had to save for a long time to be able to come to America. James's father got sick and died shortly after they arrived, but his mother was determined to fulfill her husband's dream wish and go on to the Salt Lake Valley. James was eleven years old and had three brothers: Thomas, nineteen, was crippled and had to ride in the handcart; Robert, twenty-one, helped their mother pull the cart; Joseph, four, was in James's care.

On October 20, 1856, the handcart company was camping by the Sweetwater River, not far from the base of Rocky Ridge. They had hardly had anything to eat for several days. Everyone was extremely weak, and two to three feet of snow was on the ground. It was very cold, and ahead of them lay a long, steep climb through snow—sometimes as high as the axles on the handcarts. With freezing wind blowing in their faces and through their clothes, these pioneers traveled all day and all night.

Young Joseph's shoes had worn out from walking the previous thousand-plus miles, and his little feet were numb. Joseph fell down and started to cry. James tried to encourage him to climb some more, but Joseph couldn't take another step. That's when James picked him up and began to climb the ridge. Joseph was heavy, and James had to move slowly, carrying his little brother on his shoulder, then in his arms, then over his other shoulder. The two boys fell behind the main group, but James never gave up. Sometimes Joseph would start to slip because James's fingers were frozen, and he couldn't hold on very well. So he would set Joseph down and then immediately pick him up again and continue walking.

After taking more than twenty-seven hours to get up and over Rocky Ridge, James finally saw the fires burning at Rock Creek camp. The boys had made it to safety. James had been quiet for a long time, and young, thankful Joseph couldn't get him to talk. James gently dragged his little brother over to the rest of the group and carefully set him down by the fire. James then collapsed, never to get up again. Having given everything he had, eleven-year-old James Kirkwood lay down and died.

GIVING IT EVERYTHING WE HAVE

What are we made of? Would I have done this? Could you have done this? In our day and age, the only ones who come close to understanding what it means to give it their all are our brave men and women who have served in the military and are currently fighting the global war on terrorism. Our fallen soldiers, like young James Kirkwood, made the ultimate sacrifice, unselfishly demonstrating, in the words of Jesus, that "greater love hath no man than this, that a man lay down his life for his friends."

With this inspirational story now deeply embedded in your soul, let us separate ourselves from these pioneer and military superheroes and focus on others—in an environment that is not life threatening—who are also committed to giving it everything they have—to themselves and to each other. One is a teacher and coach; the other is his student. Let me introduce you to Hank Haney. Not only is Hank a client and a dear friend, but he is also a consummate teacher and an incredible human being who just happens to be Tiger Woods's golf coach.

TIGER WOODS'S GOLF COACH

You don't have to be a great golfer or even an athlete to learn from Hank. Golf is just one of the things he teaches. To Hank, education is not the filling of a pail but the lighting of a fire. Hank wants you and me and Tiger to be lifelong learners. Hank always reminds me that education is a social process. Education is growth—not only to know more but also to be more. Education is not preparation for life—it is life itself! Hank Haney is a master of the art of execution.

In response to my question of what makes Tiger Woods the exceptional champion he is, Hank told me three things: In Tiger's world, you are either becoming better or becoming worse. To Tiger, losing hurts worse than winning feels good. And no matter what, you can't quit—it's a league rule. In Tiger's world, you either hit it exactly where you wanted to, or you don't. You don't "try" to do anything. You either make the putt and win the tourney, or you don't. No excuses. No whining. Too tough, harsh, and insensitive? Absolutely not! Sympathy doesn't help, and empathy doesn't fix the problem or change the result. To Tiger, and through my countless interviews with corporate business executives, military generals, and other successful superstars, you either succeed or fail. Period. If you fail, the next thought and step is simply, "Do something about it—immediately!"

"Immediately" means now—where you are, with what you have, and what you know. We live our lives at different speeds, for different reasons, in different circumstances. So we attain a different level of understanding along the way. This is referred to as our "current reality" or "present level of truth." The challenge is that as we relentlessly pursue greater understanding and higher truth, each successive level is usually at odds with the previous level. Consequently, we sometimes put others down because they don't *get* what we now *get*. Although this seems obvious, this one principle keeps most people from becoming champions.

Guy Kawasaki, in his book *Rules for Revolutionaries,* cautions, "Judge your results and other people's intentions. This prevents you from judging people harshly because they don't 'get it.' Most people judge their own intentions and other people's results, which usually means that they accept their own failings (because they had good intentions) but not the failings of others (because the results were lousy)."

Champions judge only their own results.

TIGER'S WORLD

This is one of the reasons Tiger's world is simple—not easy, often very hard and grueling, but definitely not complicated. What's your world like?

Most people I know say they would give anything to be Tiger Woods and have his wealth and fame. Obviously they are lying to us and fooling themselves, or they *would* give anything and everything. Tiger isn't an overnight success. He has spent his entire life preparing, increasing his present level of truth, judging only his own results, tweaking, and being a champion so that whenever opportunity presents itself, he can win the championship.

What makes Tiger different is that he eagerly faces the fierce facts of reality. Tiger knows pain is a signal to grow, not to suffer. And once we learn the lesson the pain teaches us, the pain goes away. Tiger knows that the value of something is determined by what we are willing to give up to get it, and thus, each moment and opportunity matter.

This is not the attitudinal question of whether life's glass is half empty or half full. To Tiger and Hank, this analogy doesn't even register. What if the glass is half full of the wrong thing? Regardless, the glass is still only half full. Tiger's world is about filling up the glass with only the right stuff and at all times keeping it 100 percent full. Tiger doesn't wait for failure to kick-start self-improvement. Tiger is always thinking and doing something to become better today than he was yesterday—physically, mentally, spiritually, emotionally, financially, and socially—not competing against others, but from inside the box.

BEING A TIGER

Tiger is Tiger and Hank is Hank, not because of what they do, which just happens to be golf. Way before "doing," they worked on "being." Tiger and Hank are extraordinary because of who and why they are. Once we identify and clearly define our "who" and "why," the "what we must do" becomes obvious, and the "how to do it" is easily figured out. Tiger is not the greatest golfer in the world because of his swing. He is number one because of who he is—attitude, work ethic, respect for others, and love for the game—and "why he wants it." Before you can win championships, you must first *be* a champion. And you don't get there by focusing on having fame and fortune. You become better by focusing on being whole and complete.

PROBLEM-SOLVING SKILLS

Most people can rise to the occasion once in a while and be complete long enough to win on one day, win one tournament, or be successful for a season. Champions like Tiger, however, sustain a winning level of concentration and focus and relentlessly pursue a higher level of truth every day, year after year as their current reality.

Tiger is the consummate champion on and off the course, and if we can duplicate the way a champion thinks and acts, we too can become a champion—not just in golf, but in everyday life. As I mentioned earlier, I am not qualified to write a golf book, but if I did, my title would be something like *How to Line Up Your Fifth Putt* or *Awesome Second Shots off the Ladies' Tee* or *I'm Still Away.* However, I can write and report that the game of life is like sports with out-of-bounds lines detailing the field of play, goals to shoot for, strategies, rules, objectives, penalties, hazards to avoid, scores to be posted, and rewards for the hard workers to reap.

Golf, especially, is life personified. In fact, golf teaches Decision Making 101, how behavior is linked to consequences, and that the answers really are in the box. Success in any aspect of life all boils down to mastering good problem-solving skills.

If anyone is acting out—especially your child—it is because he has something going on in his life that he's having a tough time dealing with. If he is acting out a lot, he has lots of things he has problems dealing with. If his toolbox consists only of a hammer, everything to him looks like a nail. The bigger the problem, the bigger the hammer and the harder he hits. And it's not just a phase he will grow out of. If a student doesn't understand basic math, you can't expect him to grow out of it and learn algebra. He must learn in order to progress, and progress begins at his current reality and present level of truth.

What's in your toolbox? A golfer carries fourteen different clubs in his bag because each shot requires a different tool from his tool bag—different tools for different reasons to solve different problems at different times on the course. The external, physical mechanics of club grip, setup, balance, head, back, legs, take-away, and follow-through of the swing is usually the same for every shot. Clubs and the swing are the having and doing part, and every pro golfer has basically the same equipment and picture-perfect swing. The difference between a successful and an unsuccessful golf shot—the difference between a champion like Tiger and an amateur—lies in the internal *being* part. *Being* is the hard drive; having and doing is the software application.

SPEED UP?

Being whole and complete sounds simple, doable, and right. Yet, in our high-speed world, the popular mantra of the day is that if you are not changing at the same pace the world is changing, you will be left behind. We cannot slow down the world, so we must speed up ourselves. They say it only takes a minute if you leave it to the last minute. Do you agree?

When Tiger is behind the leader in a tournament, does Coach Haney whisper, "You've got to play faster and speed up your progress"? Of course not. Yes, there is a time at the end of a match when it's do or die and you've got to take your game and intensity to a higher level, become the master of the calculated risk, and find a way to win before time runs out. But have you noticed that only champions can do this, and they can do it only because of what has happened before the tournament began?

What I'm suggesting is that certain principles are constantly at work, even if we are not. And it's these principles that keep us steady and solid and consistent regardless of how or why the emotional or physical weather changes around us. In fact, certain principles are at work even if we don't know what they are. Gravity was at work long before the apple fell and conked Newton on the head. Physics, economics, the law of relativity, chemistry, geology, ecology, and faith are the principles by which our world was created and is currently being governed. The sooner we understand these constant outside influences, the sooner we can use them to help us succeed.

For this reason, some might argue that a professional speaker and author like me should pump you up, light your fire, and motivate you to accelerate your existence. Nope. I want to slow you down! The only meaning life has for you is the meaning you give it—not based on outside comparisons, but from the inside out. I conclude this first chapter with the simple challenge to ponder and apply the lyrics to one of my songs:

In Two More Days Tomorrow's Yesterday
I used to live my life on time delay
A day behind, a day ahead, but never right away
Hurry up and wait was a road rage waste of time
Fast, slow, stop, going out of my mind

Tomorrow is the day I thought would never come
Yesterday and "used to be's" are when I got me some
The older I get the better I was, memories change
The only constant's what we rearrange

Past, present, future—really are the same
Different order, separate times, all the same game
What will be makes history, this too shall pass away
In two more days, tomorrow's yesterday
Past, present, future—all turn today
In two more days, tomorrow's yesterday

Today is the someday I longed for yesterday
Wait until tomorrow was the cheapest price to pay
The other side seemed greener, talked of glory days of play
Was caught between tomorrow and yesterday

They say timing's everything—what should be will be
Things happen for a reason, a lifetime guarantee
What goes around comes back around, just by a different name
The more things change, the more they stay the same

SUCCEED FROM THE INSIDE OUT

---

*We shall teach each other. First, because we have a vast amount
of experience behind us. Second, it is only through free criticism of
each other's ideas that truth can be thrashed out. No one is going to
compel you to work, for the simple reason that a man who requires to
be driven is not worth the driving. Thus, you will become your own
student and until you learn how to teach yourself, you will never be
taught by others.*

—J. F. C. Fuller, US Army General (to his West Point
Cadets)

All of the information in the world does not make a person
successful. It's like the guy who has three PhDs: one in philosophy, one in psychology, and one in sociology. He doesn't have
a job but at least he can explain why! We don't learn to know,
we learn to do. It doesn't do us any good to know how to read
if we never pick up a book and read. The same holds true in a
high-tech society. Without *high touch* to implement technology
through people, the information is never optimized. Someone
smarter than most of us explained this reality clearly.

Albert Einstein, in an address to the faculty and students at
the California Institute of Technology, said, "It is not enough
that you should understand about applied science in order that
your work may increase man's blessings. Concern for man himself

and his fate and the acknowledgment of the importance of every individual must always form the chief interest of all technical endeavors. Concern for that which is not tested in schools must always form the nucleus of what really matters in human endeavors. All things have been carefully placed on earth for man's discovery, and all discovery and progress comes from within us. Never forget emotion and common sense in the midst of your diagrams and equations."

What Einstein is saying is so simple. Yes, we already know it—the answers are already inside of us, but we need to be constantly reminded. Einstein is clearly and matter-of-factly stating that in a high-tech world, we should overcompensate with high touch. Technology is important but still remains only a tool. It's not about technology until it's about people. What if we allow technology to overrun us and you go to your doctor's office tomorrow and there is no human being there? All you get is a recording: "If your pain is below the waist, press one." What if you are Catholic, and when you go to confession, you find that it has been put on voice mail: 1-800-Fessupp. "If you are into bigamy, press 2. If you are worshipping the devil, press 666." Is this where we're headed? I certainly hope not!

Einstein, in the context of an IQ (intelligence quotient) verses EQ (emotional quotient) discussion, affirms the significance of EQ as the key to a successful, fulfilling existence. IQ is technical, left brain, cognitive, letter of the law, outside ourselves; EQ is emotional, right brain, imaginative, creative, spirit of the law, inside our selves. IQ is book smart; EQ is street smart. IQ is knowing how to dig; EQ is knowing where to dig, why to dig, and getting motivated to dig because of the benefits and results that come from digging. EQ is inner strength, which gives us much more stability, balance, and endurance than outer strength. EQ is what puts us and keeps us in tune with our conscience.

At the end of the day, it's not what happens to us but what we *do* with what happens to us that matters. Until we get out of the planning stage and into the *go stage*, there is no accomplishment. Until we stop confusing activity with accomplishment, there is no worthwhile *doing*. And as dumb and obvious as it sounds, until we *do,* we cannot get it done. Doing only occurs when we mix and match in equal proportion both intelligence *and* emotion, both fact *and* feeling, both talent *and* desire, both action *and* conscience.

Michael Jordan is the classic example of this. Steve Alford, former NBA player and head basketball coach at the University of Iowa, reported, "When I played with Michael Jordan on the Olympic gold medal winning Dream Team, there was a huge gap between his ability and the ability of the other great players on that team. But what impressed me was that he was always the first one on the floor and the last one to leave." Michael Jordan obviously followed his "gut" and connected his head with his heart because he knew that if the things he thought about were different than the things he did, he would never be at peace. Consequently, he did what he knew he should do.

Getting it done means taking it to the next level and growing—knowing that growth, unless it is good growth, is no growth at all. This is where leadership and management from the inside out come into play. Good growth is doing the right thing simply because it's the right thing to do. This is often identified as "conscience."

THE SOUNDS OF SILENCE

Conscience is not some mystical spiritual gift given to a select few. Conscience is an inherent human compass that always points "true north," an internal guiding light given to every man and woman at birth that we may feel truth when we hear it, recognize the difference between good and evil, and always know right from wrong. Our conscience will never fail us. Only our desire to follow it decreases as we continue to ignore its promptings and do the wrong thing. The way it works is simple. When we hear or see something or are faced with a decision, before we act, we study it out in our mind. If it is true and the right thing to do or not to do, we will know by a feeling of confirming power. We may even feel a burning in our bosom that it's true and right. It's the time in a meeting when the speaker is talking and we subconsciously nod our heads because deep down inside we know what we are hearing is the truth. It's the "good" feeling and self-administered "emotional pat on the back" that comes when we do the right thing that is never experienced when we do something wrong.

Conscience is a success-from-the-inside-out tool—a moral/ethical carpenter's level, if you will, that helps us balance out our decision-making processes. It's the key ingredient in our mortality survival kit that each of us was issued at birth. "Survival of the fittest" refers not only to physical strength but also to strength of character, moral courage, and consistent commitment to follow our gut instincts and do what we think and feel is right. Conscience is one of the most important sounds of silence. Getting in touch with it and staying in tune to its "still small voice" is the key to happiness. La Rochefoncanld wrote, "When we are unable to find tranquility within ourselves, it is useless to seek it elsewhere. By trading in our impatience for peace of mind, we have sold out not to the devil of loud noises, but to the still, calm music of Muzak."

Those who do not stay true to themselves and in tune and in sync with universal laws become weak and are eventually replaced in society by the strong and fit. From the Native American world of internal belief, we find an amazing tradition of the medicine bag. Inner strength is the prerequisite for listening to and especially following our conscience. For this reason I now have a medicine bag that hangs in a prominent, visible place in my library to constantly remind me that success comes from the inside out.

THE TRADITION OF THE MEDICINE BAG

Throughout history, cultures have looked to their holy men or women not only to heal the body but also to help them heal their souls. Tradition taught that the two were inseparably connected—that both the spirit and the body constitute the soul of man. In the Native American culture, this understanding brought about the tradition of the medicine bag. Native Americans believe that our healing and health belong to us. Others may help, but healing is an inside-out proposition.

The medicine people had two kinds of medicine bags. One was filled with herbs and compounds, the knowledge of their practice of healing. The other was each person's own medicine bag. The bag and its contents were for the purpose of keeping the person healthy. This bag was not filled with reactive medicine for the body, but rather proactive prevention medicine for the soul. It held the power to remind and inspire. The medicine of this bag was humility, gratitude, and sacred, sensitive things that connect us to the earth, universe, and humanity.

My friend and spiritual guide, Kim Nelson, who lived among and faithfully served Native Americans for two years, explained this tradition to me and presented me with my own buckskin medicine bag that I have since filled with powerful, potent "medicine." The tradition of the medicine bag is this: We ornament on the outside leather fringe or put into our bags reminders of who we are, whom we love, what we have experienced and learned, what we hope to become, what we value, and what brings us true joy and deep understanding. We are to keep these bags close and look into them often. They remind us of all we have to be thankful for and all the reasons we have to be healthy. They remind us daily of who we are and what kind of people we can be.

Because of its contents, the medicine bag serves as a motivational tool for gratitude and a reminder of why our best effort is required every day to be grateful and growing. In this intimate way, our bags not only help us heal but also keep us on the path to avoid the pain, sickness, and suffering that come from forgetting who we really are. They keep us on the right track by reminding us of where we have been, why we are here, and where we are going.

Every time and culture has had such bags: a journal, a drawer, a cigar box, a scrapbook, a treasure chest, a photo album, a special shelf, a glass case, a wall of fame. All are medicine bags for the soul of those of us who wish to know and remember who and what we are. They bring peace and true *feng shui* to our hectic lives, keeping us connected to our roots, what really matters most, and the belief that we really can become more of who we already are.

CONSCIENCE FOR ALL AGES

A classic example of instinctive understanding—being true to what is right and the reality that the natural law of conscience is always in action—is exposed every time I speak to young people. My speech is usually short and one question long. I love to ask teenagers: "If you had you for a child, would you be nervous?" Most cringe and look back at me like, "Whoa, I wouldn't even let me go out! I would have grounded myself as a baby!"

We all inherently know what is good, bad, right, and wrong, and we can truthfully judge if we want to, when we decide to. Understanding consequences is usually the motivating factor and impetus for our decisions. Life's most important answers lie inside you and me. All we need to do is trust, look, and listen.

- *Trust* that there are no mistakes in life, only lessons, and that a lesson is repeated, sometimes presented in various forms, until we learn it. If we don't learn easy lessons, they get harder.
- *Look* to see that we've learned the lesson because our actions have changed, look to see that others are simply mirrors of ourselves, and know that we cannot love or hate something about another unless it reflects something we love or hate in ourselves.
- *Listen* to every experience and person as a universal teacher, especially to those who live long, happy lives because they have a sense of humor and a sense of perspective called altruistic attitude, total acceptance, total forgiveness, and love.

Fully comprehending our conscience and realizing the power it brings into our lives validates once and for all that life's most important and critical answers are still in the box. As we previously pointed out, life has no meaning except the meaning we give it.

This is why it is so critical to associate with the right "conscience following" individuals who you can trust to help you figure it all out.

TRUST RELATIONSHIPS

Obviously if we get in tune with universal law and in touch with our conscience, our inside-out approach to business, sports, family, friends, and life will breed a desire to connect with others who are also in touch with their gut-instinct, intuitive selves. Because we cannot succeed alone or take it to the next level by ourselves, the single most important ingredient is to establish and nurture meaningful relationships with like-minded and like-hearted winners who share our passion for positive living.

Deep, long-lasting relationships are made up of one major ingredient that is generated by us and for us, and that is perpetuated exclusively from the inside out. Because we are interdependent as human beings living and working in an interdependent global society, our most important connector is *trust*. You can trust people who are so consistent that you can actually predict what they will think, what they will do, and how they will react or respond in a given situation. We trust those who consistently do what they say they will do. You trust your spouse or significant other to travel or be in mixed company out of your presence, and you feel no jealousy or possessiveness because you know exactly how that person has behaved in the past. You trust your teenager because you can predict how she will act regardless of peer pressure. You trust co-workers because they keep their promises by getting to work on time, sticking to their ten-minute breaks and forty-five-minute lunches, coming early, and staying late to help the team get the job done on time. You trust them because they are honest and do not gossip. Only when fellow employees and teammates are consistently good, honest, loyal, and helpful are they predictably positive, productive, and worthy of our full, unconditional trust.

Trust is the single most important ingredient—the starting point—of every meaningful relationship. Trust is the beginning step to building a winning team and launching and sustaining a profitable business. Without trust, every relationship is shallow and fleeting. Once you have trust and lose it, it is difficult to get back in a relationship. Trust is the ingredient that is lost the fastest and regained the slowest.

Bottom line? We only trust others if we first trust ourselves, and we only trust ourselves if we firmly believe that the answers are inside of us. Pause for a moment and think about how far reaching and profound this one fundamental truth of the universe really is. As you do, let me bolster your understanding with my favorite examples of success from the inside out.

MUSIC

The most recognizable and easily understood example of in-the-box-thinking comes from the world of music. When asked how many notes there are in music, most people reply, "Seven," and they count them out loud: "A, B, C, D, E, F, G." This answer was only correct until the fifteenth century, when a musician in Western Europe decided he wanted more options. He created a structured scale called a "chromatic scale" that gradually became the standard. He divided the seven whole notes into twelve semitones and then divided each tone into 100 parts in pitch we now refer to as "100 cents." He then added five raised ebony keys to the keyboard to keep the whole and half tones separated, organized the twelve tones into what he called an octave, comprised of the five black keys and seven white keys, and concluded his unmatched contribution to the music world by inspiring the piano builders to expand the size of the keyboard to a full eighty-eight keys, repeating the twelve tone octaves seven times from low C to a high C.

"There are twelve notes in music," the famous German composer Paul Hindemith said. "You must treat them carefully." Insightful, you say, but what does this have to do with being best or right and succeeding from the inside out? Ironically, your answer is found inside your question.

Think about it. Every song that has ever been written was penned using the same twelve notes. The only difference between one song and another is the order in which the twelve notes fall and the timing and spacing between the notes.

Wow, just think about what Johnny Cash did with three notes and what heavy metal bands do with one! So what's the difference between a good songwriter and an average songwriter? Because they both have access to the same twelve notes, the difference must come from passion, imagination, and creativity. The answers are in the box! Let me illustrate with classical music that I love and listen to often.

CLASSICAL EXAMPLES

Every piece composed by the masters oozes with passion, imagination, and creativity—deep emotional communication that stirs our souls.

Pachelbel's "Canon," Mouret's "Rondeau," and works by Beethoven, Chopin, and Vivaldi are pieces that, without words, evoke contemplation, passion, delirium, and consolation. Their intoxicating melodies require us to listen deeply and between the lines. I am always awestruck by each composer's ability to capture so much emotion through their music, introducing us to a cast of real characters jailed up inside each piece, reaching out to love and be loved.

Using only twelve notes, these classical composers arrange them into magnificent masterpieces that require us to also use passion, imagination, and creativity to interpret their meaning. There is more going on than just the obvious. The imagery and personality of each instrument, while individual, is stronger as a whole. With just twelve notes, the composers mysteriously move our mood toward the triumphant (Handel), to the melancholy (Satie), to the joyous (Mozart), each taking us into a deeper level of understanding. They paint warm, pastoral pictures such as in Beethoven's "Sixth Symphony" and sharp, vibrant images such as in Copland's "Appalachian Spring."

The twelve notes that are in every composer's "box," when used correctly, can invite us to feel—sometimes in a major key, sometimes in a minor key, but always luring us into the romantic rhythm of the beat.

I believe in the implication that music is life personified. Music comes from in-the-box thinking and feeling, and yet it is still much more than the obvious. Life should be too! Because musicians have become accustomed to concentrating on the boxed basics, they cry harder, laugh louder, feel deeper, and find more substance in the sounds of silence and the beauty in a blue cloudless sky. They see more and experience life to the fullest because they cut through the clutter of complexity and focus on the fundamentals of simplicity.

Can you imagine how wonderful our lives would be if each of us believed ourselves to be musical composers and that each new day brought with it an opportunity for us to write another hit song? Sure, some of us have already had some hits, but having a chance to write a hit song today is especially exciting to those who have written some bad songs and experienced failure.

In Nashville, we songwriters have two slogans that keep us going. The first is "75 to 1." This simply means that sometimes we have to write seventy-five bad songs we wouldn't ever play for our mother before we come up with one hit. So we keep writing. The second slogan that gives us confidence in ourselves comes from the fact that to have a platinum record means we have to sell one million copies. We songwriters say, "There are 300 million people in America. You can literally tick off 299 million and still go platinum!" Yes, writing and singing our own hit song and living the life we dream of is definitely about passion, imagination, and creativity.

All bankers, credit union executives, and brokers have access to the same economy, interest rates, and market facts and figures—the same twelve notes, if you will—in the volatile world of finance. The only difference between success and failure, great deals and no deals, extraordinary customer service and poor customer satisfaction is passion, imagination, and creativity. The only difference between an exceptional leader and an ineffective leader, an outstanding manager and an average manager, a great parent and a lousy parent, a winning coach and a losing coach, a loving family and a dysfunctional family is passion, imagination, and creativity.

Many wonder about the specific meaning of these in-the-box elements. To conclude this discussion on music, let us define them and demonstrate how they interface.

PASSION

Passion: You don't just hear, you listen. You don't just have sex, you make love. You don't just touch, you feel. You don't just play music, you become the instrument. You laugh longer, cry harder, connect deeper.

In interviewing actor Peter Fonda (son of Henry), I asked him who was the most intriguing person he had ever met. After careful consideration, Peter shared the following story. He said as a young boy, he and his sister, Jane, were living with their father in a coastal town in Spain. Because his father was so busy making movies, Peter was usually left alone and feeling lonely. Consequently, he befriended an older gentleman named Pablo Picasso. The famous artist lived and worked just around the corner from Peter's house.

Peter told me of the many times he was in Picasso's studio, watching him curse in Spanish at the paint while he dug it from containers and slapped it on his pallet. He would scream and point at it, calling it "ugly, worthless, good for nothing, stupid, and a ridiculous glob of vulgar crap!" Then, taking his brush and reverently speaking in French, he would whisper, praising and complimenting the paint as he applied it to the canvas: "You are beautiful, elegant. You are spectacular, breathtaking. I love you, je t'aime, je t'aime!"

Picasso yelled angrily in Spanish at what the paint was, but he deeply celebrated in French what it was becoming. In every sense of the word, Picasso epitomized passion. Passion is heart—not what we do but how we do it.

IMAGINATION

Imagination is what we do and will do—visualizing, tantalizing, thinking, having curiosity and childlike wonderment, seeing more than others see, reading between the lines, having insight (not just eyesight), and going beyond the map, just as Christopher Columbus did in 1492. Imagination is mind over matter. It's not changing what is, it's improving it; not changing the notes or the song, but making them more of what they already are!

CREATIVITY

Creativity is taking the imagination and arranging it into something that makes sense and works; it is passion connected to heart and mind, and taking them to a place they cannot go by themselves.

Thomas Edison had passion and imagination and continually arranged them as he relentlessly pursued his goal of creating the light bulb. By rearranging thousands of possibilities, as the old but relevant tale is told, Edison failed more than most even tried and eventually failed his way to success.

In order to take ourselves to the next level in every dimension of our personal and professional lives, we must set higher expectations and break them down into specific goals. Our passion to improve and our imagination of what our new accomplishment will be is important, but there is nothing particularly creative about setting goals. The creativity comes in laying out a plan of action to accomplish the goals—arranging the notes before we play the song.

It is important to note that passion, imagination, and creativity are not mutually exclusive events followed in a specific order, one at a time. Like the well-known Pioneering, Momentum, and Restructuring Stages of personal and organizational development, they are simultaneous events that feed off each other and that, together, create the hit song, hit personality, hit attitude, and so forth. When you gather enough hit songs ("hit people") together, you have a hit album (company, team, family). Passion, imagination, and creativity can't just be implemented once in a while. They need to be implemented every day and every moment. Being a hit songwriter, so to speak, is an all-the-time way of thinking and living. Ben Hogan reminds us of this when he said, "The most important shot in golf is the next one. Momentum is only as good as your next play."

HEALING

When we understand medicine and music from the inside-out perspective, it is easy to comprehend the process of healing.

We all know that doctors can't and don't heal anyone. Through the administration of medication and the performance of surgery, they help our bodies heal themselves. Physicians are not gods or miracle workers; they are catalysts and caregivers.

There are two kinds of healing: healing by First Intention and healing by Second Intention. Healing by First Intention is outside-in healing in which a scratch or superficial wound heals with a few stitches or with just a Band-Aid.

Healing by Second Intention is inside-out healing in which the wound is deep, the edges jagged, and the gouge uncertain. In this case, if you only stop the surface bleeding, stitch the surface layer of skin, and bandage it to heal from the outside in, underneath it all and unbeknownst to you, the wound is festering, infection is setting in, and gangrene could result in the amputation of that limb. A deep wound can only heal if we keep it open long enough so that the proper treatment can slowly heal from the inside out, one layer and one step at a time.

MEDICINE

Lewis Goodman, the world-famous professor of pharmacology who wrote the standard textbook *The Pharmacological Basis of Therapeutics,* could give a complicated explanation to doctors for prescribing medicine. Instead, as an in-touch winner, he suggested, "Don't be the first to use a new drug, nor the last to discard an old one." In other words, "Be progressive but within the confines of what really works, doing only what is right with predictable, consistent, compassionate, and kind care." Goodman was also alluding to the significance of trust.

I serve on a national charity board of directors with Dr. John C. Nelson, who was president of the American Medical Association (AMA) from 2004 to 2005. We often discuss the fact that doctors don't heal anybody. They only perform surgery or prescribe medication that helps us heal ourselves. They can suture a wound and be a catalyst to recovery, but at the end of the day, they cannot get the tendon, muscle, bone, or flesh to grow back together. Patients need encouragement and detailed direction to do their part.

When I go to a doctor, I assume he has graduated from medical school (at least last in his class) and can therefore do a required procedure. What I'm concerned with is if he really cares about my family and me. This differentiates a medical school graduate from a good physician.

As my friend Dr. Nelson traveled as AMA president, his most popular lecture included a slide and explanation of what he calls "The Practice of Medicine." The following diagram is a visual representation and graphic display of the "Box" where Science, Caring and Ethics Intersect the Place Where the Physician Becomes More of Who He or She Already Is.

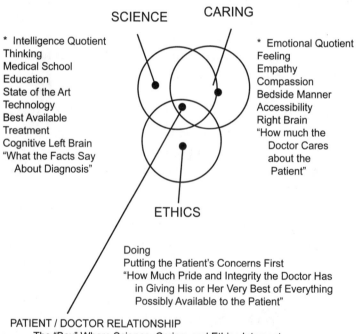

SCIENCE   CARING

* Intelligence Quotient
Thinking
Medical School
Education
State of the Art
Technology
Best Available
Treatment
Cognitive Left Brain
"What the Facts Say
    About Diagnosis"

* Emotional Quotient
Feeling
Empathy
Compassion
Bedside Manner
Accessibility
Right Brain
"How much the
    Doctor Cares
    about the
    Patient"

ETHICS

Doing
Putting the Patient's Concerns First
"How Much Pride and Integrity the Doctor Has
    in Giving His or Her Very Best of Everything
    Possibly Available to the Patient"

PATIENT / DOCTOR RELATIONSHIP
    The "Box" Where Science, Caring, and Ethics Intersect
    The Place Where the Physician Becomes More of Who He or She
    Already Is

As you can see, the Practice of Medicine requires a combination of Thinking Inside the "Box"!

In 1927, speaker Dr. Francis Peabody powerfully concluded his remarks at the Harvard University Medical School by bringing all of the complexity of medicine into an in-the-box perspective. He reminded the hundreds of physicians in his audience who were the brightest and most respected in their fields that "the secret in caring for the patient is to care for the patient." Even in the seemingly sterile "all business," astronomically expensive world of healthcare, great physicians persuade by logic and motivate with emotion—they share and explain in detail the scientific prognosis, treatment plan, necessary surgery, and predicted timetable for recovery. They let every patient know that medicine is not about money and insurance coverage. They reach out to the patient by using empathy, unexpected visits, phone calls, and love. Even in medicine the answers are still in the box.

High Performance Flying

Anybody can learn to fly an airplane, but it takes a special person who uses in-the-box answers and capabilities to be a high-performance pilot. I have experienced this every time I have interacted with the United States military. General George S. Patton put it in perspective when he explained, "Wars may be fought with weapons, but they are won by men. It is the spirit of the men who follow and of the man who leads that gains the victory. If you are going to win any battle, you have to make the mind run the body. Never let the body tell the mind what to do."

I was an eyewitness to this at the end of 2000 when I was invited to speak at the US Navy Commanders Conference at the Naval Museum in Pensacola, Florida. It was a wonderful experience. I felt deeply connected with the audience of military brass. After my speech, the admirals congratulated me and said to let them know if there was anything they could ever do for me. I didn't even have to think about it. I quickly replied that I'd always dreamed of a backseat ride in an F-18 fighter jet. Without even blinking, US Marine Colonel Eugene Frazier said, "It's done. We can do that! Your training will be tough. We will cut you no slack. You're going to have to want it bad! Most VIPs have not made it through and did not get to fly. It's a gut check that is mind over matter, will over skill!"

On January 16, 2001, I went through five long, grueling hours of intense safety and survival training at the Naval Test Pilot School at Patuxent River, Maryland, in preparation for my flight the following morning. As per my request, I wanted to experience the same training every Naval and Marine aviator is put through. All I can say is "holy cow!" My first requirement was a complete physical examination by the flight surgeon—blood, urine, eyes, ears, hernia, and so forth. I swear he checked things I didn't even have!

PHYSIOLOGY TRAINING

Then it was off to "Aviation Physiology Water Survival Training." In eighty-five pounds of full combat gear, I had to swim fifty yards—two full lengths of an Olympic-sized swimming pool (down and back)—and then tread water for fifteen minutes. After a short rest out of the pool, and with a blindfold covering my helmet, I then had to jump back in to find my way out of an underwater maze to simulate being trapped in the cockpit and keeping my wits about me to survive. I can't prove it, but from the look in the eyes of my instructors, I think they were trying to kill me, especially the East-German shot-put-champion-looking woman who squinted at me as if I reminded her of her abusive ex-husband she had hit with her truck. Three times I nearly drowned. They weren't about to just give a flight to a VIP without a fight!

SPATIAL DISORIENTATION TRAINING

Next I sat through a lecture with diagrams and a test on spatial disorientation in which they strapped me into a souped-up barstool with a seat belt, spun me around for five minutes, and had me get off and find my way to the door. (I felt like I was at a fraternity party in college!) It was then and there that I realized, "Yes, you can get too drunk to fish!"

Ejection Seat Egress Training

Next was "egress training." There I met Rambo, who, with a Southern accent, huge muscles, and a Ted Nugent guitar-solo look in his eye, asked, "Ya ever eject out of a jet before?" I sheepishly grunted a Scooby Doo *hurh?* As he walked closer, I read his nametag call sign (nickname): "Psycho." He immediately strapped me onto a tall torture-chamber-looking sled that rose to the ceiling at a forty-five-degree angle about fifty-five feet high. Smiling, he said, "Keep your head up and back, knees straight, and elbows in. On three, pull the yellow handle between your legs."

"What?"

"Three!" I pulled, and with three Gs of force squishing my body against itself, I shot up the ejection seat practice sled the entire fifty-five feet. Psycho then instructed me in the graceful art of flying and steering my parachute while I hung on straps from a ten-foot bar that turned out to be a darn good form of birth control!

I was finally cut loose, concluding our wonderful time together by roll landing off a five-foot wall to simulate a hard landing. I would surely have it if I ejected! All in all, I felt macho. The only downside of this phase of the training was that my voice was now three octaves higher!

Altitude Training

Next on the training schedule was "altitude acclamation." They took me to a room, fitted me with my oxygen mask, and simulated being at high altitude and losing air. I played a game of simply putting pegs into correct round or square holes. I thought I was doing it right. Come to find out on the video replay, I wasn't, and they documented at what altitude and point I began losing my faculties. They instructed me on what to do in case I did lose oxygen.

At day's end I was required to take a written exam on the contents and operation of every item in my survival vest, followed by a description of the cockpit gauges and "heads up display" and instructions on how to hook up and release all the oxygen hoses, communication lines, safety belts, bells, and whistles.

Why do I provide so much detail? Because I almost flunked the test! I nearly drowned three times! I was dizzy and exhausted, yet I continued on. Why? Of course, to find Kelly McGillis and date her until Nicole Kidman or Katie Holmes would marry me! But besides this, I surely did not hang in there because I'm tougher than other so-called VIP guests, and I certainly didn't do it for anyone else. I did it for me. How? The same way everybody makes a dream come true. I dug deep down inside myself where the answers and energy were ready and waiting: in the box.

PRE-FLIGHT DINNER

That night I had a full five-course dinner with Colonel Frazier at the officers club. I asked him if there was anything special I should eat for breakfast and he said, "Bananas."

"Why? Will I cramp up? Do I need potassium?"

"No. It's because bananas taste the same going in as they do coming back out."

The next day, January 17, I flew with Commander Bill Reuter—call sign "Roto"—on a ride to remember. (That's right. I put my life in the hands of Roto Rooter! Go figure!) It turned out that Commander Reuter had more aircraft carrier take-offs and landings than anyone else on base and was introduced to me as a true "Top Gunner"—one of the best of the best naval aviators. He even walked and smiled like Tom Cruise! Before we left the locker room to walk out on the tarmac, he taught me how to hold my helmet like a football in the crook of my elbow and how to walk in that "slow-mo" movie strut like I had sat on something hot and how and where to stand by the plane like a real fighter pilot when we met the photographers for the hero shots.

NINETY-MINUTE HIGH

After a full after-burner high-performance takeoff that took us straight up and over the bombing range in North Carolina in a blistering twenty-two minutes, the next ninety minutes were spent doing every *Top Gun* movie maneuver you could imagine. We dived, climbed, and dived again—with a vertical velocity of

10,000 feet per minute. We did ninety degree turns at 600 mph, and for one special simulated bombing run we climbed even higher to shoot straight down to pick up more speed (as if we weren't going fast enough as it was!). With my face smashed against the visor on my helmet and my stomach tangled in my nose hairs, we then climbed straight up to 55,000 feet, where we could actually begin to see the black sky and curvature of the earth. The breathtaking sight was interrupted when we went upside down again, flipped over to inside-out, flew in formation with a second aircraft we rendezvoused with, and again executed attack bombing runs on a makeshift ship at the Carolina practice range. Once there, we flew at 640 knots at only 500 feet off the ground, and then back up to the thin air at 46,000 feet, where we broke the sound barrier going 1.9 Mach (around 1200 mph—twice the speed of sound) and caught seven Gs in some of the final turns of the flight (seven Gs meaning seven times my 235-pound body weight being smashed against my face, back, chest, knee caps, legs, and toes). It felt like I had sat on a vacuum hose and somebody had grabbed my bottom lip and pulled it up over my head. This was all in a ninety-minute rock-and-roller coaster ride every mentally irregular lunatic yearns for, with the highlight being the opportunity to fly this F-18 for thirty of the ninety minutes!

Before I share what I learned, let me confess to what everyone wonders. Colonel Frasier was absolutely right about the bananas, and yes, I *egressed* (ejected) all five dinner courses from the evening before. In fact, I egressed a box of hot tamales I had eaten at a movie when I was nine! We were upside down so long that I am probably the only guy alive who has ever "thrown down!"

When we landed and I put my face back in the middle of my head where it belongs, I asked Roto to point out some details about the plane. He explained that the F-18 is a state-of-the-art, high-tech, finely tuned and designed machine that costs $50 million to build.

"Clark—call sign 'Hoss,'" he said (no one ever gets to choose their own call sign; I was large for the small cockpit and barely slid in). "The cockpit is crammed full of high-tech gauges, gadgets, switches, and screens. As you noticed, the control stick came out of the floor and was straddled between our knees. The stick only moved three inches forward, three inches left and right, and five inches backward. We needed to move the control stick only one inch in either one of those four directions, and it immediately changed the direction of the aircraft forty-five degrees.

HIGH PERFORMANCE SECRET

I then asked Roto how we flew this magnificent flying machine. His answer startled me. He flippantly said, "By feel."

Wow! We know the brain has two sides: the left cognitive/logical side and the right emotional/creative side. I find it interesting that we fly a high-tech fighter jet with the touchy feely right side of the brain. Still, even with the temporary bouts of nauseous hallucinations that are apparently normal when you're upside down going the speed of sound, I rank this as one of the greatest experiences and thrills of my life. Who would have ever thought that even in a supersonic fighter jet the answers are still in the box?

Shortly after this once-in-a-lifetime experience, I received a phone call from the Air Force. Colonel Johnny Weida, Wing Commander, asked if I would speak to all ten squadrons of the 388th Fighter Wing and Maintenance Groups at Hill Air Force Base in Utah. I obviously accepted as a way of serving my country. The question then came, "What is your speaker's fee?" Although the spins from my F-18 ride in January had just barely stopped that day, excitedly I humbly and immediately replied, "I never charge the armed services anything. Giving of my time is the least I can do. But since you insist, how about a back seat ride in an F-16?"

F-16 FIGHTING FALCON

I spoke in Hangar 37 to more than a thousand service men and women, and then I returned to the base on June 6, 2001, for my special ride. I had had serious knee surgery the week before I spoke and was on crutches for months. Anticipating another supersonic experience was pure torture because my excitement was difficult to contain. But the day finally came.

After three hours of safety, ejection, parachuting, and survival training, culminating in an incredible learning experience flying the F-16 flight simulator (the coolest and most expensive video game on the planet), I was ready for my second once-in-a-lifetime flight. A thirty-minute briefing oriented me to our flight plan, and we headed to the flight line. This was a unique childhood dream come true because we took off in formation, two F-16 fighter jets in tandem, side by side on the same narrow runway, screaming into the wild blue yonder! My pilot, Colonel Bill Coutts—call sign "Coutter"—took me on the most amazing ride one could ever imagine. With the other pilot and plane, we engaged in air-to-air combat maneuvers over the range in Nevada. We chased another F-16 and it chased us, breaking the sound barrier at Mach 1.1, catching nine Gs. We did loops and aileron rolls, and we went straight up to 18,000 feet to dive straight down, again flying over the ground at only 500 feet going 640 knots in a bombing run at a target, only to pull out of it, come around, and do it again!

BECOME THE PLANE

Ninety minutes later when we landed and were debriefed, I asked Coutter to point out some differences between the F-18 and the F-16. "Clark—call sign 'Hot Lips,'" he said (hey, I *am* a professional speaker!) "The F-16 is the ultimate in current air firepower. It is state-of-the-art, high technology at its finest. Every other fighter jet has a control stick that you straddle. The F-16, however, has a control GRIP mounted on the right side of the cockpit. It barely moves one-eighth to three-eighths of an inch in any direction. The throttle GRIP is on the left side."

As I discovered, you can't even tell you are moving either one of them. When I asked him how we flew this amazing supersonic machine, Coutter's answer intrigued me. "You become the plane. When you climbed up the ladder and slid into the cockpit, *did you strap into the F-16 or did you strap the F-16 onto you?"*

Think about this. High-performance success in flying a high-performance, high-tech fighter jet in the highest-risk, most pressure-packed environment in the world does not come from outside the lines or from utilizing resources outside the box. It comes from looking inside, trusting our training, making great choices, taking control, and staying in touch with our emotions and feelings. "Strapping it on" is the secret to increasing productivity in an organization, increasing sales, broadening customer service, and being a proactive "changer."

LEADERSHIP

At the end of the day, Colonel Weida swore me in as "Honorary Wing Commander" of the 388th Fighter Wing and taught me one of the greatest lessons in leadership, management, friendship, and winning team play I have learned thus far in my life. He said that in training as fighter pilots, one of the first and most basic rules was, "Take care of your wingman. Never leave him or forsake him. Constantly check his six o'clock to make certain no enemy is sneaking up behind him. We should always stay close and protect comrades in a fighter squadron. We should always be there for each other as friends."

When it comes to leadership, although it is customary to quote generals and colonels, I thought it would be important to get a perspective at the grass-roots level from the instructors who are actually teaching the leadership principles. As a leadership and character development consultant for the United States military, I have been a guest lecturer since 2001 to every new class of lieutenants and captains and to multiple classes of the NCO and Senior NCO Academies at Maxwell/Gunter Air Force Base—Air War University in Montgomery, Alabama.

The sometimes twisted and incorrect public perception that those who serve in the armed forces do so because they can't find work elsewhere is absurd. The majority of military officers and all of the US Air Force leaders are committed to their three core values of integrity first, service before self, and excellence in all they do and always do the right thing because it is the right thing to do. Consequently, I have developed some incredible friendships with some extraordinary leaders and educators and asked the frontline instructors my question, "What is leadership?"

The commandant of Air and Space Basic Course, Colonel Mark Ware (as of 2007), who is one of my dearest friends and in my opinion on his way to becoming a general, was asked about leadership. In the true nature of what makes him such a stand-out officer, Mark deflected the attention from himself and in the spirit of servant leadership encouraged me to interview some others. Lieutenant Colonel Robert Faulk, Commander of the 30th Student Squadron/Air and Space Basic Course, and Captain Yolanda Glenn, from Squadron Officer College/DEF, both responded.

ROBERT FAULK ON LEADERSHIP

To me leadership is three things best captured in a memory tool that I call Set3. First, a leader must set the example. I'll use a simple scenario to frame the topic. Is a leader going to be the fastest runner in his or her squadron/organization? As I look at a squadron where most of my staff and students are nearly half my age, I can tell you that I am not the fastest runner. Being the fastest runner is not the point. The point is that a leader needs to be out there running, running like it matters, running like he wants to win every time. The same concept applies to everything that a leader does, setting the example in both action and behavior.

A leader must also set the right environment. People want to work in an environment that is suitable from a creature comfort perspective, professionally challenging, and personally rewarding. The environment needs to be one where people trust their leader, are comfortable with that leader, and can discuss issues, thoughts, concerns, good ideas, bad practices, and so forth, and know that they will not be ridiculed or negatively impacted when they address something with the leader. I believe that setting the right environment is the most challenging area of Set3 construct in that there is a tremendous number of variables outside of the leader's control that generate both physical and mental stressors which can interfere with setting a good environment. It is easy to be overcome by these and lose your sight picture on keeping that open and trusting relationship between you and your people. Keeping your people in mind every step of the way will help to maintain the right environment.

Finally, a leader must set his or her people up for success. There are many opportunities to do so: awards, new jobs, one-of-a-kind opportunities, promotions, special recognition, and so forth. However, the process to set people up for success must be fair. Some people will do the minimum that is expected to successfully meet the tasks at hand to a minimum degree. Should they be rewarded for standard performance at the expense of someone who does the "heavy lifting"? No way! If you do that, you just marginalized your reward/recognition tools and lost your people's respect for you. Setting people up for success is more than awards, special recognition, and new jobs. It is about taking time to provide proper feedback (the good and the bad), mentoring them in a way that allows them to develop over the continuum of their lifetime regardless of what job duties they perform, and providing new avenues to lead (if they are ready and have earned it).

Yolanda Glenn on Effective Positive Leadership

Effective positive leadership can be summed up in two words: diversified thinking. A leader attracts and recruits diversified thinking, encourages diversified opinions and approaches to problems solving, and finds excitement and fulfillment in discovering diversified ways to accomplishing one mission.

Looking back, the industrial era way of thinking looked at the existences of organizations much like that of a machine. Leaders during this era were only concerned with what was needed to increase productivity. The bottom line was to get the product out the fastest way no matter what the costs. The entire organization was structured to have "orderly relations between clearly defined parts that have some determinate order." With this in mind, leadership viewed individuals to function like a machine—be proficient and dependable; or in other words, produce, produce, produce.

Leaders in the twenty-first century post-modern era are finding out this type of mindset will not work in today's society. As Dan Clark quotes in his book *Best or Right: Why Great Is Not Good Enough*, "Effective, positive leaders teach correct principles and expect their people to govern themselves." This is diversified thinking at its best. Remember, if two people agree on everything, it means one of them is not necessary. Like thinkers must agree on principles, core ideologies, and the "why" of the mission, but figuring out the "how to" is best accomplished through diversified thinking.

At the end of the day, effective positive leadership encourages people of diverse backgrounds and interests to come together for the sole purpose of achieving personal goals, realizing their full potential, and being part of something larger than themselves that provides fair and equitable opportunities. We have to re-think what an organization is conceptually and why it exists, for what, and for whom.

Diversity must be infused throughout the entire organization and enforced at each level. Leadership must ensure that future leaders are educated with this mindset. Organizations are taking on new faces. History has shown for many years that white males have predominantly occupied leadership positions; thus, the training and development has catered to the white male culture. But if leadership development practices reflect only the experiences and careers of white men, then women and people of color are disadvantaged. Twenty-first century organizations are no longer the visible, tangible, obvious places that they used to be. We are seeing the technology world show us how we can have multiple people in different places at the same time with video call or teleconferencing. American based companies now have manufacturing facilities and call centers in foreign countries. This is the wave of the future.

To be an effective positive leader means you embrace diversity and will make sure that every ethnic background and gender is afforded the same opportunities for advancement. You will see to it that your strategy has the elements of enforcement, education, and exposure to ensure its success and the success of everyone within your culture. And by understanding diversified thinking, you are able to gain a much deeper appreciation of "foreign practice" which allows you to truly think globally and act locally.

Shelton wrote, "Leaders are learners and curious about the world. They manage their egos, their fears and their impatience in order to achieve better results and to create stronger relationships." A leader cannot claim to know everything. He or she must maintain an open mind, and be willing to try new and different ideas, which foster not only innovation but creativity as well. Leadership is a lifelong learning process, which takes a commitment of both time and effort. Hesselbein added, "Most of us prefer to walk backward into the future, a posture which may be uncomfortable but which at least allows us to keep on looking at familiar things as long as we can." All in all, effective positive leadership is subscribing to diversified thinking, not as a follower, but as leader. As a t-shirt slogan reads, "If you run in the back of the pack the view is constantly the same."

JOB

Many employees, when asked about work, say they hate their jobs. They only look forward to Friday, not Monday. They complain that their job is boring. Where did they get this mediocre idea that it is their job's responsibility to make them feel rewarded, fulfilled, and accomplished? Don't they also have it backward?

When we say, "It's boring," we are admitting that *we* are boring! We are saying to our friends, family, and co-workers, "I have no passion, imagination, or creativity and I'm lazy. It's the world's responsibility to entertain me. It's my world and everything revolves around me!" Hardly. The only thing we are not in charge of is whether we are in charge.

SELLING NEEDS AND BENEFITS IS OBSOLETE

I realize the gurus have preached "need-satisfaction selling" and "benefits-based strategies" as the gospel of transactions, but they have run their course. Becoming a sales champion in any field isn't about programs of persuasion, and it requires little emphasis on the memorizing of a script. Closing any sale comes as a result of absolute product knowledge, total honesty, and integrity, coupled with a phenomenal customer-service reputation that backs up every purchase. Sounds like the answers are part of an inside-the-box process to me!

Experts teach us that no one can sell anything to anybody. Neither can anyone teach anything to anybody. We can learn and will learn—we can buy and will buy—but only when we decide. As the saying goes, "Only when the student is ready will the teacher appear." For these reasons, becoming a national or company sales champion requires that we get inside the customers' head and heart and fully understand their perspective, not our own.

The seller's perception (misconception) of why a consumer buys includes need, emotion, and the desire to improve, keep up, feel better, or solve a problem. However, consumer reports reveal that the customer's actual reasons for buying come from feeling anxious, frustrated, confused, stupid, fearful, and hopeful. Notice that the seller's perception of buying because of a problem and the customer's reality of buying out of hope are opposites. The bottom line is that customers will not buy until they feel average, stale, stagnant, inadequate, dissatisfied, or sick and tired of being sick and tired.

Apparently it's true that the dog won't move off the nail he is sitting on until the nail starts to hurt enough. Too many sales professionals think they are in the "relationship-management business" and want to be referred to as "advisers." Others think they are in the people-building business and only compliment and find the positive in an organization. Regardless, in both of these capacities, it is virtually impossible to identify enough pain to get the customer to want to buy or make a change. For this reason, sales champions and top-of-the-table performers position themselves as experts in the problem-solving business by spending their time helping customers identify their inadequacies and feeling their pain so that they may follow up with solutions to give them hope and help fix what is broken.

Yes, when you take the inside-out approach, you position yourself as a person who is genuinely interested in your customer's business and emerge as *the* "problem solver" they've been looking for. In this scenario, how can money ever become the issue? In any relationship and presentation, the salesperson is the only one who can make price a determining factor in closing the deal.

EDUCATION

In our schools, too often we test students and then jump to labeling conclusions, pigeonholing certain students as "learning disabled" or as having one of the dreaded acronyms such as ADD—Attention Deficit Disorder. It seems that if students don't understand the teacher, it's the students' fault. It seems that it's easier to change the students than it is to change the teacher or teaching method.

That isn't true. Most struggling students don't have a learning disability; they have a learning difference. Surely amidst all the legitimate cases of student learning disabilities, there are an equal and proportionate number of cases of educators with teaching disabilities. The only difference between an amazing teacher who touches kids' lives and makes a meaningful difference and a boring, ineffective, so-called teacher who isn't really teaching anything is passion, imagination, and creativity.

As a society, our lack of ability to make our dreams come true is the direct consequence of subscribing to the previously mentioned ridiculous cliché: "You've got to think outside the lines and get outside the box." We all know that happiness is not found outside of ourselves. Nor can we get results by focusing on results.

YOUNG PEOPLE

Whenever we talk of simple steps and an easy philosophical solution, some young people equate this with taking a shortcut. It's the old classroom conversation:

"How close are you to the answer?"

"About two seats away."

Young people, as well as old people, need to remember that even though the right answers are found inside the box, it doesn't mean they come quickly. It takes nature twenty years to make a strong, mighty oak tree but only two months to make a squash. What do you want to be?

Many young people are down on their neighborhoods and towns. When asked if they liked where they lived, they usually responded, "No." When asked why not, they answered, "There is nothing to do. It's boring." Where did we get the convoluted idea that it is our community's responsibility to make our lives exciting? Don't we have it bass-ackwards?

Every successful, famous, and powerful person I know grew up in somebody's neighborhood and went to somebody's high school. And some of them came from the toughest areas, poorest poverty, and most dysfunctional families in the world. They understood that it's not what happens to us but what we do with what happens to us that makes the difference. If success can happen to them, it can happen to you and me.

LOOK HARD BEFORE YOU LEAVE

In the mid-1800s, there was a gold rush in America. One man got so excited that he sold his ranch in northern California to move to southern California where he heard all the action was. He sold his property to a former army colonel and never went back. The colonel put a mill on the stream that ran through his land, and one day his little girl brought home a jar of sand from the river bed. As he sifted through it, he found some beautiful, shiny nuggets.

The man who had previously owned the ranch wanted gold. If he had stayed on his land, he could have secured all he ever dreamed of. Since that day, 38 million dollars worth of gold has been taken out of the property he sold—a stark reminder to all of us that we should always look before we go.

ONE AT A TIME

It took Michelangelo twelve years, one brush stroke at a time, to paint the ceiling of the Sistine Chapel. It took Brahms twenty years, one note at a time, to compose his first symphony. It took Sir Edmond Hillary eight days, one step at a time, to climb the 29,000 feet of Mount Everest! Stroke by stroke, note by note, step by step, line upon line, precept upon precept—this is the secret to success for all of us, especially for the young, invincible, and brave at heart!

It's not the size of the dog in the fight but rather the size of the fight in the dog that determines who rules the kennel. It's not the size of the town but rather the size of the dream that holds us back or keeps us going!

To succeed and win, we must focus and finish. Focus to *W-I-N* represents *W*hat's *I*mportant *N*ow. Then we *finish* that right now to focus on the next right now—on each and every play, one play at a time, until we finish the game. Our coaches and parents were right when they taught us, "If it's worth starting, it's worth finishing because anything worth doing is worth doing right!"

Fundamental 3

FOCUS ON PURPOSE, NOT JUST GOALS
(Dan's Own Story)

Our deepest fear is not that we are inadequate. Our deepest fear is that we are powerful beyond measure. It is our light, not our darkness that frightens us. We ask ourselves, who am I to be brilliant, gorgeous, talented and fabulous? Actually, who are we not to be? Your playing small doesn't serve the world. There's nothing enlightened about shrinking so that other people won't feel insecure around you. We were born to make manifest the glory of our creator that is within us. It's not just in some of us, it's in everyone. And as we let our own light shine, we unconsciously give other people permission to do the same. As we are liberated from our own fears, our presence automatically liberates others.

—Marianne Williamson
(as quoted by Nelson Mandela in his inaugural speech)

It's true. The answers are in the box; success comes from the inside out; what you need to succeed is already within you and your organization; the key to success is in what you possess. But people don't remember facts and figures. We remember the interpretation of the facts and figures. We want to know why and how someone was able to connect the right answers to the right questions and if we could do it too. We want to be inspired by the wisdom-filled lessons others have learned through their thrills of victory and agonies of defeat. What we want is to hear their "stories."

Everybody has a story. Mine runs parallel with how silver is cast into art. As a precious metal the silver is heated up, but because each vat of the molten metal responds differently to the same temperature, the artist has but one technique to know when the liquid is ready to be poured into a beautiful shape. Only when the artist can see his face reflecting back at him from the silver is it ready to be molded into something more.

My life is similar, in that whenever I have felt the "heat" or have been put to a test to see what I am made of, only when I've looked myself square in the eye with the proverbial "man-in-the-mirror" reflecting back at me, have I been ready to mold and shape the man I am into the *something-more-man* I need to be. In fact, it was a single experience that really forced me to get in touch with my emotions and what I believed in. Through it I discovered you have to stop and ask the important questions. That's what a midlife crisis is. You realize you're not the guy you thought you were going to be. It's someone finally stopping to evaluate his life. Most have their midlife crisis at forty. I had mine at twenty-two!

PERFORMANCE PAST

I'm a storyteller, and we all agree that no one should make himself the hero of his own story. How self-centered and ego-tistical. But because I am a professional speaker, my audiences want to know what gives me the right to speak on my topics and why they should listen. Quite the dilemma until I think of a former coach's words: "If it's true it's not bragging." Consequently, I present this up-close-and-personal glimpse into some of the char-acter-building experiences I've had in my life in the hope that you will trust me to inspire your life.

As a public speaker, I've come to realize that people don't relate to my perfections if I even have any. They relate to my imperfections. They want to know if I've ever failed and what I did about it. I wish I could tell you about the weekly televi-sion series called *47 Happiness Way* that I was in for a year as a twelve-year- old actor. I also want to tell you about being the voice of an animated character in the weekly cartoon *Dean*, but this experience wouldn't have the lasting impact we're both looking for. In sports we learn more from our defeats than we do from our victories, so for this chapter I choose to uncover the success principles in the same way.

For a quick summary, I have broken my neck, nose, and jaw; had my head sewn up eleven times and had two hernias; broken both hands, thumbs, little fingers, left wrist, and right arm; blown out patella tendons in both knees; torn cartilage repaired in seven surgeries on both knees; broken my right shoulder, requiring a three-inch titanium screw; and snapped my left Achilles tendon. In addition, five of my toughest ordeals include: (1) battling a cancer abscess in my throat at eight years of age that hospitalized me for weeks and nearly destroyed my vocal chords; (2) getting hit in the face at age twelve with a baseball pitch that resulted in root canals in my front teeth; (3) severely sunburning my feet on a waterskiing trip so that the swelling and oozing blisters kept me from walking for three days until I had to painfully cram them into my cleats so I wouldn't miss the first day of two-a-day football practices; (4) burning my body so badly on the first day of a three-day white-water rafting trip that my only option for getting relief was to tie a rope around my waist to anchor me to the shore and lay in the cold Snake River all night until the next day when I had to get back in my canoe and paddle for miles to the next evening's campsite to repeat the ordeal again; and (5) winning an inexpensive trophy.

WINNING A CHEAP PLASTIC TROPHY?

The short version of the story is that I played high school basketball for two years, and going into my last year I was told by my coach that I wasn't good enough to make next year's team. To prove him wrong, I signed up for three different summer basketball camps to improve my skills and increase my chances of making the squad. At registration of the final and most intense camp, there was a twelve-inch tall white cylinder trophy displayed next to a poster soliciting competitors to sign up for the one-on-one tournament at the end of the week. Then and there I committed to win that trophy as it would symbolize the extra effort and newly developed skill I was putting in to again make the team.

At the end of the final day of camp, the tournament brackets were posted, and luckily one of the best players in the state who had been there all week was nowhere to be found. The format was to win two out of three games, winning by two points. I lost every first game but fought my way back to win the next two games to advance round by round and eventually win the tournament. The professional players conducting the camp had a big awards ceremony and presented me with the trophy.

As I sat down, took off my sneakers, and peeled off my soaking socks to reveal huge blood blisters that had popped on my toes, my pain was circumvented by the deep joy and satisfaction I felt looking at my trophy. I did it! I set my sights and did that which was necessary to succeed. Suddenly, through the doors strutted Ricky Bordeaux, the missing superstar. He whispered to the camp director who immediately announced that it wasn't Ricky's fault that he was late and that he felt it only fair that he make me give the trophy back and play Bordeaux for the official one-on-one title.

I had to pull my soggy socks back onto my stinging feet and squeeze them back into my shoes, which I had to tie extra tight to minimize them from rubbing on my open sores. Yes, I lost the first game but scrambled from behind in back-to-back games to beat Bordeaux and win back my trophy! It probably only cost ten dollars, but if my house was on fire it would be one of the things I would save as a prized possession. It is a symbol that no matter what, I can if I think I can.

Can you see why I know without a shadow of a doubt that in life there are no mistakes, only lessons—that it's more than cliché to say it's not what happens to us but what we do with what happens that matters? Anyone at anytime in any situation can get back up and go again. If we're not failing a few times, we're not pushing ourselves hard enough.

On this foundation, let me share the one previously promised story that transformed me forever and took me down a path that I travel still today. We professional speakers call it a "signature story." It is the one experience that quickened my understanding of the law of the harvest—plant seeds, know them by their fruits, and reap only what we sow—and the single event that revealed to me the difference between best and right.

MY SIGNATURE STORY

As a high school athlete I heard from UCLA, Oregon, Colorado, Nebraska, Boise State, Utah State, Arizona State, Washington, BYU, and Oklahoma, who recruited me out of high school. I chose to follow a girl to the University of Utah. I thought I was in love. I accepted a full-ride, four-year scholarship to play football and baseball. That summer I had an invitation to try out with the Kansas City Royals Major League baseball team as a pitcher and had an invitation slot on the Hyannis Mets summer baseball team (usually reserved for college players) in the prestigious Cape Cod League in New England.

A few days after I signed my letter of intent, binding me to be a University of Utah Runnin' Ute, my girlfriend and I broke up. We almost got back together, and I blew off my big-time opportunity for summer baseball to try and make sense of everything. It didn't work, so I went south with my buddies to work until football started. Heartbroken, I learned two positive things: (1) On a sarcastic note, we need to take care of the person who is going to be at our funeral for sure, and then worry about packing the mortuary later on! (As in the airline pre-flight safety demonstration where we are told to put on our own oxygen mask before we assist another with theirs); (2) Utah is an amazing place to live because of the mountains, lakes, and streams—the fishing and skiing are great. The people are extraordinary and are family- and community-oriented. The University of Utah is a beautiful campus, and the school is one of the best academic and athletic NCAA Division One institutions in the country.

When I graduated from high school, I was six-foot-three inches, 172 pounds. I was so skinny I had to jump around in the shower to get wet! I raced motorcycles and won on the Intermountain Moto-Cross circuit and was a Golden Gloves boxing champ. I ran in three track meets on days we didn't have baseball games and beat the state 100-yard dash champion with a time of 9.9 seconds. As I mentioned, I again made the team and played point guard on our number-one ranked basketball team, and after I struggled through the ordeal of my painful sunburned feet, I was the only eleventh grade junior that year who made the team and started on our all-senior, number-one ranked football team, making the Sunkist All-America Team with ten interceptions in eight games as a defensive cornerback.

After graduation, my metabolism slowed down, and hard work paid off—during the next year I grew an inch, gained thirty pounds, and kept my 4.4 forty yard dash speed. I played receiver as a freshman and set a record, catching fourteen passes in a freshman game against rival BYU. I was moved to strong safety during spring ball, which was where I really wanted to play, but the day before practice started, I tore the ligaments in my left ankle playing in a pick up basketball game. It was put in a cast for six weeks, but after the defensive back coach called me a "whimp," I cut it off after the first two weeks, trying to play with just a good tape job. As hard as I tried, the ankle was too unstable, and the angry doctor re-cast it. This same coach made it known that he had given up on me, told me I would never play for him, and passed me off to the linebacker/defensive line coach as my last chance to make the team. Luckily the following summer I grew another inch, and through an outstanding weight lifting program, I gained another forty pounds while maintaining my forty-yard dash speed at 4.6. Starting out at third string on the depth chart, I worked harder than I had ever worked in my life and proudly became the starting defensive end that season as a sophomore. As a big, fast, intense guy out to prove my old defensive back coach wrong, I always showed up at the line of scrimmage in a real bad mood!

God bless Coach Vince Zimmer for believing in me when

others wouldn't. He has since passed away of cancer, and I will be forever grateful to him for pushing, screaming, disciplining, teaching, expecting, intimidating, pulling, and loving me into becoming more of who I already was! In my last year at the U of U, I was projected as an NFL number-one draft choice, confirmed in a letter from personnel director Ron Wolf from the 1980–81 Super Bowl Champion Oakland Raiders. I was the biggest (250 pounds), the fastest (4.6 forty-yard dash), and the strongest (bench pressing more than 400 pounds) that I had ever been. Then it happened.

Paralyzing Injury

My injury occurred on my first day of practice, when my lifelong dream of playing both professional football and baseball were alive and well. We were running a tackling drill, and two of us ran into each other at full speed. From fifteen yards apart my teammate's helmet violently hit my neck and right shoulder, momentarily knocking me unconscious. When Lyle got off of me and I came to, my eye drooped, my right side was numb, I couldn't talk, and my arm dangled helplessly at my side.

According to a physician, my eye and slurred speech resulted from a severe blow to the head resulting in a concussion where the blood vessels in my brain were stretched and cranial nerves may have been damaged. I suffered some memory loss, but my sight and speech returned to normal within minutes. However, I also cracked my seventh cervical vertebrae (which doctors didn't discover for a long time because I remained at practice, watching the rest of the drills) and severed the auxiliary nerve in my right deltoid, which left my shoulder function useless. All this in one hit, in one moment in time.

The pain was so weird and devastating that the only way I can describe it is that I felt like I had hit my crazy bone in my elbow, except that the intense burning and tingling ripped through my entire right side from my head to my toes. On a humorous note, as I lay there on the turf, Coach Halsey held up three fingers and asked me how many I saw. A fellow player interrupted, "C'mon coach, he doesn't know that!" A doctor on the field examined me and told the coach that he thought I had nerve damage, maybe even brain damage. Coach replied, "How will we ever know?" Everybody obviously laughed, which wasn't making light of my injury but rather serving as a natural painkiller that would end up being one of my greatest rehab tools—humor.

I handled the day okay, but unbearable pain hit me that night in bed. I shook and sweated and threw up, crying myself to sleep in a pool of self-pity and denial. The details are mostly irrelevant, so let me simply connect the dots. Sometimes it takes months or years for a concussion to heal. Add to that my complications. I spent time with Oakland Raiders physician Dr. Frank Jobe, the world-famous orthopedic genius, at Centinella Hospital in Inglewood, California. He treated patients from all over the world and had performed reconstructive surgery on Los Angeles Dodger pitcher Tommy Johns. (The surgery is clinically called "UCL"—Ulnar Collateral Ligament reconstruction, named after Johns, whose 1974 surgery was the first to be successful.) I also underwent tests and therapy at Craig Rehabilitation Center in Denver, Colorado. I remained numb for more than a year and went to sixteen doctors, fifteen of who projected that my arm would always dangle at my side and I would never get any better. After several EMGs and hours of ineffective physical therapy, confusion caused by one doctor putting me in an "airplane splint" with my arm braced in an up and outward immobilized position, and getting "another opinion" two weeks later that said retarding the movement on my right side was the worst thing I could do, I hit rock bottom and fell into what I thought was deep depression.

OUT-OF-SIGHT PAIN

The injury affected my whole life. I was an athlete and got a lot of attention because of it. I was somebody because I played football and baseball and enjoyed free food at restaurants, status at celebrity galas, fame, and glory. I was going to be an overpaid NFL superstar. But in a single moment, a freak accident took away my identity. Suddenly I was nobody to my coaches and nobody to my teammates and fans. Even more devastating, I became nobody to myself.

Have you ever lost your identity or at some point seriously questioned who you really are? Before you can like or love someone else, you first must like and love yourself. To like and love requires that you know and understand. I was lost, lonely, and confused.

I couldn't write—I was right-handed. I couldn't concentrate on work or education because it constantly felt like some wild animal was biting my neck and shoulder.

I used to get shocking nerve impulses in my shoulder that would shake my arm like it was plugged into a light socket. I was sitting with my family at dinner one evening when my arm flipped out and knocked a bowl of mayonnaise off the table. The next morning my younger brother showed up to breakfast wearing goggles and a batting helmet! I was afraid to go out in public, especially on a date, because my arm might blast her in the chops. I hit rock bottom, and life as I knew it was nowhere to be found. I didn't know if I even wanted to live. Have you ever felt like that? Have you ever been so down and confused that you thought you should leave your family, isolate yourself from friends, and contemplate checking-out altogether?

THE RIGHT QUESTIONS

Two Questions: Why would I want to give up and quit everything? Why didn't I quit?

I wanted to quit because I confused who I was with what I did. A lot of us do! I spoke to the fifty-one contestants of the Miss USA pageant in 1993. Tough assignment, eh? What was my message? I shared a tear-jerking experience about a young boy named Bopsy who was a Make-a-Wish kid battling leukemia. Among other things he had lost his hair in treatment and died after his wish of being a firefighter came true. Part of my message to these extraordinary women was, "You are not your body, your clothes, or your car. Is having a bad hair day really that big of a deal? Who are you without makeup, fame, and glory? What are you doing with your platform to promote the good, clean, pure, powerful, and positive? You have dreams for sale!"

On another occasion in 1988, I was flown to Kenosha, Wisconsin, to speak to former employees and their families one week after they slashed the payroll from 5500 down to 1000 workers at the Chrysler plant. Forty-five hundred men and women were out of work in one day. My message? "You are not your job or your house. Who are you? Who you are goes with you to get retrained and land another job."

Over the years, I've conducted half-day leadership retreats for the Dallas Cowboys cheerleaders at the famous "Dallas" South Fork Ranch in Plano, Texas. Many of my buddies asked what my message was. I don't remember! Actually, after I hyperventilated, I asked each cheerleader what she was going to do with her platform, fame, and influence. There are thirty-three of them, and they cheer on more than football players. As intelligent, beautiful (inside and out) mothers, teachers, models, neighbors, and friends, they too have dreams for sale. I inspired them to use their celebrity on behalf of underprivileged and neglected children, battered and abused women, literacy, adolescent obesity, and other important causes; to become more of who they already are because cheerleading only lasts a few years for most of them, but the difference they can make can last a lifetime! Their director, Kelli McGonagill, is a former Cowboys cheerleader, and truly understands their broad mission. She's a friend—beautiful both inside and out!

QUIT?

The direct answer to question number one—"Why did I want to give up and quit everything in life?"—was because I thought football and baseball were who I was. I had not realized that sports were only what I did, not who I was as a man. And as I've already stated, when we identify ourselves in terms of what we do instead of who we are, we become human doings instead of human beings. That is unacceptable if real success and lasting happiness are truly what we seek.

I learned these steps the hard way. I was pushed (actually, hit in practice). In one moment, I was faced with the emotional pain of giving up my life's dream and the identity I had grown up with. Outside, I was an athlete. Inside, I knew it was time to find a new game.

DON'T QUIT

Question number two—"Why didn't I quit?"—requires a longer answer. What allowed me to stay focused for a year of rehab, hard work, and endurance until I recovered was a combination of outside-in influence and inside-out resolve.

First, I had a doctor—the sixteenth specialist—who told me if I worked hard I could recover and get well. His name was Dr. Brent Pratley, and he was an extraordinary orthopedic surgeon who was on the cutting edge of technology and techniques, who made me laugh and hope, and who brought out my passion and imagination to do whatever I could think of that would help me get better.

Second, I had a small nucleus of great, positive friends who reminded me, "You can't quit—it's a league rule." They demonstrated that a best friend is someone who brings out the best in you. They made me laugh, didn't let me whine or feel sorry for myself, and constantly reminded me not to let what I could not do interfere with what I could do.

Third, another hero, Vice President Normand Gibbons of the University of Utah, gave me a tape to listen to. The recording was by an internationally renowned motivational teacher named Zig Ziglar. I had never heard of him and thought, "Whoa, his mom ran out of names!" Out of curiosity I listened to his forty-five-minute speech. His moving, entertaining message kick started my inside-out recovery. He eventually became a personal friend and my sponsor into the National Speakers Association in 1982.

When you break your leg, everyone can see it, wants to help, and comes to your rescue. But when you break your heart and shatter your dreams, no one sees your hurt, and everyone thinks you should just get over it. Countless people who I know had sincere intentions would come up to me and say, "I'm sorry, I know what you're going through." And I used to think, "No you don't. How could you? You don't have a clue! Let me rip your dominant arm off, bite your neck 24/7, rob you of your lifelong dream, and take away your personal identity so you can *really* see how it feels!"

Fourth, I was introduced to a six-foot-five, strong, sensitive, deeply spiritual Maori woman from New Zealand who took me in as one of her reflexology patients. Three times a week, for an hour each time, passionate and in-tune, Ellie deeply massaged my hands, feet, and paralyzed right side and shoulder. With surgical precision, she pushed and dug into the pressure points in my neck, shoulders, back, and head. Oh, baby, it hurt so good!

On an off-day from Ellie, I also went to a cutting-edge chiropractor who did so much more than the proverbial "crack" my back. For the record, I cannot say exactly what happened to me physiologically, but I can guarantee that my body did not respond to physical therapy or the suggestions from neurologists and orthopedic doctors until I had started holistic medicine; vitamin, mineral, and herbal remedies; reflexology; and advanced chiropractic treatments. Dr. Craig Buhler, in Kaysville, Utah, is definitely one of the greatest chiropractors in the world.

I did not start to recover until I integrated allopathic medicine with the natural approach to healing. I absolutely love and respect medical doctors. But with all due respect, although my orthopedic and neurosurgeon specialists have performed amazing surgeries on my broken body many times over the years, their talented and extraordinary work and prescribed medications did not heal me. They were the catalysts, but in reality, our bodies have to heal themselves. Being around practitioners of holistic medicine got me thinking about misconceptions surrounding depression and the remedy within me.

Remember that I said I "thought" I was depressed. This is extremely important to my general message: You can be *best* and transform into *right*. You can improve and become more of who you already are. The answers really are still in the box and don't change. "I'm depressed" leads to giving up in despair.

DEPRESSION VS. DISAPPOINTMENT AND DISCOURAGEMENT

Getting better mentally and emotionally was a prerequisite to recovering physically, and my improvement began when I realized there is a huge difference between depression and disappointment—a huge difference between being depressed and being discouraged. I mentioned this earlier, so let me clarify and deepen your understanding.

Yes, some people require medical help and medication for clinical depression, but most of us are not really depressed. We are only disappointed and discouraged, which we can deal with if we decide to embrace the fact that it's not what happens to us but what we do with what happens to us. *You can if you think you can* is much more than a cliché, and *If it is to be it is up to me* is more than just ten two-letter words. With compassionate, positive help from professionals, family, and friends, we can get back up and go again and again and again. It's amazing that when our attitude is right, our abilities will always catch up. Eleven-year-old pioneer hero James Kirkwood who I told you about in chapter one comes to mind.

I started getting better physically *and* emotionally only when I started focusing on purposes instead of just setting goals. (Remember this when I revisit it in a few paragraphs). I stopped focusing on having fame and started focusing on being whole. I discovered that in order to get a better answer, you've got to ask a better question, and the question I asked of each of the sixteen doctors—"How do I get better?"—was not the right question. *How* brings an outside-the-box answer. The better question was not to the doctors, but to myself: "*Why* get better?" This question generated an inside-the-box answer that took me beyond and through my pain to conclude: "Whatever it takes, I will endure to the end because this is what I am going to do *when* I get better." Although I had not heard Churchill's rallying cry during World War II, I knew his words were true. They are worth repeating again: "It is not enough to say I will do my best. We must do that which is necessary to succeed."

FOCUS ON PURPOSES, NOT JUST GOALS

Focusing on how to get better set me up for failure because each doctor had a different theory, and the pain was so excruciating that quitting before fully recovering would have been easy and reasonable. Without sounding too dramatic, when I was injured, confused, and feeling alone in the dark, I discovered that it takes courage to leap into an abyss, whether for the thrill of adventure or to move from a situation that no longer works. It's easier to hesitate, holding on to the familiar out of fear of the unknown. In the process we cling to people, positions, and possessions that are no longer sustaining. We seek a renaissance of spirit, a return to understanding that *being* is more important than *having,* and yet we lose our vitality by resisting the very steps that could help us create a dynamic and fulfilling life. Knowing *how* to get better wasn't near enough information for me to recover.

TIMELY INSPIRATION

Being afflicted for twelve months, it took me another year, one day at a time and one self-invented therapy session at a time to fight my way back from physical and emotional paralysis. All the while, I continually received chiropractic treatments, reflexology, and deep-tissue massage. I also listened to my Zig Ziglar tape.

In his rhythmic southern drawl, Zig spoke directly to me through one specific story: "A struggling oilman in Texas, in his last ditch effort to strike it rich, drilled one more time and hit a giant oil reserve so big that it gushed from the ground with such force that it literally destroyed the derrick. In an instant, the man became a millionaire. Or did he? Had not the oil always been down there? He had always been a millionaire but just didn't know it. All he had to do was dig down deeper and get out what was already there and use it for what it was meant to be used."

Can you see why this one tale meant so much to me? It pierced my mind and heart to look inside myself and hang tough long enough to drill down deep enough to discover the untapped reserve of passion, purpose, and perseverance that was stuck beneath my surface just waiting to be used.

When my friends took me to a karate tournament to give me a break from therapy, I was reminded that there is no coincidence. When a black belt attempts to break a board with his hand by focusing on the board, his hand hits and bounces back, resulting in a cut or bruise. But when he focuses beyond the board and looks through the wood, determined to make contact with whatever is on the other side of the obstacle, the board becomes a non-factor, and his hand crashes through it.

And in a third non-coincidental, I was given a book written by Captain Gerald Coffee, a POW during the Vietnam War who has become a dear friend. Captain Coffee is an extraordinary man who was shot down in Vietnam, captured, and tortured beyond belief, spending seven years locked up in solitary confinement as a prisoner of war. In his powerful and unforgettable book, *Beyond Survival,* he explains that the only thing that kept him going and gave him strength to stay true to his values and commitment to the American flag, the only thing that strengthened him to not cave into the demands of the communist North Vietnamese and admit for their propaganda that the United States was criminal and unjust in being there, was who he was going to see and what he was going to do when he finally regained his freedom. In his book he calls this motivation "faith in God, faith in country, faith in family, and faith in self."

While reading Coffee's *Beyond Survival,* I also became aware of Senator John McCain from Arizona who also epitomizes this principle of focus on purposes instead of just setting goals. He too was shot down over Vietnam. McCain's father at the time was a US Navy admiral commanding the Pacific Fleet. When the North Vietnamese found this out, they released McCain for propaganda and political purposes. However, by keeping the big picture in mind—focusing on the *purpose* of America's involvement in the war (stopping the spread of communism) and the *purpose* of building morale and strengthening his fellow prisoners—McCain told the North Vietnamese government to "bite the wall" and refused to be released.

By staying in prison with his fellow American servicemen, McCain not only fired up his comrades but also infuriated the Viet Cong. The goal was to be free, but he knew it was better to be respected and at peace with himself for a lifetime than merely popular with others and excited for the moment.

Vietnam Heroes

I recently returned from a nine-day humanitarian medical mission with Operation Smile to Vietnam, where I spent one full day in Hanoi. Because of my friendship and respect for extraordinary American heroes like Coffee and McCain, I visited the famous hellhole called the Hanoi Hilton (Hoa Lo Prison). On display in a glass case were the flight suit, helmet, and boots McCain was wearing when he was shot down and captured. As my communist guide took me to the "Museum of American Atrocities" (a small lake still filled with the wreckage of a B-52 bomber), and then to the lake that McCain parachuted into, I was proud. McCain, Coffee, and other POWs like General Robbie Risner and Charlie Plumb (whom I have gotten to know and admire), represented then and still represent today everything that makes America great and strong!

Quiet Reasons for a 95-Percent Recovery

No, I haven't forgotten the question we are addressing here: "Why didn't I give up and quit my rehab program when it became so drawn out?" I am simply giving you the abridged version to this most private battle of my life, and it is more involved than just saying, "Hard work and attitude."

Later in the book you will hear a little bit about my two-week experience in southwest Asia (Iraq and Afghanistan) speaking on twelve bases and on an aircraft carrier to thousands of airmen, soldiers, sailors, and Marines—some deployed for up to a year! One of the major things that kept them fired up and strong away from their families was their focus on improving themselves through physical fitness and weight training, as well as through continuing education classes, which allowed them to get a degree or advanced education while away from home. Every serviceman and servicewoman I met was developing greater spiritual awareness and emotional strength—their efforts fueled and motivated by the thoughts and dreams of who they would see and what they would do *when* they got back home.

I could certainly relate! Although I had my family and friends' full support when I got hurt playing ball, one of the things that fired me up and gave me focus beyond my pain and discouragement was a letter from Al Davis, the owner and managing partner of the Oakland Raiders. He is controversial in his recruiting and team-building philosophy, but he is compassionate. To this day, Mr. Davis remains one of my heroes.

His letter to me simply acknowledged that he knew who I was, complimented me on my talent, expressed sadness that I was an "All-American in plaster," and assured me that if I got better I would get a shot at becoming the player my coaches and teammates had expected I would be. He didn't have to do this, but he did. His letter turned out to be a moment of truth—a life-altering event at a critical time that taught me the power of purpose. My life, my direction, and my sense of self-worth changed because of this one man and one letter. Everyday I worked my guts out trying to come back and play at my previous level. I never won my starting job back because the coaches were afraid I would be permanently paralyzed if I got hit that hard again, but I feel good that I gained the respect of my teammates, coaches, and fans for giving it all I had.

SIGNIFICANT EMOTIONAL EXPERIENCE

My football injury and subsequent recovery are what clinical psychologists call a "SEE"—Significant Emotional Experience.

My dad's death was also one of them. A "SEE" is an event in your life that is measurable in terms of before and after it happens. You can quantify, identify, and label exactly how you thought and behaved before it occurred, and because it affected you so deeply, you now know exactly how you think and behave differently. My paralyzing football injury (both physically and emotionally) gave me a sense of urgency that I had never felt before and made me aware of opportunities, places, and things. Since this experience, I now pause, ponder, ask, and answer the same two questions in every situation, in every aspect of my personal and professional life: "Why quit?" "Why not quit?" My dad's death gave me the same sense of urgency but in regards to people and time. Since these two events I always wake up early, stay up late, never go to bed angry, read one book a week, visit one museum or monument on every trip, give one book away at every convention, call a friend and a loved one before every flight (just in case my number's called!), and phone my sweet widowed mother every day. I always "make" time when there seems to be no time to live a lifetime every day, and I leave no regrets.

Over a two-year period, I learned that you need every shattered piece in order to mend a broken heart. By healing emotionally first, I fought back physically, mentally, and spiritually to a recovery rate of 95 percent. All the feeling returned to my right side except in my right shoulder, and a small part of my right leg remained totally numb. The nerves never regenerated. We must have nerve impulse and action to keep a muscle strong or else, as in my case, it atrophies.

I went to the Raiders' training camp, but I never made my dream of becoming an NFL superstar come true. But because of my career as a professional speaker and my studies to become an expert in managing change, building winning teams, and taking personal and organizational productivity to the next level, I have stayed involved in the NFL. I have also branched out into the NCAA, NBA, and the PGA, working with teams and individual players on personal leadership that makes each of them an important ingredient in creating a winning organization. If you want to read more about my experiences and deeper philosophies, go to my website: danclarkspeak.com

I realize that listing my accomplishments is actually a pretty lame thing to do because it makes me appear to be arrogant and pompous, but I am proud of my recovery—especially when I was living in quiet desperation and managed to work my way out of it. I have lived a lifetime every day and have been given extraordinary opportunities to experience and share. But the reason I bring this up is to emphasize that all this happened—New York Times bestselling author, speaking at the United Nations World Congress, visiting with the troops in Iraq and Afghanistan, running the Olympic torch in the 2002 Olympic Winter Games, and so forth because I was injured playing football! No injury, no speaking engagements. No injury, no books (especially this one!). No injury, no reason to capture the complete essence of life, liberty, and my constant opportunity to pursue happiness. No injury, no understanding of the following truths:

- It's not what happens to us but how we find the opportunity in change and what we do with that opportunity.
- There are no problems, only challenges; no mistakes, only lessons.
- Adversity introduces us to ourselves.
- Crisis does not make or break the man or woman; it just reveals the true character within.
- No one can know how good we can become until we are tested.
- We need "Transition Experiences" in our lives. Not heart-aching, body-breaking tragedies like I experienced that we know as the previously labeled Significant and Emotional, but testing, taxing, stretching, soul-searching "wilderness" experiences that force us to look at the "man in the mirror" and allow the person we are to come face-to-face with the person we might have been.

Other speakers often ask me why exciting and amazing things like I experience never happen to them. The answer is simply that they don't make a conscious effort to seek them out and proactively put themselves in unique situations where they can take it to the limit, live on the edge, and take a spectacular calculated risk to reap an extraordinary, one-of-kind reward. Of course I did not seek my injury and it devastated me. But it did wake me up to the fact that if I got the chance to live my life over again, I would definitely want and need a similar experience to my football injury in order to learn that it's not what happens to you but what you do with what happens to you that makes or breaks you. Knowing there are no mistakes, only lessons, allows me to never fear the consequences of any endeavor as long as I do the right thing simply because it's the right thing to do! I challenge you to go for it and guarantee you will be different if you do or don't! Think about the deep meaning and long-term ramifications of this statement: Agency is never free. There is always a consequence to every thought and action, and in-action.

Now you know why I think the way I think and use the box metaphor to structure my speeches. I came back from my physical and emotional injuries because of what I already had inside of me. The answers were in my box of existing experiences and life lessons I had already learned but had forgotten. I leave you with one of my all-time favorite quotes by one of my all-time favorite philosophers, James E. Talmage:

"Promise yourself today to be strong, that nothing can disturb your peace of mind; to make friends feel there is something inside of them. Look on the bright side of everything and make your dreams come true; to think the best, to forget the mistakes of the past, and to press on to better things; to give so much time improving yourself that you don't have time to criticize others, to be too large for worries, too noble for anger, too strong for fear, too happy to permit the presence of trouble; to think well of yourself and to proclaim this force to the world—not in loud words, but in great works."

Fundamental 4

Inventory Your Box

Do not make easy hard. Wisdom is understandable. Be clear in all teachings. You cannot speak of ocean to a well frog, the creature of a narrower sphere. You cannot speak of ice to a summer insect, the creature of a season.

—Chuang Tzu

We are all familiar with the old, overused corporate training exercise using a handout with nine dots that we are supposed to connect without taking our pen off the paper. The only way we can accomplish the task is to go outside the nine dots:

I assume this is where the cliché "think outside the box" originated. But after you've completed this mind teaser, it has lost its fun and no longer generates childlike curiosity. Childlike wonderment, captured in the big eyes and giant smile of a boy or girl when presented with a big box, can hardly be described in words.

Birthday, Hanukkah, and Christmas gifts usually come wrapped in a box. Cracker Jacks come in a small box, and there's always a prize inside. On family vacations we would stop at friends' farms and pick fruit from the trees, raspberries from the bushes, and corn from the field and always take them home in a box. Take-out food and pizza also come in a box.

Anything foreign is always harder to understand than that which is domestic. After all, there's no place like home. Home is where the heart is. Home is safe and more forgiving if you stumble, fall, or fail. Houses are boxes. It's what's on the inside—the love, support, advice, and security—that makes a house a home. Likewise, a company has no value until people show up to work. The building is the container that gathers and organizes and houses the prize inside. The answers really are in the box!

HUMOR

The first thing we should do each day when we wake up and start looking around in our box is to determine what we think is laughable. There is nothing more personal, more honest, or more revealing of who we really are than a sense of humor. You can't fake laughter. You can defuse an argument, ease a stressful situation, and learn more about a person more quickly through humor than through any other form of communication. I'm not referring to jokes and joke tellers; I'm referring to everyday funny things that happen to us—those hilarious things people say and do that are all around us.

A joke is a joke: My wallet was stolen. I waited three months before I reported it. The police detective asked me why I waited so long to report a stolen credit card. I said, "Because the guy who took it was spending less money than my wife!"

That is funny, but anybody can tell a joke. Not everybody, however, can think funny and relate humorous stories. What's holding you back? Lighten up, relax, and let others into your heart and mind. Trust me, everything will be better if you'll only laugh. Because I travel so extensively, airlines occasionally lose my luggage. To keep patience alive and a positive attitude toward the situation, I always recall the man who steps up to the ticket window and says, "I'd like my bag to go to Singapore and myself to go to Denver." The lady replies, "I'm sorry, sir. We can't do that." He answers, "Why not? You did it last time!"

Laughter is internal jogging, and like exercise, having a bellyaching, rip-roaring, lip-ripping laugh at least once a day is not only good for us but also a major and important part of sustaining mental wellness and balance in life. Truly happy people train themselves to find humor in everything.

For example, my buddy and neighbor is a successful insurance salesman. He plays so much golf that he actually has friends over to show them slides of work! And no, he and my other buddies aren't always big spenders. Four of us went on a golf holiday. At the airport, the skycap asked, "Mr. Clark, does this Samsonite luggage belong to your friends?" I said, "No, their luggage is the cooler with the duct tape and the Piggly Wiggly bags!"

The other day I went through airport security. One guard frisked me so completely, we still write! Later, during the flight, the plane suddenly jerks to the left. The pilot says, "We just lost the left engine. We'll have to gain more altitude. There will be a ten-minute delay. Nine minutes later the plane jerks to the right. The pilot says, "We just lost the right engine. We'll have to gain more altitude. There will be another ten-minute delay." The man next to me leans over and says, "I hope we don't lose the last engine, or we'll be up here all day!"

I was standing in line at the airport. An elderly Southern lady was looking at a man's suitcase. It had stickers and placards from Jamaica, New Zealand, Colorado, and France. Impressed, the lady asked him, "My, oh my, have you been to all those places?" The traveler replied, "No, but my luggage has!"

Do you remember the wild, trend-setting rock and roller Frank Zappa? He had three children. He named his oldest son Dweezle (sounds like one of Santa's reindeer). He named his oldest daughter Moon Unit (what was he smoking?). He named his youngest daughter Motor Head. What an idiot. Everybody knows Motor Head is a boy's name!

All in all, it's just good to laugh. But I don't make political jokes. Too many of them get elected! When I attended my twenty-year high school class reunion, I ran into some old friends I had not seen since graduation. They hadn't changed much. In fact, some were still in high school! It was great to find out that one had appeared on national television playing the game show *Wheel of Fortune*. He was winning the game by $300 when he said, "Pat, may I buy a vowel? Could you give me a K?" Later in the show Pat mentioned, "I notice that you are keeping a personal score using both hands." My classmate proudly answered, "Yes I'm amphibias. I go both ways." Pat said, "You have a fascinating alphabet soup last name. Could you please spell it for our audience?"

Ol' Heber answered, "Yea. P, as in psychology, K, as in knowledge, W, as in write." The laughter erupted, and he couldn't finish!

Laughter is therapeutic and a necessary ingredient in the recipe for happiness. It's the best method for breaking down communication barriers and healing emotional and physical pain. Taking ourselves less seriously is the only way we can take life more seriously! Yes, happy people have perfected the art of laughter. Happy people have found escape, comfort, peace, tranquility, joy, and flat out belly-shaking release by looking within themselves and appreciating the simple fact that life's most important answers and solutions are in the box.

BUSINESS BOX

We see proof of this fundamental box thinking in every aspect of our existence. David Moore, my friend and nationally known entrepreneur and business consultant, teaches "Four Rules," explaining that if your business falters or fails, the question is: Which one or more of the four rules did you violate? All the rules are equally important:

1. Above all else, have a product or service that is better than anyone else's. If you violate this rule, you end up with only a commodity.
2. Hire and train good people, maintaining an effective sales force. Sales are everybody's business, and

customer service is not a department; it's an attitude. If you violate this rule, customer service decreases, goals and objectives go unmet, and unemployment rises. You cannot *save* your way to success. You must *work* to be profitable, not only keeping your job but also creating new ones.

3. Have adequate financial backing, such as liquidity, line of credit, and inventory. If you violate this rule, you are out of cash—and business.

4. Always know whom you are dealing with. If you violate this rule, you lose personally and professionally. The difference is trusting a brand's quality and reputation versus trusting the person who owns the shop where you buy the brand.

ENTREPRENEUR'S BOX

One of my personal heroes is the extraordinary Robert Pedersen. As an extremely successful entrepreneur, community activist, and wealthy philanthropic humanitarian, this dear friend of mine has an amazing resumé. Everything he touches turns to gold. Everyone who knows him calls him mentor or coach. A quote from American Statesman William Penn not only aptly applies to Robert, but is something he could have easily said himself: "I expect to pass through life but once. If, therefore, there can be any kindness I can show, or any good thing I can do to a fellow being, let me do it now, and do not defer or neglect it, as I shall not pass this way again."

This could actually be the Entrepreneur's Creed as it refers to the four components of the entrepreneur's box: Awareness, Ingenuity, Service, and Urgency. In high school Robert sold clothes out of his locker to fellow students as a commissioned sales rep hired by a major clothier and single handedly changed the meaning of "class"mates. In college he founded PANDA and hired and trained 400 sales people to sell home appliances, diamonds, and "extraordinary cookware." At age twenty-five he gathered together twelve people and started a wheat grinder/flour mixing company called "Magic Mill."

By creating the first and only exclusive dealership arrangement with German-based Bosch Kitchen Machines, Robert bought the North American territory which had been selling only 500 machines per month through German distribution. Robert helped increase sales to thousands a week. With his visionary ability to look not just at what something is, but to see what it has the potential to become, Robert took the hub off the motor and tinkered a bit to allow the machine to grind wheat into both coarse and fine flour for making bread. This of course nullified the ninety-day limited warranty that came from Bosch, so he replaced it with a three-year full warranty from his own company. Crazy? No. In seventeen years Robert took his entrepreneurial idea from twelve employees and one office to 9,000 employees in 175 offices and sold the company for millions.

When Robert retired, he started New Quest Technologies, creating Windows-based software that emulated the Franklin Time Management Planner. Franklin acquired it in 1992. Robert then founded LeTech International, which provided all notebook binders for Franklin. Franklin also purchased it in 1992. As a result of his vision and company mergers, Franklin was called Franklin Qwest. Robert was invited to join them as Senior Vice President of Sales and New Product worldwide and soon developed personal management software called "Ascend" as one of the first ever handheld systems on the market. With his assistance, Franklin grew from a $15 million dollar company and went public on the New York Stock Exchange to $350 million.

Robert again retired in 1995, but as the consummate entrepreneur, he created with family members the unique business he calls "Del Sol," the world's largest manufacturer of photochromatic color change clothing with over 100 retail locations in North America, the Caribbean, and Europe. To ensure he has a succession plan and a high performance internal growth process in place, Robert created "Del Sol University," which keeps his leadership pipeline full by identifying and training emerging leaders so they are prepared when they are called on to become store managers and eventually take over the company.

I enjoy being around Robert Pedersen as much as anyone on our planet. He is the perfect blend of left brain and right brain. He says, "Give me the facts and let me add the emotion. Numbers and budgets are delicious. Always keep score knowing if sales are up or down; if employees are motivated and customers satisfied, etc. This eliminates surprises and allows you to make a profit. If there is no profit it is only a hobby, not a business. Making a profit is what allows us to give back and be philanthropic." Robert is a deep thinker with an incredible sense of what's right and the timing for when it's right. He is both a successful businessman and a successful family man having never experienced the so-called out-of-balance conflict that has ruined relationships and plagued the lives of other powerful CEOs in his same bracket.

But why? What makes Robert Pedersen unique and able and willing to do all this? In a four-hour visit in my family room capped with an hour-long chat over lunch, Robert wove the many colors and textures of the threads of his wisdom into a tapestry of success that applies not only to business but to being fully alive. He quoted Edger Guest: "We become as small as our controlling desire and as great as our dominant aspiration." He then continued: "A belief in something bigger than yourself puts today in perspective. That's why I'll never sell out for cheap. I deserve more. I deserve the best. There is no substitute for being true to yourself, knowing who you are in the dark, liking yourself when no one is around, and doing whatever it takes to accomplish whatever you want. In fact, I want to have more, know more, be more, and do more today than I did yesterday. It's natural to want to upgrade. In a fast food drive-through they always ask if we want to 'super size.' When it comes to success, in one way or another we all do."

Robert continued, "Entrepreneurship is no different. All you do is share this way of thinking with others by taking the ordinary into the extraordinary. An entrepreneur is a hybrid salesperson who knows the difference between 'tellers' who use words and 'sellers' who organize a demonstration to make the product fun and come alive; who allow the potential buyer to 'try on' the product to experience the benefits which turns them into their own salesperson. At this point, price becomes less of an issue, and closing the deal almost a given because it's hard to say no to your own sales pitch."

Robert told me he hires slowly and fires quickly; trains his employees to remember people's names and to always look everyone in the eye; teaches them to keep their promises, show up on time and put in a full day's work in exchange for a full day's pay; exemplifies that they should never be afraid of trying something new and taking a calculated risk; and treats them special with an "open door" policy implying that "I'm always there for you and will listen to your suggestions because it costs nothing to have a conversation and brainstorm positive possibilities." In turn, he expects employees to represent him, his good name, and each other with class and dignity. Only when every person involved gets to the point where they refer to *the* company as "their" company will they take ownership of building brand recognition and create a superb reputation based on service before self. When this occurs, the small entrepreneurial idea that began as a crawling caterpillar who willingly engulfed itself in the cocoon of uncertainty and debt grows wings, confidently breaks out, and takes flight to become a beautiful business butterfly.

When I asked Robert to summarize his bottom-line belief that could be packaged in a box and sent to someone in need, he paused for a moment, looked away, and then taught me some pure truth: "Business guru Peter Drucker found his principles of success by studying King Solomon in the Bible. I too find no shame in also talking frankly about so-called taboo sources of wisdom and realities, like the fact that we are all going to die. How can this be shocking and thought to be out of place to discuss to so many? It is not up for discussion and has nothing to do with separation of church and state. Too many avoid the thought as if it will go away. Personally I find it motivating." Robert smiled and continued. "Do you know anyone who was rich who died? Do you know anyone who was poor who died? I'd rather die rich than poor and leave the world in better shape than I found it—physically, mentally, spiritually, and financially. Yes, rich in what money can buy, but also in the things money cannot buy.

"My father and mother both lived long, wonderful lives, and are now dead, and my amazing twenty-five year old son tragically passed away. Therefore, the way I deal with death is to remember that every today is part of the accumulation of my life and time on earth, never knowing if this today will be my last. Consequently, I make living a real joy! Every day counts. I don't want to miss out on anything. That's why I do whatever I can whenever I can to create environments at home, work, and play so others may also experience the same measure of joy and fulfillment that I do. Why? So everybody can learn that you can get what you want if you'll help others get what they want. Oh, how wonderful the world would be if everyone gave more than they took. Profits create jobs, but we are not in business to make money; we are in business to make a life and leave a legacy of leadership behind that is compelling enough to inspire others to do the same!"

Robert Pedersen truly is a hero to me and entrepreneurs everywhere. When I asked him who one of his greatest heroes was, he softly replied, "Gordon B. Hinckley who said, 'What we desperately need today on all fronts—in our homes and communities, in schoolrooms and boardrooms, and certainly throughout society at large—are leaders, men and women who are willing to stand for something. Never in the history of the world has there been a more profound need for leaders of principle to step forward.'"

BALANCE BOX

John O'Donnell, who was president of the North American Consumer Products Division of Georgia Pacific, told me: "We are all busy. Successful people's lives are especially crazy—always juggling several balls. However, as hectic as our lives appear to be, there are only four balls to juggle. Although they are not square, the number four is significant to our discussion. We need only good time-management and prioritizing skills, and we can succeed in our 'balance box.'"

The first ball in the balance box is the self-ball. It is made of a crumpled $100 bill. Do you want it? What if it is dropped and someone steps on it and grinds it into the floor with his shoe? Do you still want it? No matter what happens or what anyone does to this rolled-up, ball-shaped $100 bill, it does not decrease in value. It was and still is worth $100.

Many times in our lives we are dropped, crumpled, and ground into the dirt by the decisions we make and the environment wherein we live and work. Though at times we feel worthless, no matter what happens to us, we never lose our value. A $100 bill is still a $100 bill, regardless if it's dirty, crumpled, worn, torn, smashed, wet, dry, old, new, dropped, or juggled. You are priceless! Failure is an event, not a person. There is a difference between the person and the performance. Being up is better than being down, but in either place you are worth the same!

The second ball is the family ball. It is made of glass. We drop it, and it breaks and shatters into many pieces that can rarely be repaired. It is imperative that we keep it in the air at all times and at all costs.

The third ball is the job ball. This ball is rubber, and if we drop it, it will always bounce back—sometimes higher, sometimes lower, but it will bounce back. Even if it is stepped on and flattened, it squishes out the side, trying to escape. When it is finally released, it immediately retains its original shape and form, ready to bounce again. The rubber job ball reminds us that there is always a way. We just need to find it.

Ball number four is the faith ball. It is made of gold. It is heavy and bright and sheds light on the others. When we drop it, it leaves a dent, but it stays right where we left it, allowing us to pick it up and juggle it again and again, whenever we decide to. A a common saying is, if you feel you are getting further away from the Almighty, who moved? Not God! Remember, the ball is always where it was. The miracle of the gold faith ball is that if we drop it and dent it, as we pick it up and start using it again, somehow the movement ("faith with works") eventually smooths out the dent. And, as we juggle it, the blemish is taken away, leaving no sign we ever dropped it!

ART, RELIGION, GOVERNMENT, AND LEADERSHIP BOXES

In the world of art, all painters know there are four primary colors—red, yellow, blue, and black. Every other color is a mixture of these "boxed" colors.

The Ten Commandments constitute a box, and the Golden Rule, "Do unto others as you would have others do unto you," is a box. The constitution of the United States of America is a box that regulates and influences each American citizen every day. The Gettysburg Address and the Declaration of Independence, part of which Abraham Lincoln quoted in his speech at Gettysburg, are boxes.

All of these are good, clean, powerful, positive, productive boxes—unique in circumstance and delivery but not unique in message and structure. Each of these boxes is built on cornerstones that never change. Sure, the emphasis may change from diamonds to taste, but the standards of excellence and expectations never change.

CORE VALUES BOX

There are values, and then there are core values. I speak many times a year for the United States armed forces, particularly the Air Force. In the process of interacting with every level and rank of servicemen and servicewomen, I have rapidly developed a deep respect for everyone in uniform. The sense of duty, honor, country, sacrifice, and being all they can be is real! Sure, there are a few slugs who don't get it. But for the most part, everyone in the US Air Force is an amazing human being.

Like the United States Army, the Air Force has published an official set of core values: Integrity first, service before self, and excellence in all we do. I add a fourth: Do right. These four core values are solid, unchanging, tried, and tested. To set the tone for our investigation, let me quote from the famous USAF "Little Blue Book":

The Three Core Values make the military what it is; without them, we cannot succeed. They are the values that instill confidence, earn lasting respect, and create willing followers. They are the values that anchor resolve in the most difficult situations. They are the values that buttress mental and physical courage when we enter combat. In essence, they are the three pillars of professionalism that provide the foundation for military leadership at every level. The Core Values are much more than minimum standards. They remind us of what it takes to get the mission done. They inspire us to do our very best at all times. They are the common bond among all comrades in arms, and they are the glue that unifies the force and ties us to the great warriors and public servants of the past.

—Secretary Widnall

INTEGRITY FIRST

Integrity is a character trait. It is the willingness to do what is right even when no one is looking. It's the inner voice, the moral compass, the ability to hold together and properly regulate all of the elements of a personality, controlling impulses, and appetites. A person with integrity lives with courage, honesty, responsibility, accountability, justice, openness, self-respect, and humility. Having integrity means you are true to yourself. The following story illustrates this principle.

JILLENE

Her name was Jillene Jones. She told me *Jillene* was Portuguese for "awesome woman," and she was right. She was wonderful—beautiful, blonde, and smart, with an amazing personality. Let me take you back to high school. In a page or two you will see how many adults are still selling out, settling for mere work instead of holding out and preparing to get the job they dream about.

I wanted to go out with Jillene more than anything in the world. I was somewhat insecure and didn't want her to turn me down, so to protect my heart and ego, I asked some of her friends if she would go out with me. They all said yes. I got my confidence up, practiced my voice to make sure it was low and breathy, and phoned her. I asked her to a concert two weeks away. She said yes!

My plan was to get her to fall in love with me. I didn't think Jillene could possibly like me just the way I was, so I started asking around to find out what she did like. I was willing to change anything about myself to get Jillene to fall madly in love. I was willing to sell out and compromise my personal authenticity just to reel her in.

I spent the next fourteen days researching Jillene. I discovered Jillene's favorite color was peach. What a drag. Peach is a popular color now, but in college it was definitely uncool for a guy to wear peach. You just didn't do it. But it was Jillene's favorite color. I wanted her to fall madly in love with me. I decided to buy a peach shirt. But I didn't stop there! I bought five peach shirts, thinking long-term relationship!

More research revealed Jillene's favorite men's cologne—some exotic cologne that stank so bad that my nose hairs threatened my life. When I splashed it on, my eyes fogged up and my ears tried to bleed. But it didn't matter; it was Jillene's favorite cologne. Suddenly it was my favorite cologne. No, I didn't buy the small, date-sized bottle; I bought the huge forever-relationship-sized bottle. It cost me a fortune!

I did more research and discovered Jillene's favorite music. I liked all kinds of music, but hers was really different. Heavy, heavy metal. Sometimes I think the only reason they call it heavy metal is because the lead singer sounds like he dropped something heavy on his foot. And to think they write it all by themselves! Yeah, I bought a cassette of it. Suddenly, heavy metal had become my favorite kind of music. It's interesting how insecurity works.

The two weeks went by. It was finally date night. It was time to take Jillene to the concert. I put on a peach shirt, drenched myself in the cologne, and walked up to her front door. I stank so badly that the flowers on the front porch began to wilt.

Jillene answered the door. My preparation was about to pay off.

"Oh my gosh. I can't believe it. Nobody wears peach. Peach is my favorite color." She gave me a hug.

"Oh my gosh," she continued, "that's my favorite smell—my favorite cologne."

"Me too," I said, coughing and choking. "I can't believe how many things we have in common."

She smiled and said, "I know, I know."

I walked her to the car, opened her door, walked around the car gagging for oxygen, popped in the cassette tape, and played her favorite song. As we pulled out of her driveway, she leaped over the console and started singing/screaming to the beat, nodding her head, head banging up and down in heavy metal contortions. I joined her, nodding my head up and down until I accidentally hit her nose. As it started to bleed she yelled, "Wow, you're a great slam dancer. This is my favorite band." I yelled over the loud music, "Mine too!" We pulled onto the street and headed for the concert.

Jillene fell madly in love with me exactly as I had planned for her to do. In fact, she fell in love with me for two weeks. But something happened. I got sick and tired of being someone else. I was born to be me! I was born into this world to discover me and develop my personal preferences into a unique person that I could love and respect twenty-four hours a day—every day. And yet I had sold out to a woman! I'm not the only fool, however.

We change our hairstyles, health habits, expectations, moral standards, clothing, cologne, and taste in music just so an individual or cliquish group or club will welcome us and accept us with open arms. I went to the gym with Jillene because she liked to work out. I pretended that I enjoyed it too, when in reality I don't think people should run if no one is chasing them. And a treadmill makes me feel like a hamster! Jillene liked to dance and bowl and eat sushi. I led her into believing that I liked them too. What a phony I was! I loved to go to the movies, but she hated them and always said no. Of course, I caved in for her.

After two weeks I gave the peach shirts to my sister, and I threw the cologne away. I then got rid of the noisy music, started listening to my own tunes, and got back to doing the fun things I enjoyed. And you know what? It turned out Jillene Jones didn't like *that* me. But that was okay, because I liked me. And I have to like and love myself before I can honestly like and love someone else.

The most frightening thing about this high school experience is that it is still relevant today. Many people sell out just to get a job. When they land the job and start being real again, they hate their job, looking forward to Friday instead of Monday, thinking they are paid by the hour when in reality they are paid for the value they bring to that hour. We need to know ourselves, be true to ourselves, and hold out for the job we dream about.

The divorce rate in the United States is 57.7 percent for the same reason. We sell out while dating, putting on a show, and fast-talking each other into fantasyland. The second we close the sale, we don't have to be cool anymore. We have what we want and no longer have to put on a show to attract it or secure it. Suddenly we are authentically real, and our spouse wakes up in tears, screaming, "I didn't know you burped every morning for fifty minutes. Hit the road, you big fat slob!"

Most jobs and marriages are started and built on fantasy instead of fact, engaging someone who we are not. It's no secret why most don't last! Regarding having "Integrity First," I conclude this section with the words of Admiral James B. Stockdale:

"In 1965, I was crippled and I was all alone (in a North Vietnamese prisoner of war camp). I realized that they had all the power. I couldn't see how I was ever going to get out with my honor and self-respect. The one thing I came to realize was that if you don't lose your integrity you can't be had and you can't be hurt. Compromises multiply and build up when you're working against a skilled extortionist or manipulator. You can't be had if you don't take that first shortcut of 'meet them halfway.'"

SERVICE BEFORE SELF

To serve is to do one's duty, letting duty take precedence over personal desires. It is putting the needs of others before your own needs. It is putting God, family, and country first. Service before and above self is measured through behavior, including following rules, respecting others, and having discipline, self-control, and faith. Being a citizen of the world is determined by what you are willing to do for a stranger.

Four Star General Fogleman (who created these Three Core Values and made them Air Force policy) put them into perspective when he elaborated on the second one: "The Air Force is not a social actions agency. It is not an employment agency. The Air Force exists to fight and win wars—that's our core expertise. We're entrusted with the security of our nation. The tools of our trade are lethal, and we engage in operations that involve risk to human life. Because of what we do, our standards must be higher than those of society at large. In the end, we earn the respect and trust of the American people because of the integrity we demonstrate through service before self."

THE CIRCUS

When I was a young boy, my father and I were standing in line to buy tickets for the circus. Finally, there was only one family between us and the ticket counter. This family made a big impression on me. There were eight children, all probably under the age of twelve. You could tell they didn't have a lot of money. Their clothes were not expensive, but they were clean. The children were well behaved, all of them standing in line, two-by-two behind their parents, holding hands. They were excitedly jabbering about the clowns, elephants, and other acts they would see that night. One could sense that they had never been to the circus before. It promised to be a highlight of their young lives.

The father and mother were at the head of the pack, standing proud as could be. The mother was holding her husband's hand, looking up at him as if to say, "You're my knight in shining armor."

He was smiling and basking in pride, looking at her as if to reply, "You got that right."

The ticket lady asked the father how many tickets he wanted. He proudly responded, "Please let me buy eight children's tickets and two adult tickets so I can take my family to the circus."

The ticket lady quoted the price.

The wife let go of her husband's hand and dropped her head. The man's lip began to quiver. He leaned a little closer and asked, "How much did you say?"

The ticket lady again quoted the price. The man didn't have enough money. How was he supposed to turn and tell his eight kids that he didn't have enough money to take them to the circus?

Seeing what was going on, my dad put his hand into his pocket, pulled out a twenty-dollar bill, and dropped it on the ground. (We were not wealthy in any sense of the word!) My father reached down, picked up the bill, tapped the man on the shoulder, and said, "Excuse me, sir, this fell out of your pocket."

The man knew what was going on, and it was obvious that he appreciated the help in a desperate situation. He looked straight into my dad's eyes, took my dad's hand in both of his, squeezed tightly onto the twenty-dollar bill, and with his lip quivering and a tear streaming down his cheek, he replied, "Thank you, thank you, sir. This really means a lot to me and my family."

My father and I went back to our car and drove home. We didn't go to the circus that night, but we didn't go without.

EXCELLENCE IN ALL WE DO

Developing a sustained passion for continuous improvement and innovation will propel you and others around you into a long-term, upward spiral of accomplishment and performance. All we do means product/service excellence, personal excellence, community excellence, and resource/operation excellence. My dad used to say, "Always leave your family, friends, neighbors, job, community, parks, country, and world in better shape than you found them."

Every time I speak at Lacklin Air Force Base in San Antonio, Texas—"The Gateway to the Air Force" where every enlisted person is required to endure the six to eight week "BMT" (Basic Military Training boot camp)—my understanding of this value grows. I see postures tall, perfectly straight marching lines with equally measured out formation rows, salutes with firmness and respect, uniforms clean and sharp, boots shined, and beds made a specific way with clothes folded and hung in a prescribed designated manner. Why all this extreme discipline and conformity? Is it really necessary for the instruction to yell? Do the pushups and two-mile warrior runs really contribute to this transformation from boy to man and girl to woman? The answers are a resounding yes! Teaching Excellence in All You Do is not possible unless the student experiences excellence in everything he or she does, so it becomes a way of thinking and a daily way of life. Excellence is not a sometime thing; it's an all-the-time commitment.

COMMITMENT

There is a suicide epidemic in the world today. It affects everyone from forty-year-olds going through a life crisis to students in school. In Plano, Texas, several teenagers killed themselves in the same week. It is happening all over the country: South Shore of New Jersey; Pine Ridge, South Dakota; Orange County, California; Dade County, Florida; Toronto, Canada.

In Iowa there were one hundred suicide attempts in thirty days at the same high school. One girl died. The school brought Charlotte Ross from California, a national consultant on suicide, and me in to talk to the kids. We split up the student body into two groups. Charlotte did the left-brain, cognitive therapy presentation. I did the right brain, emotional, motivational presentation. We then swapped audiences and repeated our presentations. Finally, we gathered with counselors and health-care professionals to interview each of the students who had attempted suicide and survived.

The demographic breakdown of those ninety-nine students was enlightening: Seventy-three percent were on the honor roll. They said, "Thanks for the recognition, but I still have a giant hole in my heart. Something is missing in my life. Please help me!"

Six students were student-body officers elected by classmates. They said, "Thanks for letting us win a popularity contest, but we're missing something in our life."

Three were cheerleaders. They said, "Thanks for the attention, but it's shallow and fleeting."

Three had been varsity football players. They said, "We were injured. Our bodies let us down. Because we can't be athletes, we are nobody. There is nothing left."

In a corporate setting, they are the "employees of the month." In the community, they are the "good kids." In school, they are the stars with recognition, accolades, and constant attention. So why did they want to give up and take their lives?

Each one told us they lacked "commitment relationships" in their lives. That was the phrase they used, and it caught my attention. What is commitment? Webster defines it this way: "to connect; to trust and put in charge; to carry into action deliberately; to pledge or obligate oneself to another; an emotional two-way promise with assurance and reliance."

To me, this means a two-way deal. When you say this and I say this and no action is taken, there is no commitment. But when you do what you say and I do what I say, a commitment relationship is formed. To help us deepen our understanding of commitment, let us introduce another word: *love*. Love is commitment, not a way of feeling. Romance is not love. Think of it this way: If I love you because you are beautiful, that's romance. But if you are beautiful because I love you, that's real love.

Because of movies and music we say, "I love her so much. She makes me feel different than I've ever felt before." Feelings, emotions, and hormones are not enough to sustain a relationship.

As important as the words "I love you" are to our mental health and emotional stability, when it comes to commitment relationships, "I need you" are the most powerful words. In the context of love, "I don't love you because I need you; I need you because I love you" are the most powerful words. Think about it.

As you do, let me validate the deep yet elementary importance of *need*.

My friend was getting married. He asked me if I would write a song and sing it at his wedding. I said no. He proceeded to remind me that we were best friends and that it would be cool for me to participate in his special day. He basically made me feel important. If you think about it, everyone likes to feel important. In fact, most of us try to act more important that we really are. That's why so many people drive around with trailer hitches on their cars even though they don't even own anything to pull!

I finally gave in and wrote the song. Two days later he phoned me back to explain that the band had just canceled, and he wanted me to prepare forty to fifty songs to play as the dinner entertainment. I emphatically said, "No way!" He said, "I need you." What a drag! Had he said, "I love you," I would have responded, "I love you too; here is the number of a band." But "I need you" made me feel that I was not just good but that I was good for something, that I really mattered, that I could make a significant contribution. I couldn't turn him down, and I don't think you could have either.

I practiced and prepared my music. When my friend's wedding day arrived, I sang the song that I had written for the couple and then prepared to sing the first of the forty to fifty songs I had practiced. Before I could sing another song, however, the band arrived. There was a miscommunication. I didn't want to sing all night anyway. I wanted to eat and socialize like everybody else, so I helped the band members set up their equipment.

Now think about this. When I arrived at the wedding reception, I arrived with the attitude that my friend needed me. I would have stayed until four o'clock in the morning if necessary because he needed me. I would have waited tables, mopped the floor, and contributed in any way I could. But the second the band showed up, realistically I was no longer needed. In all truth, they could do without me. We can fool others, but we can't fool ourselves. Why hang around if I was no longer needed? I didn't. I left the reception and went home.

This is the message coming through loud and clear from adults and young people across North America, especially from those Charlotte Ross and I interviewed in Iowa who had attempted suicide and survived. Each one of them told us they knew they were liked, they knew they were loved, but they didn't believe they were needed. And when we don't feel that we are needed, why hang around?

Are you needed? In the corporate arena, when a sales champion or outstanding executive jumps ship to work for the competition, it is not always about money. There's a good chance they no longer feel needed where they are, so they go where they do feel needed. Remember, people work harder for praises than raises. The students in Iowa put on a good outward show that all was well. Most of us buy into thinking that outside attention and recognition motivate us. It doesn't, and yet we emphasize it in our marriages, personal relationships, business contracts, and athletic endeavors. But what we desperately need is to be needed. That's what keeps us motivated and hanging around.

The tough reality is that in contemporary American society, we can't afford to wait for someone to tell us or show us that we are needed. It might never happen. We could go months before we experience this crucial validation. So what do we do: give up, quit, kill ourselves? Most definitely not. Private victories precede public victories. Who are we fooling to think it is society's responsibility to give our lives meaning and purpose and excitement? It is *our* responsibility to do something on a daily basis to prove to ourselves that we are needed.

The solution, then, to commitment relationships is to participate more and get involved! We must reach out and make the move to establish and nurture commitment relationships based on action, participation, and goals. If you don't feel that you are needed at home, participate more, get involved. If you don't feel that you are needed by your children, participate more, get involved in their world, volunteer in their schools, host their parties at your home, stay in touch, and get involved in their friends' lives. If you don't feel needed in your neighborhood or world, vote, participate in charity organizations, give more than you take, and leave everything and everyone in better shape than you found them!

In a relationship, saying "I need you" is not codependency. Rather, it means, "I am okay, but I would be so much more with you. You complete me." At the beginning of the wedding, I felt that I could make a significant contribution. When the band showed up, I lost that feeling. The way we recapture it in any phase of our lives, especially in our personal and professional relationships, is to change our attitude from "What's in it for me?" to "What's in it for others?"

The best way for us to prove to ourselves that we are needed is to go out of our way to lift everybody else's performance. We could call it the "Michael Jordan factor." Let's face it; we work harder in relationships, in sports, in church, in school, in our communities, and in everyday life when we know we make a special difference to others.

NEEDED?

I was speaking to members of Our Primary Purpose (O.P.P.), a highly acclaimed program for chemically dependent teenagers in Des Moines, Iowa. At the third meeting, just for parents, a mother shared a story about her twenty-year-old son, John (who was not enrolled in the O.P.P. program). He was handsome and talented, a good citizen, a good student, a good musician, and a good athlete. He also had a lovely girlfriend and seemingly had no problems.

One day he stopped talking as much as he usually did. Thirty days passed, and his conversation dwindled to nothing. He was depressed, and his parents and girlfriend continually told him that they loved him. He knew that they loved him, and he expressed his love for them. Everyone was concerned about his well-being and wondered what they could say or do to help him, since saying "I love you" obviously wasn't enough to improve the situation.

John finally made a move. He locked himself in the cellar. Although he was down in the dim dampness for three days without food, he continued to acknowledge his parents' love for him and his love for them. His depression deepened, and his loved ones were convinced that suicide was imminent. Health care professionals were brought in, but the counseling, kindness, caring, and love were all to no avail.

On the third day of John's isolation, the local high school football coach (who didn't know what was going on in John's life) called his home to talk to him. John's mother said John was busy and took a message at the coach's request. Then she went to the cellar door and called down the stairs, "John, Coach Ivers just phoned. He said that his players voted last night on whom they wanted as their assistant coach. They said you were the greatest Pop Warner football coach they had ever had, and now they think they can win the state championship if you help coach them. Coach Ivers said they need you—he needs you! He said if you're interested you should be at football practice at 2:45 this afternoon."

Do you know what happened? John came out of the cellar and went to practice. He accepted the coaching job, and by the time he came home from his first practice, he had snapped out of his depression. He once again felt needed, wanted, and important, and he was back to his old self.

DO RIGHT

Do the right thing simply because it's the right thing to do. It's what you do when the coach is not around that makes you a champion athlete. It's what you do when the instructor is not around that makes you a champion student. It's what you do when the employer is not around that makes you a champion employee. It's what you do when no one is around that makes you a champion human being. It's keeping your word, being a man or woman of honor and, keeping your promises.

KEEP YOUR PROMISES

A young Japanese boy was to spend the weekend with his elderly grandfather. The grandfather lived in a village on the other side of the mountain, so the boy's parents took him to a train station, where they met the grandfather. The parents dropped off their son, hugged him, said good-bye, and drove away.

As the boy and his grandfather waited in line to buy their tickets, the grandfather discovered that he had left his wallet on the previous train. He didn't have any money. It was cold, and a blizzard was coming. The grandfather asked the ticket lady if she would loan him the price of two tickets, promising to pay her back later that night. Because of the Japanese culture's deep and abiding respect for elders, the ticket lady believed the grandfather and paid for the tickets.

An hour later, the boy and his grandfather arrived in the village. They walked fifteen minutes through the horrible weather and finally entered the cottage. Hungry, tired, and soaking wet, the grandfather went to his drawer and retrieved some money. "Let's go," he said. His grandson rebutted, "But, Grandfather, I'm starving and we're going back to the train station in three days. Why can't you just pay her back then? It will cost you the price of two more round-trip tickets to go now, just to pay back two one-way tickets."

Putting on a dry overcoat and handing his grandson a wool blanket for comfort, the eighty-year-old grandfather put his arm around his grandson's shoulders and taught him the lesson of the ages. "Son, we must get there tonight before the counter closes and the ticket lady goes home. This is not about money. This is about honor. I gave her my word, and we must always keep our promises!"

General Curtis E. LeMay of the US Air Force echoes the principle taught in this story: "I hope that the United States of America has not yet passed the peak of honor and beauty, and that our people can still sustain certain simple philosophies at which some miserable souls feel it incumbent to sneer. I refer to some of the psalms and the Gettysburg Address, and the Boy Scout Oath, where it doesn't get much better or clearer than: 'On my honor, I will do my best, to do my duty, to God and my country and to obey.' I also refer to the Lord's Prayer, and to that other oath which a man or woman takes when he or she stands with hand uplifted, and swears to defend this country as a proud member of our armed forces."

Fundamental 5

"STRETCH"

Learning is its own exceeding great reward. And stay the course—for great spirits have always encountered violent opposition from mediocre minds. The mind once stretched can never return to its original dimensions.

—Einstein

Stretch: an extension of the scope or application of something; an exercise of understanding and imagination beyond ordinary or normal limits; to amplify or enlarge; to reach and continue.

—Webster

When we believe the answers are outside of us we feel pressure to reactively change. However, when we know the answers are inside us we proactively "Stretch." No one likes to change but everybody likes to stretch. To illustrate: I snapped my Achilles tendon playing basketball with the guys on my street, trying to be twenty years old again. My friend and neighbor, Dr. Jim Morgan, who performed the surgery and is one of the premier orthopedic physicians specializing in ankle surgery in America, was actually playing in the game. He denies it, but I think he came up from behind me and thought, "I need a new boat," and then pushed me down. He reattached my Achilles' and put my leg in a plaster cast for three months. When the cast came off, I was placed in physical therapy. Physical therapy teaches us two things that are relevant to in-the-box thinking—two things that are relevant to every meeting and conference and person who truly and honestly wants to take it to the ultimate level, consistently win, and become more of who they already are.

First, *you've got to believe in the power of stretch.* When I go to the physical therapist, the first thing he does is warm up my weakened, stiff ankle. Then he takes the tip of my foot and bends it and stretches it to a place it has never been before. As I'm squirming there and gritting my teeth, he lets go, and my foot flips back to the same place it was before he started to stretch it.

Think about it. Is this not the reason that we discount the power of a management conference or sales rally? Our observations and experience tell us that the associated stretching is merely momentary hype that lasts only as long as the meeting.

This brings me to the second thing we learn from physical therapy. *You have to stretch before you strengthen.* And *all* the strengthening occurs in the area past the point of discomfort. I know a lot of superstar athletes, executives, and professionals in every field. We, you included, have the ability to push ourselves to the point of discomfort all by ourselves! But I know of no one who has the ability to push themselves into the area *past* the point of discomfort all by themselves. We just can't do it! Prolific players always have a coach who makes them run one more sprint; peak performing people all have someone who constantly stretches them!

Before we list examples, let us fully understand the process by examining a Vertical Stretching Scale.

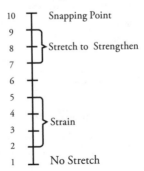

On this scale, 1 is no stretch, and 10 is the snapping point; 2 to 5 is strain by individual effort; 6 is the point of discomfort; 7 to 9 is stretch past the point of discomfort that can only be handled with support. If you go from level 1 to 7, 8, 9, or 10, you go to the snapping point, which means regardless of how much support you get, you are not physically or emotionally equipped to handle the stress. Hitting the snapping point quickly or even later on is extremely harmful because often it completely undoes the progress you've made in stretching and strengthening up to that point. Remember, it's gradual strain and stretch, line upon line, precept upon precept. A baby must crawl before it walks. Inch by inch life's a cinch—yard by yard it's hard.

The only place from which a person can grow is where he or she is. We must go to where people are physically and emotionally; only there can we gently invite them to improve. This is especially true with ourselves. Gandhi said: "You must *be* the change you want to see in the world." We must grow where we are planted and start our stretch right where we are.

Too many of us want to stretch and strengthen all at once. Too many leaders set outrageously high, unrealistic goals without giving even a modest amount of support, and then blame their people when they snap and fail.

The key to using this Vertical Stretching Scale to get the most out of others is to first start where they are; second, to inspire them to push and strain themselves to the point of discomfort; third, to stretch them past the point of discomfort and support them there until the strain and stretch are no longer stressful. Once someone has grown comfortable at the 7, 8, or 9 level, it becomes that person's new starting point. On the stretch scale they are back at 1. Now the level that once was 10 becomes level 6—no longer the snapping point—but instead the targeted point of discomfort, which the person now can handle and go beyond with support. Let me demonstrate how this works in real life.

THE FIRE

The piercing scream of sirens interrupted my morning as two hook-and-ladder fire trucks raced to the end of the street where a huge fire was blazing at Greystone Plaza. Out of curiosity, I grabbed my jacket and raced out the door. One entire five-story condominium building was engulfed in flames. In the midst of the chaos and pandemonium, the firefighters focused on evacuating those stranded on the top floor. Quickly and with surgical precision, they positioned a specially designed, state-of-the-art, high-tech ladder with one end on the roof of the burning building and the other end on the roof of an adjacent building. In the true tradition of a practiced elementary school fire drill, the occupants instinctively formed an orderly single file line, and one by one crawled across the ladder to safety. All of them went across except one man and his three-year-old son.

The man was apparently afraid of heights, and the ladder was five stories above the ground. He would not move. He *could* not move. Seeing his predicament, a female firefighter crawled across the ladder and brought his little boy to safety. She then yelled to the father, "Now you come across and save yourself." But still he did not move. Immobilized by his fear of heights, he could only stand trembling at the edge.

In a split-second decision, the firefighter did the only thing she could have done to save the man. She carried his son back across the ladder and handed him back to his father, explaining, "If your son is to live, you are going to have to save him and bring him across yourself."

He did! With his boy clinging to his neck, the man crept to safety. As the awestruck crowd cheered them on, the compassionate firefighter didn't just abandon him. She crept backward all the while with her reassuring hand on his shoulder, whispering, "Your son will live. Don't look down. We're almost there. I know you can do this. You can save him. Good job. You're his hero. Keep going. I believe in you; your son believes in you. Just believe in yourself."

As the victorious father and child reached safety, their silent supporters watching from the parking lot burst into applause. What's the message? This is a classic example of stretch—how it works, when it works, and why it works.

The fundamental principle here is that it was not in the father's comfort zone to be up so high. It was not *like* the father to cross the suspended ladder to save himself, and the firefighter knew she could not change him. But it was *like* the father to save his son. The firefighter sensed this and put the father in a situation where he could stretch, become more of who he already was, and perform at a higher level than he ever would perform by himself.

Instead of leading and influencing and stretching others from the outside in like most people attempt to do, this firefighter influenced, inspired, and stretched from the inside out, creating an environment where the father would do what he needed to do simply because he knew he needed to do it. When it comes to stretching, there is no shortcut or easy way. It takes twenty years to make a mighty oak tree and just two months to make a squash.

What do you want to be? Napoleon Hill said, "If you wished a strong right arm, you could develop such an arm only by giving it the hardest sort of use. The strongest oak tree of the forest is not the one that is protected from the storm and hidden from the sun. It's the one that stands in the open where it is compelled to struggle for its existence against the winds and rains and scorching sun."

CLIMBING MOUNTAINS

Mountain climbing is a powerful metaphor for stretching ourselves to deal with the difficulties that appear to be on the outside but are actually are from within. The mountain is not the obstacle—we are. Consider an expedition to the top of Mount Everest. One of the details that seldom gets told is the reason that most of the climbers didn't succeed. In one particular expedition, 150 men started the climb, but only three made it to the top. Why? Who chose the lucky three who made it to the summit?

As the climb proceeded, weather conditions constantly changed. Oxygen became thin, causing nausea in many. As the days crept on, many climbers questioned their own abilities. Uncertainties like "I don't know if I can make it. Is it really worth all the agony and pain? I feel too sick to go on. I'll do this another day" confronted the climbers and greatly affected their performance. Each had the choice of whether to give up and stop climbing or hang in there and keep going. So who chose the three men to go to the top? Who chose the three who were allowed to be successful, accomplish their goals, and make their dreams come true? No one did—they chose themselves!

I've interviewed several men who have climbed to the summit of Mount Everest. Their experiences are similar. They told me it took them seven years to find sponsors, buy equipment, run, exercise, lift weights, work out in high altitudes, and climb many high mountains to prepare themselves for the ultimate Everest climb. When they finally made it to the top, they only stayed fifteen minutes. Seven years of work for fifteen minutes of reward.

I asked each of them if it was worth it. Each emphatically replied, "Yes, it was more than worth it." The excitement and reward were not only found in the destination but also in the journey. Climbing mountains teaches us the fundamental steps we must follow to reap our desired rewards. Success is a step-by-step, day-by-day stretch, rising each day to rise above the previous day until we master the obstacles, the goal, and ourselves.

From a distance, mountains look majestic, beautiful, approachable, and easily conquered. Only when you stand at the base of a mountain can you fully sense its massive presence and feel intimidated. You anticipate that the climb will vary from gradual to steep, with gullies and rugged terrain that require ropes, carabineers, and technical help from your guide in order to continue your climb. You have been briefed on the dangers of sudden changes in weather, wild animals, blisters, falling rocks, and the most complicated obstacle of all, your will to win. But you worked out in the gym, got in shape, prepared, set your goal, and hired a competent, experienced guide. Shouldn't this be enough?

GUIDE AND MAP

Every climbing accident that I've heard of happened because an inexperienced climber thought he didn't need help and could accomplish a monumental task alone, or an inexperienced climber found an inexperienced guide, and they convinced each other that together they could make it. When the blind lead the blind, both fall in the ditch.

Hiring a guide who knows more than you and who has been there and done that many times is critical to the success of the mission. Guides don't help us, lead us, push us, and pull us so much when things are going smoothly. But when tough times come, we lean on them and rely on them for our survival and success. With a competent guide and a current map, you are ready to crawl across your ladders, face your fears, risk with a leap of faith, trust, dig deep, and begin your climb.

We are all familiar with the psychological climb we make when we leave home to go away to college, leave the security of home to get married, or start a new job. At the base of the mountain, we may be joining a new company or preparing for a new role within the same company. But as in physical therapy and with an actual mountain, we must stretch through our pain and climb our personal mountains in stages. Regardless of the assembled support team, supplies, equipment, expert guide, and fellow climbers, it still boils down to an individual competition between the mountain and us.

ALTITUDE SICKNESS

Some inexperienced climbers oftentimes look for the shortcut. They are unwilling to pay the necessary price by climbing to a certain level and acclimating themselves to this new higher stage before they move on. They think with money or influence they can bypass the basics and simply fly a helicopter to the top of the mountain. Experienced climbers know better; taking shortcuts can cause a potentially fatal condition called altitude sickness.

I played football in Utah at about 4500 feet and in Denver at Mile High Stadium. In hot weather and in long games we always had the advantage playing against teams from low-elevation states. When you have not spent time practicing in thinner air and acclimating your body and lungs and ear pressure, the air at high altitude makes it hard to breathe and even harder when you're out of breath and trying to regain it. This is nothing compared to climbing a high mountain.

Altitude sickness zaps your energy and slows your body *and* mind to a crawl. Deprived of air, your heart starts pounding, leaving you tired, breathless, and often disoriented. The only remedy is to climb down to a lower elevation, or your lungs will fill with fluid and you will die. There are no pills, shots, or medication that will cure altitude sickness. You must backtrack to give your body time to acclimatize. Experienced guides will tell you there is no shortcut to the summit. To climb higher you must be willing to pay your dues. During your ascent you must spend more than adequate time at each stage of the climb (at each stage of the stretch) until you reach the summit.

Without taking care of basic, yet most important, foundational needs, you will not have the attitude or stamina required to scale the mightiest peak. The more time you spend at lower, less-demanding altitudes, stretching and growing, the more stamina and resolve you will have in thin air.

CORPORATE CLIMBING

This climbing analogy is sound and obvious but not complete until we realize that for at least the past twenty years, managers have been encouraged to focus high up on the mountain via mission statements, self-directed work teams, and diversity training. These all help employees feel that their work has purposeful meaning. Total quality management, re-engineering, and continuous improvement-learning organizations all have incentive bonus programs to encourage employees to take responsibility and innovate. But have they worked?

For the short-term, yes, but as of today, most have withered away. All of these popular movements had truth at their foundation, but none really lasted. Why? An epidemic of altitude sickness spread through American corporations. They aimed too high, went too fast, and, in helicopters, snuck in at fourteen thousand feet instead of starting at the high, but not too high, 4500-foot base camp and slowly climbing to the summit.

As in the high-altitude athletic competitions that I mentioned earlier, where teams who are not accustomed to the thin air become weak, likewise when climbing a personal or organizational mountain, if we start too far up the mountain, we will die on the mountain. They say, "When the going gets tough, the tough get going." Not if they haven't paid their dues and prepared themselves physically, psychologically, and emotionally first at the base camp and then at the other incremental stages and altitude levels before the challenge of conquering the summit comes. We must crawl before we walk, walk before we run, and not helicopter past any stages of development, trying to cram our preparation like we do the night before a math test.

As in nature, you can't cram or hurry the growing of crops. They must be planted, watered, nurtured, fertilized, watered some more, weeded, and given the required number of days before they can be harvested. Climbing a mountain is like growing high-grade crops or rehabilitating through physical therapy. Stretching and strengthening beyond the point of discomfort is a step-by-step journey we must make before we set out to climb at home, at work, or at play.

ULTIMATE LEVEL STRETCHING

Some classic examples of stretching come from the world of sports. I was on a committee of the 2002 Olympic Winter Games in Salt Lake City and witnessed firsthand the Olympic motto: "*Citius, Altius, Fortius*" (Faster, Higher, Stronger). Through both individual, associate, and coached stretching, athletes from all over the world gathered in the belief that world records were made to be broken and that they could better their own past *best* personal performance.

Michael Jordan is the greatest basketball player to ever play the game. The reasons are obvious: Not only did he stretch himself, but he also stretched those he played with and those he played against. Michael Jordan's personal stretch made everybody else around him work harder and be better.

But Jordan's personal stretch wasn't enough. He needed a coach to push and pull him even faster, higher, and stronger. The power of the right stretching coach is immeasurable, as Phil Jackson proved in Chicago as Jordan's coach and in Los Angeles as Shaquille O'Neal's coach.

Basketball is a team sport, and it's easy to see how stretching and coaching can affect players and teams. Let's briefly talk golf again and illustrate one of the corners of the metaphorical box discussed earlier with Tiger Woods. As I shared in chapter one, I love golf, though I am not a great player. The other day I blasted a drive about three hundred yards and hit a guy right in the back! He pulled off the highway and came looking for me! Wrecked my whole day.

On the other hand, watching Tiger play makes my day! I first saw him live in Augusta when he won the Masters in 1997. Following that win, in a one-year period, Tiger won ten PGA golf tournaments—four of which were prestigious Grand Slam events. After winning the British Open, Tiger was interviewed on international television. One sportscaster asked: "Tiger, I was just talking to your coach, and he told me that currently you are only playing and performing at about 75 percent of your capacity and potential. Is this true?"

Tiger thought for a minute, looked the sportscaster square in the eye, and intensely replied: "Yes, it is true. And my victories this year, especially today, have not come easy." Tiger continued, "You have no idea how hard I worked. I hit hundreds of golf balls every Monday, Tuesday, and Wednesday to prepare for Thursday's opening round of each tournament."

STAYING NUMBER ONE

Tiger, the top money-winner on the tour and the number-one ranked golfer in the world, continued, "This year I have totally changed myself. I have reinvented my golf swing, I have reinvented my golf game and approach to course management, and I have reinvented myself! Every waking hour of every day I have worked my guts out to better myself, strengthen my strengths, eliminate my weaknesses, and finely tune who I am! It's rewarding to see all of this hard work paying off!"

Tiger Woods was the best golfer in the world, yet he still wanted to stretch with his coach and continue to outstretch his previous stretch to become even better. How many of us can say that? How many of us, when at the top of our game, would put even more time and effort into reinventing and finely tuning ourselves to become better than our past *best* personal performance?

Fast forward to 1999. In the first few tournaments, Tiger's name was nowhere to be seen. The press turned on him: "Tiger's lost his stripes. Tiger is no longer Tiger. Tiger's just a quick flash." What happened? In 1999, Tiger's average score per eighteen holes was 68.43. But in 2000, his average score dropped to 67.79 strokes per eighteen holes. Tiger was a better golfer in 2000 than he was in 1999. So what happened?

TIGER SEEKS ADVICE

Tiger has a coach, but he also has an adviser, whom he reportedly paid $600,000 in 2005 even though he has access to magazines, books, and websites for a fraction of the price. Tiger's adviser and caddie is Steve Williams. Tiger, like other PGA players, pays his caddies 10 percent of his winnings for the kind of customized advice that helps him improve his performance. Tiger is a solid businessman, but he also seeks advice from qualified planners, who stretch his portfolio. Tiger knows that stretching is a true principle.

I asked Tiger's friend and fellow PGA pro Mark O'Meara if Tiger was really that much better than other golfers. He shrugged his shoulders, laughed, and said, "No. Tiger is extraordinary with amazing ability, but Tiger is just willing to pay the price. Tiger just wants it more!"

Tiger decided to invest in himself and do whatever it takes to take himself to the next level—if there is one! He hired a new coach who is considered by many to be the *very* best. He brought a fresh perspective to Tiger's shot and finely tuned his swing. As of 2002, Tiger's coach has been Hank Haney, from Dallas, my friend and client, the coaching genius I've already introduced you to in chapter one. To shed some light on Hank Haney's ability to teach and stretch and help anybody get better, let me share a wonderful story to refresh your memory about the importance of hooking up, not only with a best coach (physical therapist/climbing guide) but with the right one.

HANEY AND HEARTWELL

At one of the PGA Senior Tour events at the Stonebriar Country Club in Dallas, a man named Dick Heartwell took his turn on the driving range. As Heartwell started hitting balls—using short irons first and then smashing three-hundred-yard shots with his driver—a group of the biggest names on the Senior Tour gathered around in amazement.

Lee Trevino commented, "My goal is to perfect my swing to be as sweet and smooth as Heartwell's." Hank Haney had taught Dick to play golf and had been coaching him free of charge for years. The coolest thing about Dick Heartwell's golf game is not his beautiful, flawless swing; it's the fact that Dick has only one leg. Hank Haney is a miracle worker and an incredibly intuitional being. As I shared in chapter one, he knows what he is doing on and off the golf course, in sports, and in life.

TIGER WOODS'S PERSONAL WORKOUT

A discussion on stretching would not be complete without sharing what the best of the best do and how they approach their greatness, "best-ness," and rightness. Tiger's personal physical therapist, Keith Kleven, lives in Las Vegas, Nevada, and is also a client and friend. Mr. Kleven, sixty-one, is revered by his colleagues as one of the best and most innovative personal therapists on the planet. He has tested me and worked with me to get myself back in shape from the string of major injuries I've incurred since I hit forty. He's also the one who rehabbed Tiger's knee after his surgery.

On one visit to his office he shared with me routines he has worked up for Tiger. He explained that Tiger is so intent on becoming better today than he was yesterday and that he is always changing his workout, rehab, and weight-lifting schedule—some weeks working on building more bulk in his muscles, some weeks working on speed in specific movements, sometimes working extraordinarily hard just on stamina and endurance.

As of 2006, Tiger was putting in twelve-hour days, six days a week when he was not on tour. He only scales it down Thursday through Sunday while playing tournaments. Tiger hops out of bed every morning to run four miles before eating a nutritious breakfast. He then lifts weights for one-and-a-half hours and goes to the driving range and practice greens to loosen up and hit balls. Then he heads back to the weight room to finish up with a stretching program to keep his incredible flexibility. Tiger then plays nine holes of golf—all of this before he eats a late lunch.

Afterward, he returns to the range and practice green to work on short irons, chipping, and sand traps for one-and-a-half hours. He then plays another nine holes, puts his clubs away, and divorces himself from golf for the rest of the evening. He absolutely loves a quiet, romantic dinner. Family time with his wife and socializing, laughing, joking around, and philosophizing with friends is the focus of every night. But come 7 AM, Tiger is back up and becoming better—more of who he already is.

Coach Haney explained to me that even during the grueling tour schedule, because Tiger flies in his own jet, he arrives at the new tournament location as quickly as he can. First thing early Monday morning, he is up to run his four miles, lift, stretch, hit a large bucket of balls, and eat—all before his practice round! The single most amazing part in all of this Tiger talk is that he does all of this without a personal trainer.

Every celebrity and most professional athletes have personal trainers who push them. Tiger pushes himself because he demands it of himself. Yes, this discussion is about stretching, and we established that we can't push ourselves past the point of discomfort.

Tiger goes to Las Vegas as often as possible and has Keith Kleven stretch him in his office, give him updated exercises and different routines, and push him through some pain. But then Tiger goes on the road by himself and continues to push and push until it's time to return to Keith to be stretched again.

STRETCHING IS CONTAGIOUS

I've been with Tiger up close and personal on several occasions and can verify that Tiger has strong thighs, a thirty-inch waist, broad shoulders, extreme cardiovascular endurance, and extraordinary flexibility. When you know this, it comes as no surprise why Tiger hits the ball so far and has dominated the PGA Tour for so long. So why does Tiger no longer completely dominate? In fact, why has the media turned on him, saying Tiger is no longer Tiger?

Coach Hank is quick to point out that since Tiger came onto the PGA Tour and set such a high bar, one by one, the other pros decided that if they were going to have a chance to win, they too must exercise, watch their diet, lift weights, and increase flexibility. According to Hank, now every PGA pro is lifting weights and hitting the ball longer. Now every pro hits countless practice balls every day. Vee Jay Singh overtook Tiger as the top-rated golfer in the world in 2004, and he hits balls and spends night and day on the practice tee. Rumor has it that he even wanted it more than Tiger. Then, before you knew it, Tiger, with his tenacity and his coach tweaking and working hard in 2005, came back with a vengeance and won the Masters and three other PGA events! Tiger again is the number-one golfer in the world, now having won twelve majors.

Each of us must ask ourselves, "Could I be the Michael Jordan or Tiger Woods of my industry? Could I be the one who stretches and raises the bar in my family, my neighborhood, and my children's schools? Could I stop focusing on having and doing and start focusing on being? And by simply being *more,* could I make everyone with whom I come in contact more and better to the degree that when they are away from me, they honestly say, "I like me best when I'm with you. I want to see you again"?

You can, you should, and you must! Let me introduce a special friend who did.

ROSE

The first day of my senior year in college, a professor introduced himself to our chemistry class and challenged us to introduce ourselves to someone we did not know. Before I could even move, a gentle hand touched my shoulder. I turned around to find a wrinkled, older lady with a giant smile that lit up her entire face like a Christmas tree. She said, "Hey, handsome, my name is Rose. I am eighty-seven years old. Do you want to get lucky?" I laughed and enthusiastically replied, "You incredible gorgeous babe, I'm all yours!" To which she gave me a big hug!

"Why are you in college at your young, innocent age?" I asked.

"I'm here looking for a rich husband," she joked. "You know, get married, have a couple of children, and then retire and travel."

Laughing hysterically, I begged her to be serious. Her answer was simple but profound. "I always dreamed of having a college degree, and so I'm getting one. It is unfinished business. I refuse to die at the base of the mountain with my music stuck inside me. I want to die while climbing."

After class we walked to the student union building and bought chocolate milkshakes. We became instant friends. In fact, every day for the next three months, we left class together, walked across campus to the union building, and got chocolate shakes. For at least an hour, I would sit there totally mesmerized, listening to this time machine expound her wisdom and experience as she shared her life with me.

Over the course of the school year, Rose became a campus icon and generated attention everywhere she went. She loved to dress up and even occasionally wore miniskirts. Guys would whistle at her, and she would always respond by flashing a little leg. In the third week of school she even got a tattoo on her shoulder that she loved to show off. I teased her that I was hurt it didn't say "Dan the Man." Of course, it was a magnificent little red rose.

Once a day, as Rose would walk from class to class, she would stop to rest her weary legs. It was always at the library plaza. With the huge fountain spraying and the breeze blowing mist into the air, Rose would "hold court." Within moments, one to two hundred students would be sitting at her feet basking in her wisdom.

They say wisdom is the gift of the elderly. When an old woman dies, an entire library has been lost. It was in these "Rose beds" that I learned about adversity, crisis management, and attitude. It was in this setting that I saw Rose point at a young coed we all knew was battling cancer. With a bald head covered by a baseball cap, she smiled when Rose explained, "It's not what happens but what we do with what happens that defines us." Rose taught us not to gossip and to "be loyal to those who are not present."

More than twenty-five thousand students knew who Rose was. Every person who ever interacted with Rose always left her saying, "I like me best when I'm with you; I want to see you again."

Rose was so inspirational that we had her speak at our football banquet at the end of the semester. I'll never forget what she taught us. As she began to deliver her prepared remarks, she dropped her three-by-five speech cards on the floor. How would she react? What would you have done? With her speech at her feet, Rose did not react; she responded.

With her speech scattered all over the floor, Rose leaned into the microphone and explained. "I'm sorry I'm so jittery. I gave up beer for Lent, and this whiskey is killing me! I'll never get my speech back together, so let me just tell you what I know." As we laughed, she cleared her throat and began:

"We do not stop playing because we are old; we grow old because we stop playing. In my eighty-seven years I've learned four secrets to staying young, being happy, and achieving success:

"1. *Carpe diem* with humor. Seize each day with laughter. Make people smile and feel wanted, important, lovable, capable, and that they can succeed. Realize that God has a sense of humor.

If you don't believe me, look at the person sitting next to you. They say one out of three people in America is ugly. So look at the person sitting on your left, and look at the person sitting on your right. If they are both good-looking, you're ugly!

"2. Dream. You've got to have a dream. If you don't have a dream, how are you going to make a dream come true? When you lose your dreams, you die. That's why we have so many people walking the halls of life who are dead and don't even know it! Have a reason to get up in the morning. Do something, read something, and be something *more* so you stay interesting and fully alive!

"3. Grow up. There is a giant difference between growing older and growing up. If you are nineteen years old and lie in bed for one full year and don't do one productive thing, you will turn twenty years old. If I am eighty-seven years old and stay in bed for a year and don't do anything and don't get any better or smarter, I will turn eighty-eight. Whoop-de-do! Anybody can grow older. That doesn't take any talent or ability. The idea is to grow up by always finding the opportunity in change.

"4. Leave no regrets. The only people who fear death are those with regrets."

Rose then got close to the microphone and taught us the lesson of the ages. She said, "As I've walked around campus this year, I've noticed how many of you college guys are still wearing your old high school athletic letter jackets. I wanted to tap each one of you on the head and say, 'Yo, buddy. I know you used to be a stud-muffin-hunk-of-burnin'-love, but when your horse dies, dismount! Stop living in the past. Get a life. Dream a new dream. Get a new horse. Gitty up, young men! The only difference between a rut and a groove is its depth and where it's taking you."

As we laughed, Rose concluded her short, yet deeply profound speech by sitting down at the piano and announcing that she had been taking piano lessons for the past year. She then made a lifelong dream come true, singing to an audience the song made famous by Bette Midler called "The Rose."

At year's end, Rose finished her degree and walked across the stage to receive her university diploma to a long, thunderous standing ovation. Two weeks after graduation, believing in her heart that she had run life's race, won life's fight, reached the highest measure of her full potential, and left everybody she encountered in better shape than she had found them, Rose died peacefully in her sleep.

More than two thousand college students attended her funeral to pay tribute to the wonder woman who taught by example that it's never too late to become more of who we already are—all we can possibly be. At the funeral no one mourned her death. It was a celebration of the passionate life Rose led. The service taught that regardless of our age or circumstance, each of us can stretch ourselves, seek the stretch of others, and together stretch each other in our relationships, our lives, and our world. Rose never did anything famous and never made a lot of money. She just left her family, friends, neighborhood, college, city, and state better than we were when she found us.

Is this success? Can she be put in the same category and class as the most famous and wealthy Michael Jordan and Tiger Woods? Of course! In fact, Rose is in a class all by herself. Okay, maybe not by herself. But whatever class she's in as a whole—it don't take too long to call the roll!

Fundamental 6

WHY YOU SHOULD STRETCH

In times of change learners inherit the earth, while the learned find themselves beautifully equipped to deal with a world that no longer exists.

—Eric Hoffer

Young children are famous for asking "why?" And our initial answer usually does not suffice. "Why do I have to take a bath?" or "Why do I have to go to bed?" is usually followed up with a second and third "why?" No matter what we answer, one word responses like "yes" and "no" or the classic, "Because I told you so," are never good enough. "Why" is the motivator. Continually asking "why" is the way we cut through the clutter of our existence and drill down deep enough to move from great to best and transform into right.

Mike Eruzione, team captain of the 1980 US Olympic Hockey Team that beat the Russians and won the gold medal, was asked why they were able to beat the odds and go all the way. Mike answered, "The ones who said we weren't good enough—that we were too small, not strong enough, not fast enough, and couldn't learn the European style of play in such a short period of time—were proved wrong. Wrong, not because they misjudged our abilities. Our abilities deserved seventh place. They were wrong because of the 'intangibles.' How can you measure desire, commitment, faith, passion, and courage?

They weren't able to measure those 'whys.' They weren't able to see how much heart we had, how much pride we had, why we were so close as a team, and why we were willing to pay the price that enabled us to win. You ask why we won. We asked ourselves, 'why not?'"

If we refuse to change we become obsolete. I don't know anyone who really wants to be an obsolete executive, manager, teacher, coach, parent, or friend. No one I know wants to be stagnant or remain ignorant. The challenges of a friend of mine who is an alcoholic (notice my distinction between the person and the performance) validate this and inspired my country song lyric, "Thank God I went through hell, 'cause it was the sickness that made me well." My discussion with him about his wife and beautiful daughter inspired: "Losing you will change her whole life, which should convince you to change yours!"

Charles Darwin discovered in his study of the evolution of sea turtles that it's not the strongest of the species that survive, or the most intelligent, but the ones more responsive to change. Why you should stretch is obviously about change—not about apathetically kicking back and letting your circumstances or bad habits change you, but rather about you changing your bad habits and positively managing your circumstances. Many professional speakers are guilty of this. Many times it's easier to change the audience than it is to change the speech. Some educators know they change students, so why change lessons or teaching techniques they've used since they were student teachers?

We have obsolete administrators and managers using ineffective, autocratic management styles, and we have parents using the same old, outdated, authoritarian parenting techniques they inherited from their "do it because I said so" parents. We have people who forget the Native American adage, "Short time alive, long time dead." And we have people who attend church only because of tradition rather than conviction.

Experts teach us that suicidal thoughts and tendencies are nothing more than a desperate message from ourselves to ourselves that we need a change. Too many people think that if they could just change jobs, get a raise, change neighborhoods, change their body, or change their significant other, they would finally be happy. Maybe, maybe not. But if we wait for change, it might not come. We need to take change into our own hands. *We can change* anything, anytime, anyplace, not through death or outside change but through life.

We have established in previous chapters that change from the inside out is proactive and creates power that allows us to improve and become more of who we already are. What we haven't accentuated is the reason it gives us power. The reason is simple. We succeed only one moment, one step, and one day at a time. Do you believe that one moment in time can change everything?

ONE MOMENT IN TIME

I was on a program with Henry Winkler—"Fonzy" from the old television sitcom *Happy Days*. He is one of the most amazing gentlemen I've ever met. Henry decided to take some time off and treat himself to a matinee movie. To avoid fans making a fuss over him, he entered the theater from the side exit door. He shuffled his way into an aisle and found a vacant seat.

As Henry turned to sit down, a little girl sitting in the row behind him smiled broadly, pointed her finger, and slowly said, "Fonzy." Winkler immediately snapped into the Fonzy character, flipping his hair, swiveling his hips, and glancing left and right. In his signature pose, he then pointed his finger at the girl and said, "Hey, Whoa!" To everyone's surprise, the lady sitting next to the little girl passed out!

The theater manager came in to assist the woman, who was lying in the aisle with a cold pack on her forehead. "Why did you pass out?" someone asked.

Pointing to the little girl, she replied, "My daughter is autistic, and that is the very first word she has ever spoken in her entire life!"

Why?

We know that we must stretch and change before we strength-en and that all the strengthening occurs in the area past the point of discomfort—no pain, no gain. Change is nothing more than improvement. We also know that change can occur rapidly from the outside in and force short-term, emotion-driven change. But to sustain long-term change and continuous improvement, our motivation must come from inside out in a specific step-by-step process.

When we ask, "Why stretch?" and answer, "Because we can—not because it is expected by others but because it is demanded of ourselves," we are admitting that we will initiate change and change our comfort zone—not by going outside the box but by expanding the size of our comfort-zone box and becoming more of who we already are.

Organization feels good. It is calm, it is status quo, and it is steady. To stretch means you will disrupt the organized, disor-ganize, and reorganize. Change always happens on the edge of chaos. A simple visual matrix will help you see and remember the four steps to anticipate and measure your stretch and change:

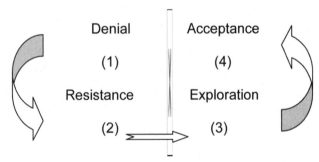

Most managers expect an unreasonable quantum leap from step 1 (Denial) to step 4 (Acceptance). When we finally snap out of Denial on our own as a result of an *intervention*, we must face Resistance from others and ourselves—deal with our pain—and then conduct an Exploration of all the pros of the change. After thirty to sixty days, we are ready for an Acceptance of the stretch and change.

We can't expect a quantum leap, shortcut change in ourselves. But if you have a "you ain't seen nothing yet, the best is yet to be" attitude, it's amazing how exciting, exhilarating, and energizing change becomes. If we remember Walt Disney's observation, we answer the question "Why stretch?" with "Just because I can!": "There are not many heights that can't be scaled by someone who knows the secret of setting high expectations, dreaming big dreams, and working hard to make them come true. Because what we expect to happen will greatly determine what *will* happen."

WHAT GOES AROUND COMES AROUND

A unique directive was initiated at a high school in northern Utah, where students with a physical or mental challenge were fully integrated into the mainstream classes and curriculum. To make the directive work, the administration organized a mentor program that teamed up one special-needs student with a main-stream student, who would help and mentor.

The school athletic director presented the idea to the cap-tain of the football team. John was a tall, strong, intense young man—not the patient, caring type needed for this kind of pro-gram. He made it clear that this wasn't "his thing," and he didn't have time to be a mentor. But the athletic director knew it would be good for John and insisted that he volunteer.

John was matched up with Randy—a young man with Down syndrome. The minute they were introduced, they became insep-arable. Reluctant and irritated at first, John literally tried to lose Randy, but soon John welcomed the constant company. Randy not only attended every one of John's classes and ate with him at lunchtime, but he also came to football practice with him.

After a few days John asked the coach to make Randy the official manager responsible for the balls, tape, and water bottles. At the end of the football season, the team won the state cham-pionship, and John was named state MVP. Randy was presented with a school letter jacket. The team cheered as Randy put it on. It was the coolest thing that had ever happened to him. From that day forward Randy never took it off. He slept in his jacket and wore it throughout each weekend.

Basketball season started, and John became the captain and star of the team. At John's request, Randy was again named the manager. During the basketball season they remained inseparable. Not only did John take Randy to special occasions—like dances as a joint escort for his girlfriend—but he also took Randy to the library to tutor him in his classes. As he tutored Randy, John became a much better student and made the honor roll for the first time in more than a year. The mentor program had made that school year the most rewarding year of John's life.

Then tragedy struck in the middle of the state basketball tournament. Randy caught a virus and died suddenly of pneumonia. The funeral was held the day before the championship game. John was asked to be one of the speakers. In his talk John shared his deep, abiding friendship and respect for Randy. He told how Randy had been the one who had taught him about real courage, self-esteem, love, and the importance of giving 100 percent in everything he did. John dedicated the upcoming state finals game to Randy and concluded his remarks by stating that he was honored to have received the MVP award in football and the Leadership Plaque for being the captain of the basketball team. "But," John added, "the real leader of both the football and basketball teams was Randy, for he accomplished more with what he had than anyone I've ever met. Randy inspired all who knew him."

John walked from behind the podium, took off the irreplaceable, twenty-four-carat gold state football MVP medallion that hung around his neck, leaned into the open casket, and placed it on Randy's chest. Then he placed his leadership plaque next to it.

Randy was buried in his letter jacket, surrounded by John's cherished awards, as well as pictures and letters left by those who admired him. The next day John's team won the championship and presented the game ball to Randy's family. John went to college on a full athletic scholarship, eventually earning a master's degree in education. Today John is a special education teacher and volunteers ten hours a week for the Special Olympics.

THE OLYMPIC TORCH

One moment in time really can change forever. I experienced it time and again as a member of one of the Olympic committees during the 2002 Winter Games. Of all the venues I visited and the fourteen events I attended, my most significant experiences centered on the Olympic torch and the ritual meaning and magic of the Olympic flame.

One of the greatest honors I've received came when I was nominated to carry the Olympic torch on February 7, 2002, in Roy, Utah. General Motors was the international Olympic torch relay sponsor, and Chevy Trucks selected me as one of only 11,520 torchbearers worldwide to carry the torch over a route that covered 13,500 miles across forty-six states (including riverboats and canoes) on a journey that took sixty-five days.

Each runner proudly held the thirty-three-inch, three-and-a-half pound butane-fired torch, and each—cancer survivors, handicapped, sick, dying, old, young—had a story. A high school student ran in front of his school wearing the shoes his brother had worn the day he had been killed at that spot a week earlier. One man who ran on my day was a local firefighter who was running for his father who had lost his life as a firefighter at the World Trade Center on September 11, 2001.

I was the final runner on day sixty-four, which meant instead of carrying the torch the standard quarter mile, as most other runners did, I ran the last half mile and got to relight the caldron mounted in the back of a special truck that transported the flame to downtown Salt Lake City for safe keeping until the next day's magnificent opening ceremonies.

Two weeks before I was to carry the torch I, like every other torchbearer, received a white running suit fitted to my size with an accompanying letter explaining the sacred significance of the Olympic flame. The letter boldly proclaimed that the flame had a soothing, mystical effect on world peace when it was put on display during the Olympic Games, but that the flame's transforming power was experienced and felt mostly by the torch runners themselves. The letter referred to us as "Keepers of the Flame."

Our orientation described the symbolism found in this specific torch: the rough finish (portraying the strength and pioneering spirit of the rugged old West), meshing into the shiny polished surface (portraying progress through high-tech in the twenty-first century), connected by the Olympic theme, "Light the Fire Within" (portraying life in the present). The orientation ended with the reminder that when a torchbearer carries the flame, he and the flame become the world's single most significant symbol of peace, hope, and good will toward men at that single moment in time.

Following the orientation we were put on a small bus and taken to the points from which each runner would step off the bus, stand in the road with his own torch held at a forty-five-degree angle, receive the flame from the oncoming torchbearer, run his segment, pass the flame onto the next relay runner, and reboard the bus to be returned to our families. At the orientation we were formally introduced to the individual who would be passing us the flame.

LIGHT THE FIRE WITHIN

I was runner number 92; runner number 91 was a serious, formal, yet delightful Chinese diplomat who headed the committee of the 2008 Olympic Games to be held in Beijing, China. Having a small four-foot-eleven-inch Chinese communist pass the flame to a six-foot-five-inch blond, blue-eyed American capitalist was a wonderful context for putting our differences aside, coming together as human beings to fairly compete, and creating peace on earth. The power of the flame exposed cultural commonalities, and cultural commonalities eliminate ridicule, prejudice, and anger. Cultural commonalities remind us that we are all part of the family of humanity!

My experience was phenomenal and metaphorical in nature. As thousands of onlookers watched, cheered, chanted "USA," and waved miniature American flags, a police officer on the motorcycle escort turned on the gas container in my torch, and I stood in the middle of the road with my torch held out with both hands. The approaching torchbearer was instructed to stop, keep our torches eight inches apart, and let the flame leap from his torch to mine. His torch was then extinguished by the officer, and I ran off as the single keeper of the flame, representing everything the Olympic Games are about.

Think about it. This flame brought ninety-three countries together; ironically, people from ninety-three countries died in the World Trade Center terrorist attacks only a few months before.

RELAY INSPIRATION

Having been moved by my experience, I interviewed the young lady on board our shuttle bus who had been in charge of the entire sixty-five-day torch relay. I milked her for stories that proved true the power of the flame. With tears in her eyes, she related several experiences regarding her responsibility as director of the relay to make sure every scheduled torchbearer showed up on time. If one canceled at the last minute, she would have to find a qualified replacement, orient him to the significance of being a keeper of the flame, fit and outfit him in the required white running suit, and take him to his relay segment.

When one man with cancer received his letter stating that he had been nominated to carry the torch, he immediately put the date on his calendar. Against the advice of his doctor, he started training to be in shape when the day came. His cancer quickly spread, and his training threw him into a coma. The lady in charge of the relay was notified, and while she was arranging a replacement runner, the man miraculously came out of his two-week coma on the morning he was to run. He was delivered to the pick-up point in an ambulance, assisted to the middle of the road with his torch to receive the flame from the oncoming runner, had his torch ignited, and proudly ran his quarter-mile segment.

No one could believe it, and everyone cheered as they witnessed the inner strength exposed and supported by the spirit and power of the Olympic flame. As soon as the man lit the next runner's torch and his torch was extinguished, he collapsed in the road and was put back in the ambulance. Seconds later he lapsed back into a coma and died soon after arriving at the hospital.

Go, Billy, Go!

When the torch relay went through Houston, Texas, one elderly woman phoned to cancel the night before her run. Early the next morning the relay director drove along the relay route, prospecting for some possibilities when she happened upon an elementary school. She parked the bus, went inside, and asked to speak with the principal.

With a huge sense of urgency, the relay director said she needed someone to carry the Olympic torch in about two hours and that the torchbearer would run directly in front of the school building. She asked the three people in the office—the principal, the counselor, and the secretary—if they could think of someone who could use the experience to help change the lives of others. Immediately they began spouting names of faculty; the principal was even nominated.

The relay director interrupted them and said, "I need the name of a young student who struggles at school with his grades, who sits alone and is terribly lonely, who other kids make fun of, who has been given up on by the teachers, who has a horrible home life, and who has low self-esteem."

All three fell into a moment of dead silence and then simultaneously blurted out the name of a poor, scruffy, skinny little ten-year-old fourth-grade boy. They immediately called Billy to the office, where he was informed of his selection. His mother was notified and invited, permission was granted, and Billy was taken out to the bus to a closet full of every-sized running suits, and directed on how to hold and carry his torch. Billy was also told about the importance of the Olympic movement and the special significance of carrying the torch—that he would be one of the most important people on the whole earth for the time he was the keeper of the flame.

Unbeknownst to the faculty or students that Billy would be running, school was dismissed and small American flags were distributed to faculty and students, who joined the thousands already lining the streets to cheer on the forthcoming torchbearers. As the shuttle bus drew closer, the crowd went wild. The torchbearer was running a quarter-mile behind, which allowed the bus to stop in time for the announcer to call the name of the new runner over the sound system, for the runner to be let off the bus, and for him to stand in the road and hold his torch out to be ignited by the approaching runner.

Billy's name was announced, and the usually dirty kid emerged in his spectacular running suit, holding the magnificent Olympic torch, which was almost as long as he was. Fellow students and faculty gasped, "What is this? Who let him do this? Did he steal the suit? Oh my gosh, call the police and report an imposter! He must have stolen the torch!"

As Billy's torch was ignited and he started to run, somehow his name filtered through the crowd. Some people suddenly started chanting, "Bill–y, Bill–y, Bill–y!" One by one the skeptical, negative faculty members realized at that moment that little Billy was the world's ambassador of peace, that he alone epitomized the power of a positive dream. They couldn't help but join in with their support, chanting "Bill–y, Bill–y."

Fellow students couldn't hold back either as they too began to understand, shouting, "Go, Billy, go. Keep on truckin', Billy. You're the man!" Billy's proud smile got so big and wide that he could have eaten a banana sideways!

Billy completed his quarter mile, lit the next torch, had his extinguished, and reboarded the bus to be taken back to a parking lot to meet his mom. The students and faculty returned to the school.

Two days later, the relay director received an email from the school principal. "You have no idea what you have done for Billy, his family, and for me, our teachers, and students. None of us will ever be the same. The Olympic spirit and the power of that flame have helped us look for the good, not the bad, to be positive, tolerant, loving, forgiving, and definitely less judgmental. We have been reminded that every kid matters. We now understand the meaning of 'Leave no child behind,' that everyone can make a significant contribution if we'll just believe in them and encourage them to let go of the past, succeed in the present, and prepare for the future. Thank you, thank you, thank you! This one moment in time changed us all. *P.S. Billy no longer sits alone!"*

FLIGHT-ATTENDANT STRETCH

Something most of us are familiar with is the preflight demonstration that flight attendants do prior to takeoff. Why don't I pay attention? Because it's always the same. But what happens when a flight attendant stretches? What happens when the flight attendant looks inward and digs deeper to be more and do more than the written presentation? Do we notice such stretching?

Once I was flying on Delta Airlines into Dallas, Texas, when we hit huge wind turbulence. The plane was knocked around violently in the sky. When we landed, the plane hit the runway hard, we bounced, then hit again, bounced, then hit a third and final time, skidded, and screeched. In response, the flight attendant came over the P.A. system and said in her thick southern drawl, "Welcome to Dallas, Texas. If you enjoyed your flight, tell your friends you flew Delta Airlines. If you did not enjoy your flight, tell your friends you flew Southwest."

Everyone suddenly tuned in, laughed, and listened. She then said, "And please remain seated with your seat belt fastened while Captain Kangaroo bounces us the rest of the way to the gate." Now we were rolling with laughter. Is this stretching contagious? An elderly woman, walking with her cane in the aisle in front of me, stopped at the door and asked a uniformed man, "Are you the pilot?" He smiled and proudly answered, "Yes, ma'am." She then asked, "Did we really land, or did we get shot down?"

We stretch because we *can* stretch.

Those of us who fly know that Southwest Airlines is the first airline that inculcated "making flying fun" into their job description and corporate culture. The other major airlines state that the flight attendants are there for your safety. Yes, but they should first be there for customer service and customer fun. It took the industry a while, but look at what this stretching did to influence the rest of the airline industry—not just in personality expectations but also in pricing and on-time delivery. Airlines were forced to stretch and internally change if they wanted to compete! We are the same way. Sometimes we must stretch—we have no choice. But when stretching comes from inside the box with the understanding that why we stretch is because we can, it's all good!

BORN OR MADE?

Don't you think at minimum we should always be grateful for what we have, say please and thank you, and address our elders with respect? Please don't tell me this is a stretch. Why we do this is obvious, isn't it? Isn't it obvious why we should not burp in public or pass gas around others and not use vulgarity in mixed company, and why we should greet people with eye contact and a firm handshake, and always do what's right simply because it's the right thing to do? We're not born with class and sophistication. We learn it and practice it and live it. Table manners are a little thing but so important. And everyone should always open doors for others and especially let an older or disabled person have a seat. Respect for authority and other people's property, space, and time is a sign that we respect ourselves.

Inside-out change and internal stretch say we would never wait for someone to remind us of fundamental etiquette. On our own, we should always be on time, keep promises and commitments, and most important, always be the role model family and friends can look up to. Why? Simply because we can.

Let me share a personal experience for illustration. It begins with a song I wrote called "Special Man" that used to get radio play. I quoted the first line earlier and now share the entire tune.

Special Man

A little boy wants to be like his dad,
So he watches us night and day.
He mimics our moves and weighs our words,
He steps in our steps all the way.
He's sculpting a life we're the model for,
He'll follow us happy or sad.
And his future depends on example set,
'Cause the little boy wants to be just like his dad.

A special man talks by example,
Takes the time to play and hug his lad.
A special man walks by example,
The very best friend a growing boy ever had.
Any male can be a father,
But it takes a special man to be a dad.

He needs a hero to emulate,
He breathes, "I believe in you."
Would we have him see everything we see?
And have him do what we do?
When we see the reverence that sparkles and shines,
In the worshipping eyes of our lad,
Will we be at peace if his dreams come true,
And he grows up to be just like his dad?

(Child): I'm just a little guy doing my best,
With me God isn't through.
Don't lose your grip and yell "grow up,"
That's what I'm trying to do.
Folks shouldn't bring a child to earth
If they won't guide us through.
But because you have, I love you, Dad,
And I know you love me too.

This song is about my dad, S. Wayne Clark. He always set a high, powerful, positive example for me to stretch by challenging me to grow and improve from the inside out. As a special man, my dad always understood the importance of one person acting at one moment in time. He understood that influencing others was based on a mindset of what goes around comes around. My dad was, is, and always will be my hero. My relationship with him is captured in words he gave to me upon which I can build my own father-son relationships: "A boy is a bank where we deposit our most precious treasure, hard-won wisdom, and dreams for a better world. The future is his, and through him, the future is ours." In this vein, before I tell you my story, let me share two of my dad's.

AMAZING MAYO

As I mentioned earlier, when my dad was taken to the hospital for exploratory surgery and came out not only diagnosed with malignant cancer but also given only six months to live, my family was sad and frightened. An attending physician who was a friend pulled me aside and explained that Dad was so sick and his vital signs were so weak that he might only last a few weeks. He didn't even have strength to walk and was confined to a wheelchair.

Fast-forward one week as one of Dad's doctors attended a lecture by a physician who presented a paper on carcinoid cancer—my dad's rare disease. During the seminar he heard of a special program at the world famous Mayo Clinic in Rochester, Minnesota, that Dad qualified for. As one of twenty-five experimental patients with a six-month life expectancy, Dad flew back to Rochester, and we went with him. The Mayo Clinic immediately stood out from all other hospitals. There was no wait at admissions, and my dad was made to feel like he was the single most important person who ever walked in the door. Presidents, kings, rulers, and celebrities all come to the Mayo Clinic, and as one of hundreds of patients, each receives extraordinary care.

My dad was carefully wheeled into a large, sterile room with no furniture in it. There we met Team Mayo—twelve polished professionals all dressed in their uniforms. World-renowned chief oncologist Dr. Scutt took charge and softly and politely introduced each of his eleven colleagues as his equal. There were no ego trips or pecking order. He introduced the nutritionist, then the dietician, then the orthopedic specialist, and then the physical therapist. He introduced another oncologist, an abdominal/intestinal specialist, nurses, nurses' aids, and even a music therapist certified in natural herbal organic treatment.

All were equal and important to the care of my dad because each brought a unique outlook and expertise from their training and education. This first impression bolstered the level of confidence we had in the doctors and their treatment as they made it crystal clear that Mayo was not about any one of them—it was only about making my sweet dad well!

Dr. Scutt knelt in front of my dad's wheelchair and said, "There is a difference between dying of cancer and living with cancer. What will it be?" My dad's sad face slowly lit up with the first smile since his surgery. As the positive energy and confident conversation of hope continued, color came back into his cheeks, and his hollow eyes got back their glimmer. Seven days later my dad walked out of the Mayo Clinic on his own with renewed physical and emotional strength, stable vital signs, genuine hope of healing, and a real understanding of how they were all going to help him fight off his horrible disease if he would lead the fight himself.

My dad went on to live six and a half years and was the only one of the twenty-five experimental patients who lived beyond the six-month prediction. Every twelve weeks my dad went to Mayo for seven days of tests and treatments. He said he fought hard because he wanted to give all he could to Mayo and help them advance their specialized treatment for carcinoid cancer. Because of my dad's successful, long-term care, the FDA approved the drug given to him for regular use in other hospitals in the United States. My dad loved the Mayo Clinic, and so do all of us in the Clark Clan. Thank you, Team Mayo!

The "Mayo Way"

A second story my dad shared was about flying back to Mayo by himself for a week of tests and treatment. What he experienced epitomizes the polished, professional, and compassionate service rendered by absolutely everyone in every department. Our family affectionately calls it the "Mayo Way."

Dad was to be tested by a special echocardiograph. A tube is inserted in the patient's esophagus so that the operator can view the heart from a closer point than the heretofore echo and traditional cardiograph would permit.

The machine to be used had been newly developed and had not yet been acquired by other hospitals in the United States. In due course, Dad was lying on the table. The incredible Dr. A. Jamil Tajik, his assistant, and a nurse who would take care of the intravenous injections were hovering over Dad.

"After preparations got under way, including the spraying of my throat to make it numb and more receptive to the black tube, Dr. Tajik asked me if I had any of my family with me," Dad said. "I told him that I was alone. He said there were some risks in using the machine that he had to advise me of. At the end of the tube was a mirror-like tip through which the action of the heart was relayed to a screen. The good doctor explained that as he attempted to thrust the tube down my throat he might cut the esophagus, or he might even cut the heart." I asked him, 'What then?' and he replied that I could die on the table. With a deep breath, I knew I could trust a Mayo doctor and agreed to the procedure. The first try the tub would not go down. He pulled it back up, and the second time he was successful."

Dad concluded, "I presume that the nurse noticed a tear in my eye that dropped and ran down my check as we proceeded with the test. She promptly and gently held my hand and began to whisper and assure me that everything would be all right. I had never felt the need for third-party support as strongly as I did at that moment. And in the 'Mayo Way,' that dear nurse, whose name I will probably never know, gave me, through her soft, confident voice and compassionate, tender touch, a beautiful fulfillment that I would be fine. As I lay helpless on that uncomfortable bed a thousand miles from home, she refused to let me feel alone."

DAD'S LAST DAY

My story, as I referred to it, that I always use as an intimate and powerful illustration of the second cornerstone of the metaphorical box, is also about my dear dad. As I explained, my dad battled cancer for six and a half years—a rare cancer in his intestines, stomach, and liver called carcinoid. As the pain mounted and Dad's last day was approaching, I was hopeful that I could be by his bedside when he took his last breath. But that didn't happen for me. I had to fly out for back-to-back engagements. I was in Seattle, Washington, to give two speeches to two large groups—one at meeting on Friday morning, the other at a convention on Saturday.

I was staying out of town at the Seattle Airport Marriott Hotel. It was early Friday morning, October 12. I had shaved and showered and put on my coat and tie when the phone rang. Thinking it was my ride to the convention, I picked up the phone and almost flippantly said, "I'll be right there." Fifteen seconds of silence later my younger brother's voice pierced the quietness of the call, "Danny?" Shocked, I tentatively answered, "Paul? What's up?"

Another fifteen seconds of silence started my heart pounding out of my chest. Then Paul confirmed my greatest fear. "Dad passed away this morning at 7 AM."

I sat down on the bed, and the tears immediately started to flow. I asked, "How is Mom?" He said, "Good." I said, "Give her a big hug and a kiss for me, and tell her I'll phone her in a little while." Paul then asked me the gazillion-dollar question: "What are you going to do?" What would you do?

After a moment of consideration, I said, "I'm going to go make my speech. That's what Dad would want me to do. He always taught us to only make commitments that we can keep and to always keep those commitments."

I thought it through out loud as I continued to talk to Paul. "I can't imagine what it would be like to be the meeting planner with more than 2,500 people sitting in the audience and not have the speaker show up. Dad always taught us to keep our promises. I need to stay here and speak and spend the night, speak tomorrow, and then hustle home. God knows I need your support, and hopefully I can give you some of mine. I know that you and the rest of our family and Mom's huge circle of friends will comfort Mom and each other. Mom will understand that my decision is exactly what Dad would want me to do. I'll talk to Mom later today and will see you tomorrow."

I hung up the phone and broke down crying like a baby. My dad, my hero, was gone! And I was ripped and wrenched with the pain of regrets. Every thought and word was, "I wish I . . . If only I had . . . " For the record, I've done a lot of pretty cool things in my life and have had an exciting time. But I would trade it all for just one more day with my dad. I miss him very much and have too many regrets!

As an author, I love to interview people, especially elderly people (elderly meaning someone older than I am!). When I interview older people, I am often told that they do not have regrets for things they did; they only have regrets for things they did not do. Do you? Will you? I did. I still have regrets, and it's a living hell. They say religion is for those who are afraid to go to hell. Spirituality is for those who have already been there. I am a much more spiritual being now. Religion teaches that hell comes to the unbeliever after death. But I also believe that hell is where the man I am comes face to face with the man I could have been. I still have regrets regarding my dad and don't wish regrets on anyone.

THE BELLMAN

Fifteen minutes had gone by when the phone rang again. This time it was my ride. I told him I would be right down. I went into the bathroom, splashed some water on my face to freshen up, left my room, and entered the elevator. As the elevator doors began to close, the corner of a bellman's cart crammed its way through the narrow opening and the doors binged back open. On the elevator came an overzealous, way-too-cheery, psycho bellman. He pushed his cart to the middle, forcing me back to the rear corner. Trying to avoid eye contact, I stood with my head down, hands clasped in the "elevator position." As the doors closed he blurted, "Yee-haw! Whoa! Did you see the beautiful sunshine today? I've lived here in Seattle all of my eighteen years, and it's rained every single day. You must have brought the good, happy weather with you. How ya doin'?"

Not looking up I said, "Fine." He kept staring at me until he again blurted, "No, sir, you're not fine. Your eyes are red and a little puffy. You've been crying." Instinctively, I replied, "Yeah. I just found out that my dad died this morning, and I'm really sad." The bellman said, "Whoa," and went hauntingly quiet until the doors opened at the lobby. He went left, and I went right.

Fast forward to the introduction of my speech. I had to dig deeper than I had ever dug in my life to rise to the occasion, but I did, and I made my speech. At the end of my speech I told the audience I would conclude with a song from one of my albums. I told them the reason I was singing it was that my dad died that morning, and it would be the first time he had ever heard me sing it in public. It was a song I wrote the day my dad came out of cancer surgery when they gave him six months to live. My dad told me it was his favorite song I had ever recorded, and I ended up singing it at his funeral.

Will I See You Again?

There's a feeling stuck inside me 'bout a leader of life's band.
You're the one who showed me how to play, and whispered, "Yes, you can!"
You taught me life and living love; your wisdom was my friend.
Will I see you again?
There's a memory-making motion 'bout a beacon burning bright.

*You're the one who turned my troubled times from darkness into
    light.*
Your guiding ray unveiled the way, you counseled 'til the end.
Will I see you again?

You always cautioned at the door, "Remember who you are,"
'Cause I guess you saw in me what I could be.
I needed you to need me, and you stretched a helping hand,
Unselfishly, so tenderly left footprints in my sand.
You let me understand.

*There's a notion nestled in me 'bout the rules of the Master
    Man,*
*Even though you lost the battle here, you won the war, His
    plan.*
I'll miss your hugs and eyes that grin, but we'll meet once more
So long 'til then.
When I see you again?
Yes, I'm gonna see you again.

I finished the song and had the driver take me to the Seattle
Aquarium. Why the aquarium? To run from change? To avoid
pain? To stop the stretch? Absolutely not! Rather, to create a
special ambiance and safe environment in which I could think
and feel and focus on what matters most. It's the same reason
that a corporation or organization has a meeting off campus at a
nice hotel or resort—to get away, gain perspective, and recom-
mit to the most important issues and people.

That night at the aquarium, I "questioned and answered"
myself and thoroughly evaluated my innermost beliefs and feelings. In the tranquil setting of water and slow-swimming beautiful creatures, I remembered that we are all going to die and that
we have to deal with it by living every day to leave no regrets. I
contemplated my own mortality and asked the better questions
to get the better answers like, "Where did I come from? Why am
I here? Where am I going? Does character count? Surely there is

a reward for obedience, so what will the judgment judge? Did my parents sign a divorce certificate the same time they signed their marriage certificate ('until death do us part')? Or is there a higher universal law officiated by a higher authority in which marriage is performed for time and all eternity and families can stay together so I can see my dad again? If families aren't forever, then what's forever for?"

A lot of the principles I knew suddenly made more sense like, "Pain is a signal to grow, not to suffer, and once we learn the lesson the pain is teaching us, the pain goes away." Short time alive—long time dead. We should do things that won't just help us when we are alive but that will also help us when we are dead. Having learned the lessons by reflecting on my strong theology that, yes, I would see my dad again, I had the driver take me back to the Seattle Airport Marriott Hotel.

Here is where you come into my story. Here is where you either accept or reject my challenge to be like the Delta flight attendant, to be like Tiger Woods, to stretch and change from the inside out and be more than you're expected to be.

I walked into the hotel room, and there on the chest of drawers was a basket of fruit. Not your basic basket delivered from the hotel gift shop with the colored cellophane cover, ribbon bow, and small sterile stamped card from the manager that seldom gets your name right—"Thanks for staying with us, Ralphie." This basket was a broken basket, slightly smashed on one side. It appeared as if it was a last-minute gesture with no resources available.

Whoever delivered it was obviously into presentation because the crinkled portion of the basket was turned toward the wall and covered by a big, silky, rubberized leaf that had apparently been picked off the fake tree in the lobby. In the basket were two oranges and an apple that had a little bite out of it. (No exaggeration!) Now I don't think the deliverer got hungry on the way up to the room and snacked on it. I believe that he was into presentation and had found this huge, luscious, polished, red Washington apple that was perfect for his presentation. He couldn't help it if it had a crunch taken from it. The good definitely outweighed the bad, and the color was important. The fruit basket also had in it a big, ripe tomato and a long, thick carrot.

THE NOTE

Most important, in my basket was a hand-written note that said, "Mr. Clark, I'm sure sorry your dad died. I was off work today at 5 PM, but I came back tonight so I could be here for you. Room service closes at 10 PM, but the kitchen has decided to stay open all night long so they can be here just for you. If you need anything, just call and ask for me. Signed, James—the bellman in the elevator."

James was not the only one to sign the card. Every single employee that night at the Seattle Airport Marriott Hotel signed my little card. I have it matted, framed, and hanging in my office!

Let's put this experience into perspective and briefly rekindle the lesson learned. Here we have James, an eighteen-year-old young man, the youngest person on the entire employee payroll, who "gets it." Here we have James, the lowest-paid person on the entire employee payroll, who "gets it." Gets what? Service above self, stretch, inside-out change, improvement to become more of who he already is, in-the-box thinking, and behavior that exceeds external expectations, being more than he has been simply because he wants to—motivated by the simple fact that he can!

What James gets we all need to get: that age has nothing to do with success. We can't honor our elderly enough and need to pay big bucks for experience, but age is not a factor. Some of the greatest songs you will ever hear were written by young men and women. They have access to the same twelve notes as the old songwriters do. James also gets the process for creating loyal customers. We all know that the only place from which a person can grow is where he or she is. We must go where they are physically and emotionally. Only there can we gently invite them to grow. James reached out to me and created loyalty to his employer. As a professional speaker, I am always booked at the same hotel where they hold the meeting, and most of the time the hotels are posh where the towels in my room are so fluffy I have a hard time getting my suitcase closed. But every time I speak in Seattle, I try to stay at the Airport Marriott, even if I have to rent a car at my own expense.

To conclude, let us visit one of the lessons of the terrorist attacks of September 11, 2001. What motivates someone (a firefighter, a police officer, a soldier) to run into a burning building to save and assist someone they don't know? On United flight 93 that crashed in Pennsylvania, what motivated those few men on the hijacked plane to say, "Let's roll," and do something brave, courageous, and extraordinary to change an otherwise more horrible outcome? Was the motivation money, a raise in pay, better benefits, recognition, a promotion, or a sales trip to the Bahamas?

In the authentic, big-picture world of what matters most, what it's really all about is stretching and changing and being more—everything we were born to be! We initially stretch ourselves, but with the help of a "physical therapist of the mind, spirit, and soul," we stretch each other *and* keep the stretch alive. It really is true. When the water in the lake goes up, all the boats rise together!

Fundamental 7

HOW YOU SHOULD STRETCH

The weaknesses of the many make leaders possible and necessary. We are strengthened when we know what they know, with hope and faith in things that are not seen, which are true.

Is the twenty-first century really about high-speed changes and technological advances? Yes, and how exhilarating and exciting. This is not a contradiction to my previous statement that my job as a professional speaker is to slow you down. This book is designed to slow you down long enough to gain perspective and find the true purpose and meaning of life that only you can give it. But unless we all proactively keep our internal stretch changing at the same rate as our external techno-stretch, we will plummet to a low level of reactive personal insecurity fueled by pressure and worries of the unknown. Only proactive control of our stretch allows us to rise to a high level of personal power and control of our destiny. In other words, high-tech change is great and welcomed, but it remains only a tool.

What if we allow technology to completely overrun our society and tomorrow you go to your doctor's office and there is no human being? All you get is a recording, "If your pain is below the waist, press one." What if you are Catholic and they put the entire confessional system on voice mail? "1-800-Fessupp. If you are into bigamy press two; if you're worshiping the devil press 666." Is this where we're headed? I certainly hope not. Skillsoft, Microsoft, Oracle,

Sisco, Hewlett Packard, Novell, Word Perfect, SAP, Samsung, and other companies are cutting-edge, global leaders in technological research and e-learning development. But they are successful because of their passionate, creative, and imaginative people.

"How" is obviously the plan—the "getting-from-here-to-there" part of every endeavor. It's the most personal and unique part of execution. We can and need to share our "whys" and reasons. Objectives and goals get us on the same path and moving in the same direction. But each of us has our own unique walk and style and way in which we accomplish the whys. We hear the same music yet dance differently to the same beat.

In the early 1940s, Cal Farley started the famous "Boys Ranch" for troubled teens in Arizona. For decades, his what, why, when, and where results have been phenomenal and conventional, while his methods for turning these boys' lives around have been unconventional. What makes Farley's teaching philosophy based on unconditional love, giving responsibility, and expecting obedience so legendary are his how-to's:

- Shine a boy's shoes and he'll stay out of mud holes.
- With a boy, the tone of your voice in how you say something is more important than what is said.
- The boy who has done just as he pleases for twelve to fourteen years isn't easy to saddle and bridle in just a month.
- Performance, not pedigree, establishes a boy's rating.
- The wildest colts make the best horses when properly trained.
- To handle boys, be honest, be positive, be fair, be consistent.
- Don't take your boy to a psychiatrist; take him to the woodshed. Then use a little sugar to keep him from growing sour.
- Any boy from the alleys, given a home, some fresh air, and shown how to raise his standard of living by merely conforming to a few rules of good citizenship will never willingly go back to his old way of life.

As we have already mentioned, in our twenty-first century world of high-tech we must overcompensate with high touch. How we stretch has always been and will always be through people and on a team or in the corporate setting. The stretching is most often initiated by the leaders.

THE LEADERSHIP TOUCH

Steve Murray, consultant, author, and editor of the publication *REALTrends*, has surveyed hundreds of realtors across America. Two of his questions are relevant here: What is more important in your company—results or people? How do you know? Among the responses Steve shared with me, the employees of one of the largest real estate companies in Connecticut all agreed that their CEO is an extraordinarily personable, loving, and compassionate leader who genuinely cares about each of them and their families more than results. And how do they know this? On September 11, 2001, the barbaric terrorist attacks on the World Trade Center obviously left the lives of surviving family members devastated forever. In this one Stamford-based real estate company, twenty-three agents lost a mom or dad or brother or sister. One female agent lost her husband and both of her sons who worked together in the same Trade Center office. Her whole family was wiped out in a single moment. The company president didn't just phone these employees up and say, "If there's anything I can do, let me know." He and his wife jumped in his car and immediately raced to each of their homes to mourn with them and make sure they had meals brought in and help with their children and other personal matters.

We all can pretend to care, but we can't pretend to care the way this corporate leader cared. He attended all twenty-three funerals, helped with all of the details, and stayed extra close and "on call" in the weeks ahead. It's the human touch and the physically being there, not words of sorrow or strength, that facilitate the healing power of the universe. My song "I just Stayed to Help Her Cry" suddenly made more sense in the context of this story. And because at some point you do have to get on with your life and keep running the business, when it was time to work and focus on profits, the hundreds of employees never forgot what their leader did, and they increased productivity with a deeper sense of loyalty!

STRETCHING FACE TO FACE

We've got to take advantage of every opportunity to communicate face to face and heart to heart. Too many people at work email when their co-worker is only a short distance away. Teenagers would rather text each other than call on the phone to have a personal conversation. I've been on stage speaking in a large ballroom to a large audience, where the audio-visual setup included an IMAG system of television-type cameras that projected me live on a huge screen so the people in the back could see me. The odd and troubling part of this scene is that people sitting in the first five to ten rows who could see me up close and personal were not looking at me. They were watching me on the giant projection screens! The answer to how we stretch is personal communication.

In a previous chapter I mentioned that the average person speaks four hundred to eight hundred words per minute and yet thinks eight hundred to twelve hundred words per minute. Thoreau's words of living life in "quiet desperation" are true. I will establish the importance of communication by devoting all of chapter 15 to the subject. However, because this chapter is about intimate connection, I will quickly present some details to take this Cornerstone discussion to a deeper level.

GENDER DIFFERENCES

Stretching occurs not between machines but between people—often between men and woman. For this reason, there is a gender difference you should be aware of.

Communication experts have documented that men speak approximately 12,000 words per day. Sounds like a lot until you compare it with women, who experts say speak 25,000 words per day. To concede that it's okay for women to talk more than twice as much as men seems harmless until we realize that when men have used up their 12,000 words, they shut up, shut down, and shut off.

If a man has used all 12,000 of his words during the day at work, when he comes home he doesn't want to talk anymore and in reality, has nothing left to say. However, the woman has had a great or poor experience at work with perhaps some additional children's responsibilities and has spoken 12,000 words during her hectic day. When she gets home she has so much more that she wants to talk about.

Another man who is aware of this word-total formula is willing to alter his natural male tendencies to listen and respond to the remaining 13,000 words crying to come out of his wife. Listening, understanding, and intimately connecting another human being is the only way we can stretch ourselves and take our personal and professional lives to the next level. The way to turn a house into a home is through open and right communication. Stretching with family members and using correct and empathetic communication skills build strong families. Transforming a team of *best* players into a team of *right* players begins and ends with clear and complete communication. Stretching begins and ends with inside-the-box human touch—first connecting in a deeper, purely authentic way with ourselves and then with others.

I have already discussed music and the twelve notes that have been used in writing every song. Let me briefly mention the power of the lyric. In the English language, there are only twenty-six letters in the alphabet. Yet every word is an amalgamation of the letters. Change the order and you change the meaning. G-O-D is something omnipotent and magnificent; D-O-G is a lovable, loyal, four-legged companion.

Stretching requires that we first get in touch with ourselves—our thoughts, passion, creativity, imagination, hearts, and emotion.

We determine how we stretch, but as we established, we can only take ourselves so far. How we stretch is determined by people—our individual, personal, intimate interaction with ourselves stimulated by another. I wrote the following story that songwriter Don Schlitz turned into a wonderful hit song and amazing music video recorded by superstar Kenny Rogers called "The Greatest." Music is a powerful stretcher!

MUSICAL STRETCH

A father promised that he'd play baseball with his son after work if the boy practiced all day. When the father arrived home, they went to the backyard.

"Show me what you can do," the father said. The little boy shuffled his feet, threw the ball up in the air, took a swing, and missed. "Strike one," said the dad.

The son repositioned his feet, threw the ball up again, took a second swing, and missed again. His father said, "Strike two."

More determined then ever, the kid dug deeper, threw the ball higher, and took a third mighty swing. He missed again, spun completely around, and fell on the ground. His father said, "Strike three, you're out. What do you think about that?"

The youngster stood up, brushed himself off, and said, "Man, am I a good pitcher!"

Of all the songs I've written striving to stretch myself and others, my song "A Real Man" is my favorite:

A Real Man
I need a man,
Who knows happily ever after
Is a day-at-a-time proposition,
A man who knows makin' love
Is not a three-minute composition.
It's a slow dance, full of romance, a walk on the beach in the sand.
It's having a whole conversation, just by holding my hand.
He would stir deep desire that sets me on fire
To be with him all that I can.
No, no I won't settle for anything less than a real man.

Chorus
A real man's strong in stature, firm in faith, and kisses slow,
He sometimes cries, and when we hug, he's the last one to let go,
Worshipping the ground I walk on, he's my biggest fan,
There's nothin' like being loved by a real man.

I need a man
Who knows honoring me and my dreams
Is a macho disposition,
A man who knows "I love you"
Is a more than words rendition.
It's roses for no reason, secret love notes in my drawer,
It's making me his equal, yet he always gets my door.
He would never raise his hand to me, he believes in who I am,
Yea, I can be more than I thought I could be,
With a real man.

He talks to me through touch,
I'm swept away in every clutch,
We're lovers but our friendship's true
I like me best when I'm with you.

When I quote these lyrics in a speech or when women hear it performed, they usually cat call, whistle, moan, clap, and get that urge to smoke! They love these words, which inspire them to find a "real man" with such stretching possibilities. When men hear this song, they usually cringe and, with a scowl, moan, "Oh, perfect—put the pressure on!"

I was interviewed on Country Music Radio and was asked how a linebacker could write a sensitive, insightful, love song like "A Real Man." I answered, "It was easy. I just made a list of things I wasn't, and I decided I could stretch and change and be more than I ever had been before. I knew the only place from which we can grow is where we are. I knew I had to see who I am and say who I am before I could stretch who I am, and I did. I decided I could set a higher personal bar and a more passionate standard of inner excellence, and I did. I am stretching and changing because I can. And how am I stretching? Through a deeper understanding of others and myself and through more constant and frequent feedback.

INCREASING FREQUENCY OF FEEDBACK

Feedback is the breakfast of champions. It determines our direction and destination. When NASA shot a rocket to the moon, feedback determined its direction and destination. When it went off course, the astronauts heard "bleep, bleep, bleep," and either electronically or manually the course was corrected. So what would happen if NASA had launched the rocket and waited ninety days to check up on it like some do in the corporate world with their quarterly reports? The rocket would be headed toward Uranus and would require extra work, effort, time, and money to bring it back in line. We all know that the quicker we recognize weakness or misdirection, the easier it is to fix it and get ourselves back on track to reach a desired destination.

Increasing our frequency of feedback allows us to change our behavior before it's too late and become more of who we already are. To illustrate, let me compare two winter Olympic events that take place on the same ice rink: figure skating and hockey. First let me discuss figure skating. I don't think it's a sport as much as it is an amazing extravaganza. Yes, they are athletes—strong, flexible, and balanced—but it's more entertainment than competition because there is no feedback.

FIGURE SKATING

During the Olympic Winter Games in Salt Lake City in 2002, I attended the figure skating finals. As two figure skaters' names were announced over the PA system, they emerged from behind the backstage curtain area, smiling and holding hands. Curiously, I watched as they skated to their places in the center of the ice. In seconds, they posed a John Travolta one-arm-up-*Saturday-Night-Fever*-disco pose, signaled the music to begin, and off they went. After spinning each other around a few times, leaping, doing triple axles, and one-legging it down, they ended their routine four minutes later in the same spot where they began.

"Utterly amazing," I mumbled. "Graceful, classy."

As they skated off the ice, I noticed the audience gave an appreciative, polite, sophisticated applause but then contentedly waited in dead silence. Everyone sat quietly for sixty seconds until I finally spoke up. "How did they do?" The stranger sitting next to me said, "Don't know yet." I countered, "Why?" The man explained, "The scorer's table hasn't flashed the judges' scores yet."

I was baffled. Everyone had just sat there watching a routine for four minutes, and we didn't even know what we just saw! (How many of us sit at our desks at the end of a workday with the same shocked look, wondering what happened?)

As the minutes of waiting passed, I could see behind the curtains backstage a broadcast on the arena big-screen TV. The two skaters were holding hands, out of breath, and sweating. A sportscaster interviewed them with classy questions like, "So, did you fall on purpose?"

Suddenly the silence ended for both the spectators and the skaters. The scorer's table finally flashed the judges' scores: 4.5, 4.5, 4.6, 1.2 (from the Russian judge!), and 8.6 (from the paid-off French judge who forgot there was only a maximum 6 points possible!). Now there were tears; the skaters were devastated.

"What a tragedy," I thought. "All those hundreds of hours, all those years of training down the tube. Their dreams of world championships and Olympic gold had slipped away." The score-keeping system had no way to adapt or adjust during the performance. The feedback measurement came at the end of the task when it was too late to change anything. I pulled out my pad of paper and wrote down my observation: *Increasing our frequency of feedback allows us to change our behavior before it is too late!*

HOCKEY FEEDBACK

The next day I attended the gold medal hockey game. As the match began, I couldn't help but contrast figure skating with ice hockey. I asked my two buddies, "Do hockey fans sit quietly with their arms to their sides? Do they wear sport coats and ties, dresses, and pantsuits in a sophisticated, reverent experience like I had just witnessed at the figure skating exhibition?"

"No way!" they all shouted in unison. "Hockey fans bring their own pucks so they can throw them at each other," one friend observed. The other blurted, "People spill drinks instead of drink them, the organist plays tunes that have never been written, and people eat popcorn they don't even own." I added, "Yeah, and the players get into it several times a game as they drop their gloves to rearrange one another's faces. A lawsuit was recently filed in New York because two fans climbed over the glass and beat up the opposing team's coach. That's right, guys," I smirked. "Do you realize that ice hockey is the number-one cause of prison riots in North America? It's true. The prisoners are locked up watching hockey on TV, and they become uncontrollably mad when they see a hockey player get a five-minute penalty for the same offense that got them thirteen years!"

Before we knew it, the fast-moving game had progressed to the end of the final period. That's when I realized the correlation between figure skating and hockey as they relate to the dynamics of feedback. In figure skating, the feedback is hidden and comes too late in the routine to help that performance. However, in hockey, everybody—the fans, the coaches, and especially the players—have constant feedback. Everybody can see the clock tick off and know at all times the score and time remaining. Everybody always knows at which precise moment the game will end. If one team is behind the other by one goal with a minute left to play, the coach doesn't quit and say, "I can't take it. We lost. Buy me a hot dog." Instead, because of dynamic, up-to-date feedback, the coach adjusts, takes out the goal keeper, puts in a sixth attacker to tie up the game, and sends it into overtime.

After I dropped off my buddies, I headed for home. With my mind and imagination now in high gear, it was easy for me to evaluate other examples of the importance of feedback. In business management we can't afford to wait until April to find out how we did in January and February. In sales, we can't afford to wait until the end of the month to find out how our totals versus quota ratios ended up. In family life, the time for parents to keep a child off drugs and teach sexuality and moral responsibility is not when that child is eighteen. It's a daily task beginning when the child is two and then three, four, five, six, seven, eight years of age. Feedback teaches, preaches, guides, and alters behavior before we lose or go off the deep end.

"I need to remember," I reminded myself, "that it's better to build a fence at the edge of a cliff than to park an ambulance at its base. It's better that our children crash their tricycles and learn from affordable mistakes when they are young than total the family car when they're teenagers. Athletes know that the game is won not on game day but in practice!

MEASUREMENT SYSTEM

We must stop and ask ourselves, "Is my system of measurement feedback more like figure skating or ice hockey? Do I know what's going on at all times so I can quickly make essential choices along the way? Or is change, positive and especially negative, always a surprise?"

In the 1994 Winter Olympics, Alberto Tomba, the top-ranked ski racer in the world, finished a lousy, embarrassing, twelfth place after the first slalom run. But because of feedback, he knew exactly what he needed to do down to the hundredth of a second, and he went all out in his second and final Olympic run. As Tomba crossed the finish line, this time he led the entire field until he was beaten by one-tenth of a second by the final racer. Tomba finished an unbelievable second place and won the silver medal.

Feedback affects our relationship with time. Are we in control or out of control? Have we established rules and measurements in the home regarding the performance of our children? Do we pay attention and solicit feedback on curfew, hours studying, minutes per phone call? Are we dealing with life day-by-day, gate-by-gate as Tomba did? If not, why not? And if not now, when? Increasing our frequency of feedback is so vital that it must be broken down into its most basic forms. All three forms inspire us and better equip us to become more of who we already are.

THREE TYPES OF FEEDBACK

Three types of feedback organize what we need and what we must do.

- *Factual feedback* constitutes the cold, hard facts of our current reality—data to which we assign accountability without blame. Accountability is positive feedback; blame is negative feedback. You cannot increase a person's performance by making him feel worse. Factual feedback tells us what the score is, how far for a first down, and what yard line the ball is on—information that allows us to measure the progress toward reaching the goal.

Ski racer Tomba knew the exact time he must beat. Only then could he do something about it. Factual feedback is neither positive nor negative. It's just the facts!

- *Motivational feedback* is the cheering crowd and encouraging coach who tell us, "You can do it—go for it." Motivational feedback triggers adrenaline and endorphins and emotion to dig deep and compete. Motivational feedback is necessary to get us to hustle. As a professional speaker, I have realized that most convention attendees want less information and more motivation and acknowledgment that they are doing a good job. Motivational feedback must not only celebrate excellence and winning, it must also celebrate improvement, which stimulates more improvement.

- *Educational feedback* is correctional coaching, which changes and improves Tomba's ski run or our job performance at work. It's the teacher telling the child, "I love the way you attempt this math problem, but this is the change you must understand and implement to get the correct and desired answer."

If we increase our frequency of receiving all three forms of feedback, we will not only be able to change our behavior, but we should also be able to pick the most appropriate behavior at the right time to positively effect the outcome of a task, event, or game.

CHOICE

Feedback gives you a choice. A classic illustration of choosing the right thing to do occurred at a college basketball game. The teams had gone back and forth, changing leads the entire evening. Finally only three seconds remained in the game. One team was behind by one point and called a final time-out. Then the whistle blew, and play resumed. A player on the team behind by one threw the ball in bounds. A second teammate caught the ball, turned, and shot. The ball was airborne when the buzzer sounded. The game ended as the ball ripped through the net for the win. The team down by one had won by two. Pandemonium erupted.

Two points? When the player caught the inbounds pass, he didn't turn and take a short jump shot. He turned and threw the ball like a baseball the whole length of the court to the other basket ninety-three-and-a-half feet away! Talk about a three-pointer! That's not a real high percentage shot. What would the coach have said to him had he taken that shot in the middle of the first quarter? "Calm down! Why don't you bounce it a while next time before you launch another one? Mandatory drug testing from here on out!'"

But the coach was not upset. Neither were we, the fans; nor were his teammates. So why was it okay at the end of the game to shoot a full-court shot but not at the beginning? Because of his exposure to up-to-the-minute correct information, the player was able to alter his actions and behaviors and match them to the specific needs required at that specific moment to be successful in that given situation. Given the situation, the player had to go for broke. Increasing the frequency of feedback not only allowed him to change his behavior before it was too late, but it also allowed him to pick the most appropriate behavior to keep the dream of winning the game alive. As an aside, I must also tell you that this hero player had missed his previous eight shots.

The same thing happened in the 1970s when the Lakers were playing the seventh game against Milwaukee for the NBA championship. One of, if not *the* best pure shooter in the history of the game, Jerry West, had missed twelve shots in a row. But he sank his thirteenth shot at the final buzzer to win the game! I wonder what the coach's feedback was that allowed both of these players to do what they had to do in the closing seconds?

I'm no expert, but it's obvious that we repeat that which is rewarded. Consciously or subconsciously, we duplicate what is emphasized. Obviously, both coaches emphasized the positive and reinforced their belief and confidence in these players throughout the entire game—especially when they failed. For this reason, the players remained confident and capable to rise to the occasion when it mattered most. Remember, champions aren't great all the time, but they are great when they need to be.

POSITIVE VS. NEGATIVE

But increasing feedback isn't enough. It must be positive feedback. Garbage in, garbage out; stupid is as stupid does! We remember what we see, and for some reason we have an inherent way of acknowledging our failures way before anyone else has to point them out. Psychologists tell that it takes eleven positive things to balance out a single negative thing we hear or see. It's a fact that feedback positively or negatively affects attitude, work ethic, commitment, performance, and participation. Positive input breeds positive output 100 percent of the time.

DISNEY SERVICE

Years ago I was at Disneyland with my family. At Disneyland, it's amazing how positive feedback is at the heart of total quality control and customer service. Just as I stood in line to go on Space Mountain, a Disney employee handed me a time card. When I was still in line an hour later, another employee took the card and documented how long I had been holding it. As I finally boarded the ride, I commented on how absurd the long wait had been.

I was intrigued by the possibilities that this feedback might generate, and I decided to check up on how quickly they could implement a change. I trust that this information was evaluated and acted upon immediately because the next day with more people at the park, I went on the same ride at the same time of day, and I only had to wait twenty-seven minutes. I pulled some strings and was able to make an appointment with a manager at the end of the day to briefly discuss my observations. She explained to me that through their intense and constant measurement-feedback system, they can tell that people willingly wait in line for longer periods of time or leave certain ride lines to go elsewhere depending on their age, the outside temperatures, and time of day. This allows Disneyland to add or subtract cars and personnel to better handle the crowds. Because of continual feedback, they know how many people on average attend the park each day of the week during each season, holiday, and special event. This allows their customers to drive the business and determine the standards for daily service based on supply and demand.

ACCEPT, REJECT, IGNORE

Believe it or not, this is important stuff for us to know and utilize on a daily basis in both our personal and professional lives. For example, I remember a leadership conference in a workshop full of thirty students where the instructor told us that she was selecting three students to leave the room with her assistant and go down the hall to the resource library. She carefully picked out specific students with specific personalities who she knew could handle the feedback that was to come. She told the three students they had five minutes to get their thoughts together about leadership and that she would bring them back one at a time to give a two-minute talk. They were excused.

When she knew they were safely out of listening range, she stepped close to the remaining students and whispered, "Here's the deal. We are going to play 'Accept, Reject, Ignore.' No matter what these students say in their speeches, as the first is brought back into the room, cheer, encourage, agree with, and fully accept her. At her conclusion give her a standing ovation.

"When the second student comes back, totally disagree with everything he says, and reject his words with verbal abuse. Say, 'No way. I don't agree.' Boo him when he concludes.

"When the last student comes in, totally ignore the fact that he even entered the room. As I introduce him, already be talking with the person next to you. A couple of you get up while he is speaking and exchange books, look out the window, and throw away trash. No matter what, everyone must totally ignore him, and never make eye contact!"

As the first speaker began, she was nervous, shy, and intimidated. But as the cheers of encouragement and total acceptance came, her confidence quickly grew, her posture straightened, her countenance changed, and she smiled. Her words articulately flowed from her lips the entire time. She spoke for five minutes and would have gone on for fifteen minutes had the instructor let her.

As the second speaker began, he immediately got angry and defensive. His voice rose, and after thirty seconds he actually fired back at some of the negative comments with his own rude rebuttals. At the two-minute mark, we had a loud argument on our hands. The instructor had to stop his speech and ask him to sit down. The first speaker sat there confused and sympathetic, yet proud of her performance. Without any cue from the instructor, she stood up to defend the second speaker and encouraged all of us to cut him some slack, saying that what he said was really profound.

The third speaker then entered and began talking. After thirty seconds he stopped, his posture slouched, and he just stood there and waited another thirty seconds. When no one acknowledged him, he angrily said, "Excuse me, hello. I'm up here giving my speech." He patiently waited another thirty seconds, but when he realized that he was still being totally ignored, he simply said, "Thank you," gave up, and sat down in his seat. The first speaker just sat quietly in shock while the second speaker defended this last speaker by angrily slamming the class for having no class, pointing out how sad the speaker was, and telling us that we should be more sensitive and supportive.

When the smoke had settled, the instructor invited all three speakers back to the front of the room and confessed that we had pulled a dirty trick. She explained the planned responses to their remarks and asked each of them how they felt when they were speaking and how their experience had affected the way they treated their peers who had participated with them. The first pointed out that positive feedback was energizing and empowering. She wanted to keep speaking. The second was still ticked off and pointed out that negative feedback is also energizing but in a discouraging way that makes you feel that you are being punished for trying. The third speaker explained that receiving no feedback and being ignored is more devastating than negative feedback. "You don't even know how to respond because there is no one and nothing to respond to," he said.

We all agreed. Everyone is crying from within, "Praise me, accept me, reject me, punish me, but don't you dare ignore me. Notice me! And if I can't get attention for doing something positive, I am going to get attention for doing something negative! I need attention. I'm important too!"

Increasing our frequency of feedback is not enough. Our feedback must be positive. What it boils down to is this: Feedback, negative or positive, dictates our behavior and results. When we hear and see something over and over again, we remember it. When we do it over and over again, it becomes a part of us forever. If we just keep doing what we're doing, we'll keep getting what we've been getting. Practice makes permanent. Only perfect practice makes perfect! Let us give only positive, helpful, constructive feedback in all that we do.

When we increase the frequency of feedback, our measurement system becomes a dynamic decision-making tool instead of an outcome report. When performance is measured, performance is improved. When performance is measured and immediately reported back, performance improves at an accelerated rate.

Tactful Feedback

Obviously feedback is most critical to peak performance. It's a communication process of giving and receiving. Many have studied how to tactfully give feedback so that the person receiving it will be most likely to act on it. There are three categories of people: subordinates, peers, and superiors.

There are only two ways to tactfully share feedback. First, group subordinates and peers together and ask permission.

"May I suggest something that will benefit you?"

"Why yes," he says.

"You have lettuce in your bicuspid and should probably remove it." Or, "You should tie your shoe so that you don't trip and fall."

The tactful approach to giving feedback to superiors reminds them and gives them credit for what they already know.

"As you know, John is willing to help you work out the hassle with your computer. May I call him?" Or, "As you know, that crate is way too heavy for one person to lift. May I get a dolly?"

How do we stretch? Not by taking time and making the effort once in a while. Going to the gym once a month isn't going to help you at all! Stretching must be an ongoing commitment and realization that strengthening occurs in the area *past* the point of discomfort. When we keep the stretch alive, miracles manifest themselves to help us improve and become more of who we already are. This is my sequel story and follow-up short film to "Puppies for Sale."

Puppy Love

The young boy who had been wearing a steel brace on his left leg for four months walked through the front door of his home with a newly purchased puppy in his arms. The dog didn't have a hip socket and, when placed on the floor, it walked with a serious limp. The boy's selection of a physically challenged puppy intrigued his parents. The boy had been down, but with his new companion at his side, his parents sensed a revitalized spirit of hope and enthusiasm emerging from his soul.

The next day the young boy and his mom went to see a veterinarian to find out how he could help his little dog. The doctor explained that if he stretched and massaged his puppy's leg every morning and then walked with him at least one mile per day, the muscles around his missing hip would eventually strengthen to the point of no pain and less of a limp.

The dog whimpered and barked out discomfort, and the boy winced and hassled with his leg brace, but for the next two months they religiously kept to their massage-and-walking regimen. By the third month they were walking three miles every morning before school began, and they were both walking without pain.

One Saturday morning when the boy and dog were returning from their workout, a cat leaped out of the bushes and startled the dog. Breaking loose from his leash, the dog darted into oncoming traffic. With a speeding truck barreling toward his dog, the boy instinctively ran into the street, dove for the dog, and rolled into the gutter. He was too late. The dog was hit and lay on the street, bleeding profusely from the mouth.

As the boy sat there crying and hugging his dying dog, he noticed that his leg brace had bent and popped loose. With no time to worry about himself, he sprang to his feet, picked up his dog, cuddled it close to him, and started for home. The dog quietly barked, giving the boy hope. His jog turned into an all-out, adrenaline sprint.

The boy's mother rushed him and his suffering pup to the pet hospital. As they anxiously waited to see if his dog would survive the surgery, the boy asked his mother why he could now walk and run.

"You had osteomyelitis, which is a disease of the bone," she said. "It weakened and crippled your leg, which caused you to limp in severe pain. Your brace was for support. It wasn't necessarily a permanent condition if you were willing to fight through the pain and hours of therapy. You responded well to the medication, but you always resisted our encouragement for physical therapy.

"Your father and I didn't know what to do. The doctors told us you were about to lose your leg. But then you brought home your special puppy. It was amazing how you looked out for each other day after day and seemed to understand one another's needs. Ironically, as you were helping him, you were also helping yourself to strengthen and grow. You obviously no longer need the support of a brace, and today you discovered it."

Just then the operating room door slowly opened. Out walked the veterinarian with a smile on his face. "Your dog is going to make it," he said.

The boy learned that when you lose yourself, you find yourself. It is more blessed to give than to receive.

Inspirational Heroes

Dan believes that we should be willing to pay any price and travel any distance to associate with extraordinary individuals. Over the years, he has associated with some of the most influential people on our planet. Each relationship has left a lasting impression on him with words of wisdom itemized in the captions. Each experience has helped him to realize that the answers are in the box.

Top left: Larry King—Life's about asking the right questions.
Top right: Zig Ziglar—How to become a polished professional.
Bottom: Dan "trekking" for three days on the Oregon/Mormon Trail.

Dan with Al Davis, Oakland Raiders owner

Top right: With NFL Oakland Raiders owner, Al Davis.
Bottom left: 6-foot-5-inch, 250-pound Defensive End.
Bottom right: College student-athlete.

THE BEST IS YET TO BE

Top left: Bo Jackson—Excellence in everything you do.
Middle left: At a Raiders camp with Howie Long.
Top right: With Raiders Hall of Famers Art Shell and Fred Biletnikoff.
Bottom: Jim Craig and Mike Eruzione—Heart matters more than talent.

Top left: Dan in the cockpit of an F-18. He went 1.9 Mach at 55,000 feet where he could see the curvature of the earth.
Top right: After catching 9.4 Gs and going 1.3 Mach in an F-16.
Bottom left: You fly a high performance jet with the emotional right side of the brain.
Bottom right: Dan flying with the US Air Force "Thunderbirds" Demonstration Team.

Top: Dan in the back seat of an F-15 going 660 knots at 1000 feet.
Middle: Dan speaks to troops all over the world.
Bottom: Dan is the Honorary Wing Commander of the 388th Fighter Wing at Hill Air Force Base.

Top: Dan took 30,000 packages of Juicy Fruit gum to give to the troops in Southwest Asia.
Middle: Speaking to security forces in Iraq.
Bottom: In Afghanistan speaking to the troops

Top: Captain Gerald Coffee—Have faith and keep the faith.
Middle: Senator John McCain—Believe in something larger than yourself.
Bottom: Tuskegee Airmen—Judge by character not by color.

Top right: With Music Mogul Dick Clark.
Middle: Songwriting friends Mike Reid, Chuck Cannon, Billy Dean, and Tim Nichols—Life is about writing your own songs.
Bottom: Righteous Brothers—You are the message.

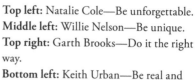

Top left: Natalie Cole—Be unforgettable.
Middle left: Willie Nelson—Be unique.
Top right: Garth Brooks—Do it the right way.
Bottom left: Keith Urban—Be real and vulnerable.
Bottom right: Dionne Warwick—Be elegant.

Top left: David Foster—It's not what you say but how you say it.
Top right: Kenny Loggins—Be true to yourself.
Bottom: Jessica Simpson—Use your influence for a good cause.

Top: Wayne Gretzky—You learn more from listening and watching than from playing.
Middle: Michael Jordan—The last few minutes matter most.
Bottom: Mohammad Ali—Never forget what got you there.

Top: Cal Ripken Jr.—Consistently never say never.
Middle left: Jack Nicholas—You can if you think you can.
Middle right: Phil Mickelson—Feel and touch give you the competitive advantage.
Bottom: Johnny Rutherford and Al Unser—Know when to speed up and when to slow down.

Top: President George Bush—Look beyond the issue to find the guiding principle. **Middle:** Colin Powell—Causes change; character and commitment never do. **Bottom:** Rudy Giuliani—Crisis reveals the true character within.

Top left: Bill Marriott—Success is never final.
Top right: Henry Kissinger—Diplomacy and negotiations are the keys to conflict resolution.
Bottom: Buzz Aldrin and Frank Boreman—Always look at life from a big-picture perspective.

Top left: Dan's dear old friend.
Bottom left: Henry Winkler—One moment in time can change forever.
Bottom right: Running the Olympic Torch—World peace is possible.

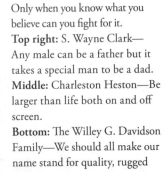

Top left: General Hal Hornburg—
Only when you know what you
believe can you fight for it.
Top right: S. Wayne Clark—
Any male can be a father but it
takes a special man to be a dad.
Middle: Charleston Heston—Be
larger than life both on and off
screen.
Bottom: The Willey G. Davidson
Family—We should all make our
name stand for quality, rugged
individualism, and class.

Fundamental 8

WHEN YOU SHOULD STRETCH

Today is yesterday's pupil. To disdain today (it is the first day of the rest of your life) is to prove that yesterday has been misunderstood. Remember, the only life which a man can lose is that which he is living at the moment.

—Marcus Aurelius

We must see who we are and say who we are before we can stretch who we are and change where we are. I believe that it's easier to act our way into positive thinking than to think our way into positive action. If we decide we are going to stretch, we should ask the questions: "If who, why not me? If when, why not now?" Sound familiar?

It's against human nature to stretch (remember the dog won't move off the nail he is sitting on until the nail starts to hurt enough). Stretching becomes easy or difficult based on the people we surround ourselves with. For example, I was invited to speak at my old high school. I was flattered and intimidated at the same time. I was introduced and walked out on stage of the auditorium. I immediately made eye contact with some of the faculty members who had been teachers when I was a student. You should have seen their faces. "Oh no, who let him back in here? The three years Dan was an eleventh grader almost killed us all!"

People don't want us to change, stretch, improve, or grow because in order for them to connect with us on the same level, they must also stretch and improve. Although it was all those years ago, my high school teachers expected me to be the same irresponsible kid I was the last time I was with them.

As an inspirational speaker, I always ask myself if my resumé and introduction is the same this year as it was last year. If so, I might make an effective teacher or trainer but a lousy inspiration. I was in a program a while ago with someone who climbed Mt. Everest more than twenty-five years ago, and I thought, "Cool photos, but what have you done lately?" Is your resumé the same this year as last year?" I want my gravestone to read, "He died while climbing," "He croaked while doing," or better still, "He'll be right back!"

We must always look at death not as an exclamation mark but only as a comma. We must look at time and life not as hours, weeks, months, and years but as right now. "Some day I'm gonna" doesn't make it. "I shoulda, coulda, woulda" is no way to live life. We must *carpe diem*—seize the day—and welcome every opportunity to stretch and become more of who we already are. This doesn't mean we work to acquire more things or build worldly treasures but rather that we build better relationships and acquire more memories with our loved ones, who truly matter most.

MAKING MEMORIES

It was the holiday season, with the big three—Halloween, Thanksgiving, and Christmas—just ahead. My father was battling cancer and was very ill. Afraid that he wouldn't be around for Christmas, I wanted to make that year extra special. I thought the perfect gift would be a grandfather clock, hand built by me. It was one of the things he had always wanted but could never afford. Although I had never built anything that complex, I felt that it would not only make my dad proud of me but also be something that he would treasure.

I purchased a magnificent self-assembly kit and immediately devoted my time to the overwhelming task of putting it together. Every day after work I went to my brother's house to secretly work on the clock. Three hours a day, six days a week I labored, trying to figure out the complicated instructions. As the clock started to take form, the anticipation and internal excitement were almost too much to bear. I was really proud and couldn't help visualizing how appreciative and amazed my dad would surely be when he unwrapped the masterpiece. On October 10, I finally finished the clock and wrapped it with a big red bow, ready to be delivered in a couple of months on Christmas Eve. The next morning I left on a trip to Washington.

Two days later the phone rang in my hotel room. It was my brother. "Dad just died," he cried.

That was a sad and brutal Christmas for me. Mom had a gorgeous Christmas tree; there were gifts galore. And there in the corner of my mother's living room stood the tall, solid oak grandfather clock that I had spent sixty-three hours building. But there was no Dad! The present meant nothing without Dad there.

Not a day goes by that I don't regret the time I spent on that clock, now knowing that I should have spent those final, most sacred hours at my father's side. If you look around, most people use people and love things when they should actually love people and use things. What a fool I was to think a *thing* would make him happy. Things don't make people happy. Time spent together with loved ones does!

KEEP SWINGING

Stretching cannot just be a sometimes thing; it must be an all-the-time thing. We must approach every day and every situation having learned from the past and realizing that no matter what our past has been, we have a spotless future. We must realize that some things are tough, but we must remember that the difference between a successful person and an unsuccessful person is that the successful person will do what the unsuccessful person will not do. The successful person does not want to do it either, but he does it anyway. A movie illustrates this profound principle.

In *A League of Their Own,* the true story of the first-ever all-woman's professional baseball league, the coach, played by Tom Hanks, catches his star player, played by Gina Davis, sneaking away at night. He confronts her, asking, "What are you doing?" The player answers, "I'm quitting. I don't need baseball anymore." The coach replies, "Don't quit. You'll regret it for the rest of your life." The player says, "Baseball just got too hard." The coach responds, "What do you mean, it got too hard? If it were easy, everybody would do it. The hard is what makes it great!"

BO KNOWS BASEBALL

They say the hardest thing to do in sports is to hit a round baseball, thrown by a pitcher sixty feet, six inches away that is going ninety mph. Yes, the hard makes it great. The hard in *A League of Their Own* refers to the mental and emotional hard. As in life, you must swing the bat to get a hit. Everything begins with a swing. In fact, most of the time, with the exception of the pitcher, the value of each player is determined by how well he hits the ball.

The difference between an average .200 hitter (two hits in every ten times at bat) and a superstar .300 hitter (three hits in every ten times at bat) is only one hit in every ten times up to bat. On average, when a batter gets a full count—three balls and two strikes—the difference between a .200 hitter and a .300 hitter becomes only one hit in every sixty pitches!

This concept also applies in life. Becoming a superstar requires only one more effective sales call in every sixty sales calls—one more effective interaction with every sixty customers, one more effective communication with a family member, friend, or foe. The difference between good and great in every aspect of life is just a little bit of extra effort—a little more passion, imagination, and creativity, a little stronger desire to focus and finish what you came to do: figuratively keep swinging until you hit the ball!

Years ago, I was at a pro baseball game in Anaheim, California, between the Kansas City Royals and the Angels. As I sat there in the stadium, I was also tuned in to the radio broadcast of the game with my radio headphones turned up loud and clear so I could get a more detailed account of each player's stats.

Suddenly the stadium announcer blurted over the sound system: "Bo Jackson, number sixteen, center fielder for the Royals will be the next batter." Every eye focused on the dugout. My heart started to pound. Suddenly this massive, buffed and cut, larger than life mythical character strutted onto the field. As he sauntered up to home plate, the radio announcer in my headphones explained, "Bo Jackson is currently in a batting slump as over the last three games he has struck out ten times in a row!" Bo's team was behind by one run, with one runner on base and two outs. Jackson dug in at the plate and stared down the pitcher as if to say, "I dare you to put it right here."

What happened? On the very first pitch, Jackson's mighty swing pounded the ball high over the center field fence—a five-hundred-foot home run that sailed out of the stadium and into the parking lot. That turned out to be the game-winning run.

As Bo trotted around the bases, with his teammates cheering his heroics, I began to philosophize, "How many times have we been led to believe that what we've been in the past makes us who we are today?" No. What we've been in the past isn't nearly as important as what we hope to become in the future. Bo Jackson just proved it.

If our past makes us who we are today, Bo would have stayed on the bench in the dugout saying, "I don't want to do this anymore. Bo don't know!" But because of his understanding that the past must be analyzed, learned from, and then left behind—that each at-bat is independent from every other at-bat—Bo stepped up and became a champion. We can't be afraid to swing the bat. And if we miss? Learn why, practice, and keep swinging. Now is the time to stretch.

RESCUE AT SEA

In a small fishing village in Holland, a young boy taught the world about rewards of unselfish service. Because the entire village revolved around the fishing industry, a volunteer rescue team was needed in cases of emergency. One night the winds raged, the clouds burst, and a gale force storm capsized a fishing boat at sea. Stranded and in trouble, the crew sent out an SOS.

The captain of the rescue rowboat team sounded the alarm, and the villagers assembled in the town square overlooking the bay. While the team launched the rowboat and fought its way through the wild waves, the villagers waited restlessly on the beach, holding lanterns to light the way back.

An hour later, the rescue boat reappeared through the fog, and the cheering villagers ran to greet them. Falling exhausted on the sand, the volunteers reported that the rescue boat had to leave one man behind because there wasn't enough room in the boat. Just one more passenger would have surely capsized the rescue boat, and all would have been lost.

Frantically, the captain called for another volunteer team to go after the lone survivor. Sixteen-year-old Hans stepped forward. His mother grabbed his arm, pleading, "Please don't go. Your father died in a shipwreck ten years ago, and your older brother, Peter, has been lost at sea for three weeks. Hans, you are all I have left."

Hans replied, "Mother, I have to go. What if everyone said, 'I can't go; let someone else do it?' Mother, this time I have to do my duty. When the call for service comes, we all need to take our turn and do our part." Hans kissed his mother, joined the team, and disappeared into the night.

Another hour passed, which seemed to Hans's mother like an eternity. Finally, the rescue boat darted through the fog with Hans standing up in the bow. Cupping his hands, the rescue team coordinator called from shore, "Did you find the lost man?" Barely able to contain himself, Hans excitedly yelled back, "Yes, we found him. Tell my mother it's my older brother, Peter!"

SEPTEMBER 11, 2001

Sometimes stretching right now is not a choice. But with the realization that it's not what happens to us but how we deal with what happens to us that makes or breaks us, stretching right now is often the key to success. Country singer Alan Jackson asks in his hit song, "Where Were You (When the World Stopped Turning)?"

I was speaking the morning of September 11, 2001, in Allentown, Pennsylvania, to a citywide early-morning leadership breakfast, sponsored by the local chamber of commerce and the Health Care Hospital community. When I concluded my remarks, I was whisked to the airport to catch my flight to JFK airport in New York to catch my nonstop flight home to Salt Lake City. We boarded our Delta Airlines jet and taxied out only to be immediately turned around and hurriedly sent back to the gate. We were then firmly asked to get off quickly and to remain in the gate area.

When we re-entered the waiting room, television news was reporting the first plane crash into the World Trade Center. While we were standing there, the second plane hit the other tower, soon to be followed by the attack on the Pentagon. Delta's ticket counter is next to the United Airlines counter, and soon the six United employees were in tears upon hearing the news of United Flight 93 being hijacked and crashing into Somerset, Pennsylvania, not far from Allentown.

I was taken back to my hotel, where I desperately tried to re-book a flight, rent a car, catch a bus, or take a train. However, the entire county's mass transportation system was shut down until further notice. Stranded with the burning desire to be back home with my family, I phoned a national trucking company called England Trucking, headquartered in Salt Lake City. I talked to the dispatcher to see if he had a driver going west. He called me back and said I was in luck—that a driver would meet me in the lobby in twenty minutes.

Like clockwork, a truck cab pulled up outside. Disappointed, I asked him where the trailer was. After all, I thought that a childhood fantasy was about to come true: "Eighteen-wheeler, roll on, roll on. This is Beaver Cleaver checking for Smokey Bears. I read you, Pork Sausage, come on." So I asked him what was going on.

He laughed, and we drove thirty minutes to Hershey, Pennsylvania, where we hooked up to a huge trailer loaded with 43,000 pounds of Hershey chocolate bars.

Suddenly I didn't mind if we crashed or ran out of gas! Our route took us 76 south to I-70 west, and in the next two-and-a-half days, we drove 2,640 miles across America the beautiful. I had never seen America this way, and with no airlines flying or trains running and with F-15 and F-16 fighter jets patrolling the skies, I would never experience anything like it ever again.

Our route took us past Somerset, Pennsylvania, where United Flight 93 had crashed over the mountain, and I wondered if I would have stepped up. Would I have given my life, said, "Let's roll," and put up a fight to save another building and thousands of lives from being destroyed? Do I have what it takes, and is my life in order to be a hero?

The long drive took us past Terre Haute, Indiana, where Timothy McVeigh had been in prison and executed for his terrorist Oklahoma City bombing. It was then that it hit me that McVeigh had attended a Christian church in his youth and was a war veteran. He had forgotten that America is not people or buildings but rather an ideal. He had attacked that which allowed him his freedoms in the first place.

FREEDOM

My friend US Air Force General Hal Hornburg has helped me understand that we all not only need heroes, but more important, we also should all *be* heroes. Every time I've been on a program with him, Hornburg takes a few minutes to make his case. Typically, most young people choose actors, models, and sports figures to look up to emulate. As we grow older our values shift to admire those in society who make significant individual sacrifices for noble and just causes. There is no better or finer hero than the military veteran who has endured mental and physical hardship in the defense of America's freedom. America is losing hundreds of World War II era veterans every day. An entire generation of heroes is dying, and we must not let the memory of their commitment, sacrifice, and service die with them. They willingly paid the price so that we could enjoy the prize when they were gone. Freedom is not free, and everybody needs to be reminded of it daily.

General Hornburg, General Tommy Franks (US Army), and my friend General Johnny Weida have all expressed that the very most important thing any of us can do is to remember every single day of every year for the rest of our lives exactly how we felt, what we thought, and how deep our resolve became the day the terrorists attacked the Pentagon, United Flight 93, and the World Trade Center. The memory of that horrific day will serve to keep America's citizens grateful for peace and liberty. All of us must remember that it is better to fight our foes on foreign soil than in New York City, Pennsylvania, and Washington, DC. We cannot afford to let ourselves or our neighbors and friends become lackadaisical about our freedom and forget about the importance of supporting our brave and selfless military men and women who take the fight to the enemy wherever and whenever they pose a threat. Yes, our soldiers are afraid for their lives. But they are more afraid of living without guaranteed rights, peace, liberty, and justice for all, so they volunteer to serve and fight their way through their fear anyway.

CORONA

I was honored to be the keynote speaker at the US Air Force four-star generals' conference called "Corona" in November 2003. It was amazing to become friends with many extraordinary officers and gentlemen. If you could visit with them, you would find each one to be classy family men who find no glory in war. Rather, they find glory in an unwavering commitment to excellence, high moral character, and dedicated service that they see daily in each of the men and women who serve under their command. They find glory in growing more leaders who absolutely live by integrity, sacrifice, and loyalty to the cause of liberty. Because freedom is not free and somebody has to defend it, these men of principle are ready to do whatever it takes, whenever and wherever it takes them.

David Boorstin describes these true heroes perfectly: "Though thou art able to tear the scalp off an elephant, if deficient in humanity, thou art no hero. The hero is distinguished by his achievement; the celebrity by his image. The hero created himself; the celebrity is created by the media. A hero is a man or woman who does what he or she can."

Let me put all of this into perspective by sharing an experience I had at the Iwo Jima Memorial in Arlington Cemetery, Virginia.

ONE OF THE FEW GOOD MEN

My experience one Saturday afternoon at the Iwo Jima Memorial Monument made it perfectly clear that our Revolutionary War for life, liberty, and the pursuit of happiness changed the trade, commerce, opportunities, standard of living, and history not just of the Western Hemisphere but also of the whole world. When the taxi pulled up to the memorial, I got out and told the driver to wait. I only wanted to read the plaque, take a photo, and return to my hotel.

As I walked around the circular drive, I noticed that all of the other tourists were gathered to one side, standing off in a state of shock and awe. I looked over and there, sitting in a wheelchair, was a young, clean-cut man proudly wearing a gold United States Marine Corps T-shirt. His right arm had been blown off and was freshly bandaged. His left arm was also blown off, and one leg—stitched, stapled, and skin-grafted together—was also bandaged.

A solider and his wife were attending to him and were quickly preparing to take his photograph. When they said, "Okay," the young Marine struggled to stand on his feet, determined and quaking with more pride than I had seen in a long while. He stood tall and straight, flexed his neck, and bowed his back for the picture. With tears streaming down our cheeks, each of us tourists (about twenty) started to reverently clap and give this courageous young man a standing ovation.

Losing strength, the young Marine collapsed into his wheel-chair, and his friends pushed him to their car to take him back to the hospital. The young Marine looked over at us, saluted, said thank you, and turned to go.

"Thank you," he said. No, "Thank *you*," I thought. I couldn't refrain myself. Humbly, I caught up to him and with all the love and respect I could muster, I introduced myself, explained that I was emotionally moved and inspired by what I had just experienced, told him that he was a hero, and thanked him for his sacrifice and service. He asked me what I did for a living. When I told him, he said he had read one of my books. That opened the door for me to ask him if he would share his story.

"My name is Corporal James Wright—my friends call me Eddie—United States Marine Corps, one of the few and the proud," he said.

Eddie was twenty-eight years old with a serious girlfriend and was in his second tour of duty in Iraq when he was wound-ed. A tour lasts six months, with an additional month to overlap with new units arriving.

He told me that he was the only Marine at Walter Reed Hos-pital. His friend Robert Storm, also a Marine who had already done two tours in Iraq and was soon returning for another seven months, had flown out from Camp Pendleton in San Diego to visit him. Eddie's accident happened in April. It was now May, and he was excited to be out of the hospital and in the fresh air for the first time since he left Iraq.

HERO JAMES "EDDIE" WRIGHT

Eddie was in a reconnaissance battalion that went out on patrol at least once every day. Their job was to constantly show a presence of strength and security in the toughest parts in and around Baghdad. When reports of insurgents came in, his unit would be sent to the firefight.

A patrol was usually six vehicles—all armored-up Hum-vees—called a platoon, with four Marines inside each vehicle and a machine gunner on top. This particular day they were on the west side of the city when they came down a road and realized all hell was about to break loose. You know an ambush is coming because suddenly the busy street goes vacant and people hurry off like rats scampering on a sinking ship.

The insurgents greatly outnumbered the Marines and opened fire in what is called an "L" ambush, with the bad guys shooting from two sides. Eddie was sitting in the passenger rear seat and stuck his SAW (squad automatic weapon) outside and returned fire. Suddenly a rocket-propelled grenade hit his door. The huge explosion blew Corporal Eddie's right hand off and his left arm off at the elbow. His right leg was ripped apart, destroying thigh muscle and the ability to move his right foot.

His company commander was killed, and though Eddie was gushing blood and dying by the minute, as second in command, he had the responsibility to take charge and lead the platoon out of the firefight. Marines are taught to fight through attacks, and because it was an "L" ambush, Eddie's platoon had to continue toward the insurgents before they could turn around and fight their way back out. Under Eddie's courageous and unbelievable leadership, they not only killed every one of the attacking insurgents, but they were also able to get back to base with only one dead and a few wounded.

Visualize this if you can. Eddie's arms and part of his leg are blown off, and he still rises to the occasion because others are counting on him. While losing strength, he still yells out orders and directions to his teammates to fight the hard fight, win the battle, and return with honor. For outstanding bravery, going beyond the call of duty, and absolute heroism, Corporal James "Eddie" Wright—United States Marine Corps, "one of the few and the proud"—was awarded the Bronze Star, the fourth-highest award given in the armed services and presented by President George W. Bush.

It was a sunny Saturday afternoon, but this one day made me more proud, more patriotic, and more dedicated to giving more of myself to duty, honor, country, community, schools, charity, family, and friends. I asked Eddie if he was bitter. He struggled and shook and again stood up out of his wheelchair on his one good but weak leg, looked me square in the eye, and said:

"No sir, I'm not angry. But unless we stay there and finish what we went there to do, I sacrificed my body and left my arms in Baghdad for nothing! I chose to be an American solider. All of us currently serving in the military are volunteers who enlisted during war. We all knew what we were getting ourselves into. None of us is complaining. I wish parents like that blonde lady organizing anti-Bush and anti-war demonstrations who lost her Marine son would shut her mouth. She's embarrassing her dead son, who is proud he served and willingly sacrificed his life for freedom!

"It's a great feeling to believe in and be part of something that is larger than yourself! I am proud to be a Marine and honored to serve my country. If they would let me go back to Iraq, I would go in a minute to be back with my unit. I love and miss those brave men."

Afterward, we had our picture taken together. That photo is the most important photo hanging on my "Wall of Fame."

NOT ALONE

Eddie's girlfriend, Donnette, stuck by his side; they are now engaged to be married. Today he has prosthetic arms. His right leg is healing, although he will walk with a limp for the rest of his life. Eddie told me twice how lucky he was just to be alive and how thankful he was to have played a small part in bringing freedom, the right to vote, opportunity, and justice to the wonderful Iraqi people.

When I asked him what message I could deliver to the world on his behalf, Eddie looked me in the eye, choked up, gritted his teeth, and said, "Tell them to stay strong and no matter what, not to quit. Tell CNN to report only the truth. The media should not make it look like and sound like the terrorists are winning, because they aren't. Tell the celebrities to shut up—they don't know what they are taking about. Remind US citizens that Islamic fundamentalists have vowed to kill all infidels and Americans, and that it's better to fight them over there than in New York City, Washington, DC, and the plains of Pennsylvania.

"Remind Americans that freedom is worth dying for, so they should never take it for granted. And no matter what, we should finish the job we started, or I and every other Marine, airman, sailor, and soldier who lost their limbs or lives in Iraq and Afghanistan will have done so in vain. Everybody on earth deserves to be free—not just Americans and our coalition of friends. Our responsibility is not just to ourselves but also to the whole world. Most Iraqis I've met smile and wave and say, 'God Bless America.'" I say it too: "God Bless America!"

I have become friends with Eddie and Robert, and we keep in touch. Every time I see a soldier, I always stop to shake their hand, think of Corporal James "Eddie" Wright, and say thanks!

Having seen the pure devotion and pride that this young man had in being a United States Marine and realizing his excitement to get his photograph taken in front of a World War II memorial as one of the "few and the proud," I must pay tribute before I conclude. Let us never forget the sacrifices so many have made day after day, year after year, dealing with the bad guys in war after war so you and I can be free to enjoy our freedoms.

History Never Lies

Every time I speak in Washington, DC, I try to break away to visit museums and monuments like the Iwo Jima Memorial. The Holocaust Museum is emotional and mind-boggling, and I love the reverence and sacred memories displayed in Arlington National Cemetery during the changing of the guard at the Tomb of the Unknown Soldier. I am always moved by the sea of white gravestones lined in perfectly straight rows in every direction as far as the eye can see.

So much sacrifice. For what? Freedom. Every soldier gave everything he had and made the ultimate sacrifice. He backed up his words "Liberty or death" with complete and total service above self. Military cemeteries at home and abroad are stark reminders that Americans have always been willing and prepared to fight the battles of those who could not fight their own. We have learned that we cannot enjoy peace living alone, that our own well-being depends upon the well-being of other nations far away.

I often see men reaching out and touching the "Wall" of the Vietnam Memorial, connecting with a name of a fallen comrade, shedding tears, kneeling in sorrow, and walking away past the street protestors who desecrate the American flag. All of us—Democrats and Republicans, liberals and conservatives, Jews and Gentiles, Protestants and Catholics, Latter-day Saints, Seventh-day Adventists, Unitarians, atheists, agnostics, pacifists, isolationists, conscientious objectors, and every other American citizen—should be thankful for our extraordinary, brave, and dedicated men and women in uniform.

THE SOLDIER

Father Edward O'Brian declared: "It is the soldier, not the reporter, who gave us freedom of the press. It is the soldier, not the poet, who gave us freedom of speech. It is the soldier, not the campus organizer or the fanatical off-the-wall college professor, who gave us freedom to demonstrate. It is the soldier who salutes the flag, who serves under the flag, whose coffin is draped by the flag, who has given the psycho, insensitive, irresponsible protestor freedom to burn the flag."

WHY NOT NOW?

To solidify the four-corner box detailed in the last four chapters, I conclude with deadlines and urgency.

One night I was talking to my father on the telephone when he taught me an important principle of success.

"Dan," he said, "I was just watching a professional basketball game on television. Do you know what? They ought to just give each team 100 points and let them play the last few minutes of the game."

"Why, Dad?" I asked.

"Because more happens the last two minutes of the game than the rest of the entire game."

"Why, Dad?"

"Because they have a deadline, and running out of time creates a state of urgency, and urgency creates emotion, which converts into adrenaline, energy, and, finally, into second-wind hustle, which creates change. As they say, Dan, 'In the absence of emotion there is no change.'"

Always intrigued by my dad's wonderful wisdom, I asked him if this principle of urgency also applied to life. He chuckled and explained, "You tell me. If I asked you to come over to my house right now at 11 PM in this snowstorm to bring me my mail, would you do it?"

"Dad, I'm so tired. It's been a long day," I said. "I'd probably talk you into letting me bring it to you at my convenience sometime tomorrow."

"Right. But if I called you up and said I was having a heart attack, would you drop everything and race over here?"

"Of course I would!"

"See, with a sense of urgency, we can increase our energy and performance to do whatever we need to do in school, sports, and life! We should never make the lame excuse, 'I'm too tired.' Not if we want something badly enough!"

DO YOU HAVE DEADLINES?

My dad then concluded and summarized the lesson for me as he always did: "If you think about it, we get more things accomplished the day before we go on spring break or vacation than in all the weeks leading up to the holidays combined. You cram for a test and learn more the night before the test than the entire semester. I guarantee if you were worn out and already in bed but someone called you and said they had ten nights of free lodging and passes to Disneyland, but you had to be there tomorrow or they would expire, you would get up, wash the car, plan the trip, buy the food, pack your bags, load up the car, drop off the dog, go to the bank, fill up with gas, and say good-bye to everybody all in the two hours before you had to leave!"

IS ANYTHING URGENT?

As you know, my dad battled cancer for six-and-a-half years and died on October 12, 1990. I never thought he would. One day my dad asked me if today was my last day on earth, would I sleep or complain or be negative and difficult to be around? Or would I be positive and productive and loving and leave my friends and family in better shape than I found them? He then really hit home by asking if I would die trying to be somebody I was not. He said, "If you spend your life trying to be me, who is going to be you?" He always said I would make a lousy somebody else.

Leonardo da Vinci validated my dad's observations when he wrote, "Iron rusts from disuse, stagnant water loses its purity and in cold weather becomes frozen, even so does inaction sap the vigor of the mind." There is no better real life example of this than seeing strong trucks, out of action, sitting in a parking lot not being used for the purpose for which they were created.

Recently I saw two such trucks headed for the same destination, one bringing cement and the other bringing lubricating oils—the one emblematic of construction, the other of operation. It struck me that cement is symbolic of that bond which binds us to other people; the lubrication is symbolic of the "oil of peace" that eliminates friction among employees and co-workers and produces cooperation and toleration among humanity.

Like the trucks, we should do what we're designed to do and be all we were born to be: strong, never out of action, always serving others by bringing to the world strength and cooperation. Remember, to get good at doing pushups one must simply do pushups; bathroom faucets break more from lack of use than from overuse; in a war, fighter jets can only contribute when they are flying. Act don't react; succeed, don't survive; dream, don't accept; live, don't exist; stretch, don't wait.

According to my dad, if we only had one day to live, we would live it with urgency. So why not live every day as if it were our last? Remember, we are supposed to be here on earth right now at this moment in time. These last four chapter reminders about Why, How, and When to Stretch are fundamental things we can all do. The answers have always been and still are in the box.

Fundamental 9

BECOME MORE OF WHO YOU ALREADY ARE

Do one thing each and every day that scares you.

—Eleanor Roosevelt

When an archer misses the mark he turns and looks for the fault within himself. Failure to hit the bull's-eye is never the fault of the target. To improve your aim—improve yourself.

—Gilbert Arland

Those of us who have taken golf lessons know there is a huge difference between a pro who teaches golf to people and one who teaches people to golf—outside-in versus inside-out instruction, changing versus improving, and becoming more of who we already are. Experts agree that people will improve performance, increase productivity, and take all aspects of their lives to the next level more through encouragement and example than through demand, and more for recognition than for money. But they must be ready.

Yes, we need direction, hope, reward, and a shared vision from outside in. Vision without action is a daydream; action without vision is a nightmare. And, yes, we need a system of success so we can stay on course and measure our progress. And if it breaks down, know exactly where to look to fix it. But no system in the world will work unless we do. It's doing what the teacher says but remembering that it's what we do when the teacher is not around that defines who we *really* are.

WHO ARE YOU REALLY?

J. Stone wrote: "The most visible and powerful creators are those artists whose medium is life itself. The ones who express the inexpressible without brush, hammer, clay, or guitar. They neither paint nor sculpt. Their medium is just being. Whatever their presence touches has increased life. They see and don't have to draw. They are the artists of being fully alive."

This is beautiful, yet one fundamental question continually lingers year after year, generation after generation: If achieving success and happiness is really this simple, if genuine meaning and significance and the purpose of life are found not in having fame but in being whole, then why are so many people still looking for themselves and trying to define who they really are? Why is this simple personal development process continually so difficult for so many? It's because they are making it too difficult. Duh! There are only two reasons people do not improve themselves: wrong questions and wrong answers. Let me illustrate.

QUESTIONS AND ANSWERS

A college professor asked his students to list what they thought were the Seven Wonders of the World. Out of the hundred students in the lecture hall, the general consensus was:

1. Egypt's pyramids
2. Great Wall of China
3. Grand Canyon
4. Taj Mahal
5. Rainbow Bridge at Arches National Monument
6. Niagara Falls
7. Geysers in Yellowstone Park

(St. Peter's Basilica and the Golden Gate Bridge were also mentioned).

While gathering the votes, the professor noted that one student had not yet finished her paper. He asked the girl if she was having trouble answering the question. She replied, "No, I'm not having trouble with the answer; I'm having trouble with the question. Why only seven? According to whom and what criteria? What does 'wonder' mean to you, and is it different for me?"

The professor responded, "Tell us what you have, and maybe we can help." The girl hesitated and then read, "I think the real Seven Wonders of the World are to see, to hear, to taste, to touch, to laugh, to feel, and to love."

The room was so quiet you could have heard a pin drop. The professor took a deep breath and replied, "Wow! This is the most profound lesson we will learn all year. And isn't it pathetic that out of the 101 people in this room—me included—that only one of us, only 1 percent, understands that the things we overlook as simple and fundamental truly are wondrous."

This story provides three powerful reminders:

- The most important and precious things in life cannot be bought or built by hand.
- Before we look for answers outside of ourselves, let us first look within.
- Life is not about answers; it's about questions.

If you really analyze it, life is nothing more than just a string of back-to-back questions linked together and fueled by our curiosity and commitment to uncover the whole truth. In the four "wilderness" cases previously discussed, it is obvious that each person progressed only when he asked the right question, and he thrived in and through the wilderness only when he got the right answer. Only when we ask the right questions can we get the right answers and progress to the next right question.

For example, in the corporate world, the popular thing to do is to publish organizational "mission" and "vision" statements, make a list of "core values," and solicit "commitment." To do so requires the correct questions. A mission statement answers "Why do we exist?" A vision statement answers "What do we want to be?" Values clarification answers "What will we do?" Personal commitment answers "What will I do?"

Asking the right questions reveals that the mistakes we make are temporary, but the lessons they teach us are permanent. Here are two of my favorites: "True laws sometimes sleep but never die" and "Life is not measured by the number of breaths we take, but by the number of moments that take our breath away."

Yes, right answers are everywhere. Truth has always existed. The hard part is constructing the proper questions that reveal the truth. Too many people try to get the right answers from the wrong questions. That's as absurd as believing you can discipline the wrong people to do the right thing. It's not going to happen. Remember, to get a better answer we must simply ask a better question; to understand more about human beings, we must fully comprehend what it means to be human; to live a more meaningful, purpose-filled, peak-performance life, we must first challenge our belief system and the status quo, and then sometimes go against the popular flow.

I don't know about you, but I have been where my friend, the great blues guitarist Jonny Lang, sings about when he asks:

Why am I fighting to live if I'm just living to fight?
Why am I trying to see if there ain't nothin' in sight?
Why am I trying to give if they won't give me a try?
Why am I dying to live if I'm just living to die?

Do you see what I mean? Just the right answers to these four lyrical questions would be enough to change attitude, commitment, performance, participation, work ethic, passion, ability, and desire to take control!

RIGHT ANSWERS ARE NOT ALWAYS THE SOLUTION

Right answers are critical, but at the end of the day, as odd as it sounds, right answers don't necessarily solve the problem. For example, consider the answer "Don't drink and drive." It's right, yet many people still drive drunk. Only right questions solve problems. To produce a more specific answer, we must pose to each and every person who will drive under the influence a more specific question: "Why must you drive right now?" Followed by,

"Is there another way or form of transportation?" Which, if nothing else, produces a better answer: "Because I haven't been drinking, I will help you get to where you are going safely." I realize this shallow discussion is about behavior, but because we must crawl before we walk, I begin here to encourage your fundamental belief that we can question and answer our way to solutions to any dilemma life presents us.

"WHY, WHO, WHAT, HOW" QUESTIONS

Before we answer any more questions, let me point out that questions beginning with "why" and "who" are more emotionally charged than "what" or "how" questions because "why" and "who" questions are historical in nature. They take us back in time. "Why did this happen?" "Why must you drive drunk now?" "Who screwed up?" They plead for reasons, but they breed excuses. We all despise excuses and get annoyed when others use them on us, but the fault is usually with the one asking the wrong "why/who" questions. They are simply answering the question we asked.

Instead of asking people to live in the past, we should ask future-oriented questions like, "How can we fix this?" or "What can we do right now to stop the decline and turn this around?" Notice that these inquiries invite people to live in the present, encouraging positive statements about how things can be done better in the future. Notice that these questions are not about how to be a different person, but about how to become more of who and what we already are. A powerful example of this is found in China.

THE MAGLEV TRAIN TO SHANGHAI

Trains, in any country, are taken for granted and deemed a common occurrence. Rails cover the land and are looked at as slow and uneventful and perhaps unnecessary. However, when deciding on a better form of transportation, the Chinese government didn't ask what is a better way than the train. Instead, they asked, in what ways can we make the train better? On a regular day it takes one-and-a-half hours on a bus to get from the

Shanghai airport to the downtown city center. With the many variables of traffic, pollution, millions of people crossing the bustling streets, and always unexpected delays, making a better bus was not the answer. They could not control congestion. However, with infrastructure tracks already in place, they could control improving the railroad.

The Maglev Train is the world's fastest passenger train. As a futurist rail, it rides on a magnetic cushion of air. Using technology that has been around for decades, the Chinese train is free from resistance due to the electromagnetic field it creates. It literally lifts up, thus eliminating resistance, allowing it to travel at speeds exceeding 300 miles per hour. From the time the doors close, it accelerates up to full speed within thirty seconds and travels the same distance it took one-and-a-half hours on a bus to cover in just nine minutes. No exhaust, no pollution, no delays—just a futuristic fast train ride cooler than the coolest of all Disneyland rides, just a modern-day version of the classic children's story *The Little Engine that Could* who puffed, "I think I can, I think I can" until he did, and became more of who he already was!

LANGUAGE KEEPS US FROM IMPROVING

The second reason people find it difficult to improve themselves is the crazy, confusing communication used by our leaders to give us our answers. Have you listened to the way we talk these days in our corporate "foreign language"? The buzzwords that were planted a few years ago by the business educators and trainers turned out to be noxious weeds that have overrun the garden, choking off the simple, beautiful explanations and blossoms of truth.

"At the end of the day," our "interface" must be "win-win" with "synergy" even though we have "redeployed people" because the "paradigm" shifted from "Generation X" to veterans who "value add" with "core competencies" being "on the same page" that then creates a "customer-centric" organization. Oh, and of course you are no longer a sales professional; you are a "consultant solution provider" and "relationship manager" who must "re-engineer" or get "right-sized" away.

As my daughter Nikola would say, "Are you joking me?" The newest buzzwords fresh off the press are just as brutal: When co-workers engage in discussions during their "water cooler games" about the "smell test" determining the success of a new product, they must use "fresh eyes" and resolve to "pick the low-hanging fruit." Give me a break!

It seems that everywhere and in every way we are taught and expected to talk in cutesy riddle-like clichés, making things more difficult than they need to be. The other day I saw an issue of *Cosmopolitan* with the cover headline: "76 Ways to Seduce a Man." Hey, it ain't that tough! Whatever happened to the never fail, time-tested wink and a breathy "come over here." Why does positive thinking have to be "attitudinal conditioning" or "neuro-linguistic programming?"

TASTE, EXPRESSION, OPINION

This communication confusion also plays out in our personal and family relationships. Yes, everybody is entitled to their own taste, expression, opinion, and interpretation, but nobody is entitled to their own bias of truth or right and wrong. Let's back up the discussion we had about this in chapter one with a family life example. All families have argued over a child's appearance—makeup, jewelry, body piercing, and tattoos. We must choose our battles and not argue over self-expression, individual tastes, or passing fads.

If you are in a park throwing a Frisbee with friends and you see some punk rockers with orange and green and purple Mohawks and your buddy's hunting dog suddenly stops and goes on point, mistaking the hair for a flock of birds with that look in its eye that says, "Shoot those things," relax, respect differences, and get over it. There is no such thing as a bad kid, only bad behavior. William Shakespeare wrote in Romeo and Juliet, "What's in a name? That which we call a rose by any other name would smell as sweet." Whatever we label people, remember that a human being is a human being. Looks can be so deceiving, as can titles.

LABELS AND TITLES

First Lady of Utah Mrs. Mary Kaye Huntsman created a national movement called "The Power in You," the premier school/family/community program in the country focused on mental health and self-esteem issues and why and how we should remove the labels we place on one another. I highly recommend that you pull up the website www.powerinyou.org and contact the office to learn how you can implement this program in your school district.

Labels come from comparing something or someone to something or someone else, and hinder our personal and professional development at all levels. For example, the answer to the question "What is success?" depends on comparisons. Opinion and passing phases in our "work-in-progress" life are just that and only that. They change as the comparisons and competition changes.

However, if our children are suggesting that they will do something irreversible to their body and harmful to their health, or they are becoming sexually active, parents have an obligation to say something, provide loving counsel, and intervene, because promiscuity is wrong and harmful. This is not opinion; it is irrefutable truth. Obscenity, racism, sexism, anti-Semitism, hatred, and lies about history, people, and places are not "expressions," and they are unacceptable in establishing self-identity.

Opinion is different and separate from fact and mere expression. Stating opinion is "self-expression"—the residual of finely tuning our likes and tastes, the vital ingredient in developing our "unique factor" and "brand of one" that sets us apart from all others. More important, self-expression is one of the key developmental steps on the path to personal conviction and integrity, and to standing up against wrong and standing for right.

Understanding the differences among fact, taste, and opinion is not only critical for young people but for adults as well. No one I know is perfect, and every so often we all screw up. Therefore, we need to know what's right as well as how to act when we don't do the right thing. The question is not whether we will be wrong or do wrong, but what we will do to make it right when we do mess up. When we stumble, we can't go too long before we fix what's broken. We must take action.

No matter how difficult or embarrassing, we must immediately do whatever it takes to make restitution. Opinions, expressions, and tastes change. Right does not. Truth is always truth.

BUSINESS MARKETING

Like discussions over taste and expression, there can be no right opinion in marketing until facts are revealed and measured to determine success or failure. Right, in marketing, is only about one thing: did you increase sales, generate more profits, grow more market share, exceed your production and delivery quotas, and meet shareholder expectations and investment goals? If your ideas created this jump in value, you were right. If your ideas did not accomplish your goals, you were wrong.

When Taco Bell aired their Mexican Chihuahua talking-dog ads, polls showed that they were the most popular commercials on television. Taco Bell made people feel good and listen to an adorable dog, but over the course of the few months this Chihuahua ad ran, sales did not increase, and neither did the bottom line. Taco Bell did not sell more food; however, the purchase of little brown Mexican Chihuahua dogs increased at all pet stores nationwide. They were great entertaining advertisements, and if entertainment was the goal, the ads were right. But the goal was for the company to make more money; therefore, the opinion of whoever thought the ad would sell more burritos was wrong.

IS THE OPINION OF YOU WRONG?

What is your goal for you? And what if your opinion about how to achieve that goal is wrong? Is your goal right in that it helps you stretch toward reaching your ultimate capacity and full potential as a human being, or is it wrongfully focused on just being best compared to others? In the context of the previously stated, "We cannot exceed our *potential;* we just misjudge it." We should not be impressed by how much money someone makes or by what kind of car someone drives or the size of someone's house.

If you are making $50,000 a year and could be making $100,000, if you are driving this car and could be driving that car, if you are living here when you could be living there, I am not impressed.

However, given your circumstances, education, and opportunities, if you should be making $50,000 a year but are making $100,000, and if you should be living in a small house driving a cheap car but are living in your dream home and are driving your dream car, I honor you and respect you. I *am* impressed! You inspire me.

Of course, material success is only one aspect of life, and the goal is to balance out our lives. But you can't just click off the pursuit of excellence in *all* you do. Maximizing potential and winning are not a sometime thing. They are an all-the-time thing. Reaching your full potential as a human being is inspiring to everyone. Remember, in sports, sales, marketing, and customer service, you may not be training and pushing yourself to maximize your potential and reach the full measure of your existence, but others are. When you meet them, they will win. On the other side of potential, if you are a workaholic, you are no different than an alcoholic or drug addict—being gone is still being gone, whether it be physically, mentally, chemically, or emotionally.

If you could vote on election day but don't, if you could get an education but don't, if you could balance out your life but don't, if you could be honest but aren't, if you could exercise and eat right but don't, if you could be more involved in your community but aren't, then shame on you! No one respects you or is impressed by you. You should be embarrassed and chastised and decide on your own to be more of who you already are. Not for me but for yourself and your loved ones.

I knew a guy in high school who had an IQ of 167, always got the highest score on tests he never studied for, and was valedictorian. He killed himself after high school graduation because he never competed against himself. Understanding and striving to reach our full potential is a wonderful, noble thing! So be you! My dad always told me, "You'll make a lousy somebody else."

Determining what your goal is for you (not what you want

to accomplish, but who you need to be in order to accomplish it) is made possible only when you identify exactly who the actual, 100 percent authentic you really is. Only when you do this can you begin to become more of who you already are.

PIONEERING, MOMENTUM, RESTRUCTURING

The experts say 85 percent of what we remember is visual, and at least half of us learn through documented flow charts and diagrams. Consequently, let me explain personal and professional development in the most elementary terms. In every endeavor both individually and organizationally, there are three phases:

- The pioneering stage
- The momentum stage
- The restructuring stage

These phases are not mutually exclusive but rather simultaneous events that will lead every person and organization to increased productivity and maximum efficiency and effectiveness. Consider the following diagram:

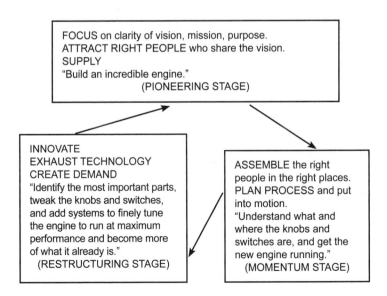

FOCUS on clarity of vision, mission, purpose.
ATTRACT RIGHT PEOPLE who share the vision.
SUPPLY
"Build an incredible engine."
(PIONEERING STAGE)

INNOVATE
EXHAUST TECHNOLOGY
CREATE DEMAND
"Identify the most important parts, tweak the knobs and switches, and add systems to finely tune the engine to run at maximum performance and become more of what it already is."
(RESTRUCTURING STAGE)

ASSEMBLE the right people in the right places.
PLAN PROCESS and put into motion.
"Understand what and where the knobs and switches are, and get the new engine running."
(MOMENTUM STAGE)

CIRCULAR PLANE PERFORMANCE MODEL

If you study this process and implement it, you will cut through the clutter of your life, identify needs, initiate resources to fill the needs, focus on what really matters most, and improve. (Notice that it is a constant process of continuous improvement—no complacency or apathy). The interesting thing is that this circular model also works on a linear plane.

Linear-plane process has always been suspect because if things start going badly, they will continue to go badly.

However, if you proactively take charge by starting on a positive, effective note and begin with the end in mind, through increased frequency of feedback you will turn effective into efficient, maintain the positive course, and literally simplify your process as you go. The classic example of this linear model is the Wal-Mart Supply Chain Model.

WAL-MART SUPPLY CHAIN EFFICIENCY

In a nutshell, Wal-Mart thought they sold Tide laundry detergent. Consequently, Wal-Mart's store shelves were stocked with every kind, size, and "flavor" of Tide, and Wal-Mart's warehouse inventory was overstocked in large quantities—Tide with Clorox, Tide without Clorox, Tide for hot water, Tide for cold water, Tide for whites only, Tides for colors, and so forth. The supply chain was clogged and bogged down, precious working capital was *tied* up (excuse the pun) in unnecessary inventory, and maximum profitability suffered.

To optimize efficiency in the supply chain, Wal-Mart and Tide got together and monitored which of the specific "flavors" of Tide were actually being purchased. Even though they broke it down to regions and individual stores, it turned out the customers were confused by all the choices and mostly purchased one size and kind—large powder for cold-water washing. Suddenly Wal-Mart realized that instead of "selling" customers and telling them what they wanted and needed, they should listen, become distributors, and deliver exactly what customers wanted.

In supply chain/warehouse management we must always look at inventory as a stack of real money just sitting there collecting dust. On this linear plane, Wal-Mart eliminated the inefficiencies of unnecessarily handling goods and the necessity for long-term warehousing. Wal-Mart no longer has warehouses but rather "distribution centers," or clearing houses, that do nothing more than capture the exact demand of each product and regulate the shortest, fastest, most direct supply route from manufacturer (supply) to customer (demand). No speculation, no delay, and no waste of time, money, space, or employees.

Linear Plane Performance Model

MANUFACTURING	WAL-MART DISTRIBUTION	CONSUMER
Supply	Assemble	Demand
(Supply/Focus/ People/Pioneering)	(Assemble/Process/ Momentum)	(Demand/Innovate/ Technology/Restructure)

I'm sure it is clear by now how these organizational systems also apply in our personal and professional development. Whether we look at life in a circular or linear way, our primary purpose is to cut through the clutter of all the unnecessary choices presented to us daily and identify what we really want, what we really need, and what really matters most. The goal becomes to tweak and streamline our ability to optimize our personal strengths to get everything out of others and ourselves in the most direct, efficient, and effective way.

This is the simple yet profound secret to Wal-Mart's success and validation that continuous improvement in both our personal and professional lives always has been and always will be about inside-out internal excavation based on asking the right questions that bring right answers. Because geographic reloca-tion doesn't really change much of anything—no matter where you go, there you are; and because the purpose of life is to be you—you're going to make a lousy somebody else. Let us con-clude this chapter with a process that actually demonstrates how to drill deep within ourselves, one success principle, one attri-bute, one trait that we want to develop at a time. One of the most important is character. Becoming more of who you already are starts with character. The following exercise is a simple game of "connect-the-dots" linking one right question to the next until we exhaust the discussion on what is, why we should, when, and how to develop character.

CHARACTER COUNTS

Question: What is character?

Answer: When education, skill sets, and experience are equal, character is the differentiating factor that sets one indi-vidual apart from another. When the weak beat the strong, char-acter is the determining reason. Survival of the fittest is not just about physical prowess; it is also about inner strength and mental toughness. The great football coach Vince Lombardi said, "Men-tal toughness is sacrifice and self-denial combined with perfectly disciplined 'will' that refuses to give in. This persistence is char-acter in action."

Question: "How do we develop character?"

Answer: Hang around with people who have character.

One of the men I admire most is Thad Gaebelein, an army major who taught military history at West Point and is an in-structor at the Merchant Marine Academy. He was an infantry officer and an assault helicopter pilot who knows more about character and how to develop it and live it than anyone I've ever met. I take pride in calling him my friend.

Thad has taught me that character development is nothing new. Aristotle left us with his four virtues: wisdom, respect, cour-age, and moderation. Ancient Hebrew writers such as Micah in the Old Testament taught that we must have justice (integrity), mercy (kindness), and humility (meekness).

Even the ancient Greeks discussed character. Whenever something happened, good or bad, the popular cry was "fate." The great philosophers rebutted this and proclaimed, "Character is destiny." They did not say, "Fate is destiny." Fate is something happening to you over which you have no control. Destiny is you deciding to take control.

The next obvious sequential question in this line of exploration: How does character help us take control?

Answer: Character is the sum total of everything we do and say—the sum of all of our choices, both grandiose and mundane. For this reason, character directly affects our destiny more than any single attribute or trait. Character defines us as an individual. Character helps us make the right choices. Look around. What organizations teach character education, which empowers and enables their members to live good, proactive, lives? The Boy Scouts of America is top on the list. Yes, I previously quoted their character-building philosophies, but we should all remember to "Be Prepared" and to be "trustworthy, loyal, helpful, friendly, courteous, kind, obedient, cheerful, thrifty, brave, clean, and reverent."

Many people have talent and the capability to succeed, but they lack character. Most organizations have mission and vision statements, have identified values, and have solicited personal commitment, but they lack the character to live them. With character we can always do the harder, right thing instead of the easier, wrong thing.

IS CHARACTER CONSTANT?

As we continue in this search, the next obvious question is: When do we know we have character?

Answer: How we react to diversity exposes our character. Winning is extremely important, but how we win—and lose— is more important. Those with character consistently win even if they have to come from behind because they know winning isn't a sometime thing; it's an all-the-time thing. Character isn't turned off and on. Those with character know it's about who they really are and what they do when no one is around. This allows them to be authentically real when others are around.

Question: How does character affect others around me?

Answer: The most important ingredient to leadership is character. With character, a leader can get others to follow and do what they don't want to do. And when they have completed the task, they thank the leader and love him for expecting them to do it. Leaders with character discipline not to punish but to teach, counsel, and improve. Developing character is the critical component to being a champion in every way, every day.

One of the greatest of all American four star-generals and leaders, General John Jumper, former Chief of Staff of the United States Air Force, explains, "Our most meaningful memories will be the times when our character, integrity, persistence, stamina, and fortitude were most challenged, and we had the courage to do the right thing."

As you now pause at the end of this discussion to fully digest the power and effectiveness of a question-and-answer process—how it works and why it works—isn't it interesting that becoming more of who we already are really only requires a desire and firm commitment to simply do the right thing? When I asked General Jumper what he means by "doing the right thing," he told me, "Living a higher law."

Question: "What is living a higher law?"

General Jumper answered: "Doing the harder instead of the easier, taking the high road less traveled."

Question: Why?

Answer: "It's where we discover the meaning of duty, honor, country, integrity, service, excellence, sacrifice, patriotism, love, and the promise of heaven."

Fundamental 10

PREPARE FOR LIFE'S STORMS

We are all, it seems, saving ourselves for the senior prom. But many of us forget that somewhere along the way we must learn to dance.
> —Alan Harrington

The world needs dreamers and the world needs doers, but above all the world needs dreamers who do.
> —Carmen Snow

One universal principle and natural law states: "There is opposition in all things." We have heretofore discussed going from great to best and best versus right. Let's go deeper and discuss right versus wrong. Why is there 'wrong,' and who says so? Why can't we just live and let live and all get along? The answer obviously lies in our acknowledgment that America's founding fathers had a spiritual understanding of why the world was formed, why America was discovered, what our purpose is on earth, and where our place is in it.

The US Declaration of Independence states: "We hold these truths to be self-evident, that all men are created equal, that they are endowed by their Creator with certain unalienable Rights, that among these, are Life, Liberty, and the pursuit of Happiness." In other words, the greatest gift we have is our agency to do things of our own free will and choice. The fact that the Founding Fathers acknowledge freedom of choice to be at the core of our existence assures us there is an opposition in all things. If not, where is the choice? We never act for ourselves without being enticed by one thing or another.

In the story of the Garden of Eden, there was the "forbidden fruit" in opposition to the "tree of life"—the one being bitter and the other being sweet. Without life there would be no death, without corruption there would be no incorruption, without happiness there would be no misery, without darkness there would be no light.

Why, when we find good, do we also always find bad? Why, since recorded history began, has there been a clash of values with one civilization pitted against another, with evil continually doing everything it can to disrupt, corrupt, invade, and overthrow good?

There are philosophical and theological answers to these questions that I will not confirm or deny. What I'm seeking is a general consensus that every culture and society has people who contradict the core values and sense of what's right and wrong in that society. Consequently, these individuals must be dealt with in an extreme manner to avoid chaos and destruction, and to maintain peace, freedom, and safety for all others.

Scott Peterson in California and Mark Hacking in Utah killed their wives. Susan Smith strapped her two little children into their car seats and pushed her automobile into a lake. Fourteen-year-old Elizabeth Smart was abducted from her bedroom during the night by a man who had worked as a contract laborer at the Smart home. A superstar singer was arrested on multiple counts of child abuse and criminal molestation. Two teenage students opened fire on fellow students at Columbine High School in Colorado, killing thirteen. Timothy McVeigh blew up the federal building in Oklahoma City, killing 168 men, women, and children. Hitler murdered six million Jews. Stalin murdered millions of Russians. In the "killing fields" of Cambodia, Pol Pot murdered millions. The list of evil goes on and on.

As hard as it is for some to comprehend, especially those of us who grew up in good neighborhoods, there really are bad neighborhoods and evil people who want to hurt someone or something. There really are smart, intelligent, hard-working people who could be honest, productive, positive contributors to society, but instead decide to spend their entire day and night figuring out how to hack into a computer mainframe, how to destroy computer software operating systems, and how to embezzle millions from business and screw their friends in investment scams. Some people actually believe their calling is to perfect identity theft and sell it to others to defraud financial institutions and governments. And the real mind-boggler is the fact that there are fanatical religionists who wake up each day, and all they can think about in between their five prayers to their God is how to kill an "infidel" American.

Elizabeth Smart was held hostage and psychologically and sexually abused for nine months until the "good" police officers were tipped off by "good" citizens and Elizabeth was rescued from the "bad" man and his "bad" wife. John Walsh, host of his powerful television show *America's Most Wanted* aired the photo sketch of the possible abductor nine times until Elizabeth was finally saved. Mr. Walsh had a handsome young son, Adam, with an entire life of dreams and accomplishments ahead of him, who was kidnapped and murdered, and was among the thousands of missing children who never come back. Because of this experience, Mr. Walsh has dedicated his life to rally the "good folks" in the world to stand up to the creeps.

The question for each of us is, when is it our turn to stand up for right? If we are weak, isn't it time to get strong—physically, mentally, spiritually, emotionally, financially, socially, and especially as a family? If we are unsure, isn't it time to get prepared? Have we forgotten that pressure is not something that is naturally there, that it's created when you question your own ability, and when you know what you can do there is never any question? When we are prepared, when we know what we believe to the point of conviction of the heart, we shall not fear life's storms and can sleep on a windy night.

Sleep on a Windy Night

A young man came a calling, he was answering the ad.
The farmer needed hired help, so he promised all he had.
The farmer asked, "Why hire you?" He said, "I'll do what's right,
You'll never have to worry, I can sleep on a windy night."

Late that evening clouds rolled in, disaster dead ahead.
The farmer called the lad for help, but he was asleep in bed.
He raced out but the gates were tied, the yard was fastened tight.
Everything was safe and sound until the morning light.

The farmer smiled, knew what he meant, he could sleep on a windy
*   night.*
You can sleep through the night, if inside your skies are blue.
Takin' care of business before business takes care of you.
No matter what the forecast, if prepared there is no plight.
While others stay awake and stir, you can sleep on a windy night.

A traveling man was lonely, left his room to get a drink.
She caught his eye and flashed some thigh, his flesh began to think.
A storm was raging, lust was caging him and squeezing tight
But he didn't stay, with his wife away, he'd rather sleep on a windy
*   night.*

Back at home with kids tucked in, the weather turned real bad.
The frightened children climbed in bed and snuggled up to dad.
"Willthehouseblowdown, willthewindowsbreak, ordidthebuild-
*   er build it right?"*
Everything's secure; we're safe and sound until morning light.
He said, "I am the carpenter, you can sleep on this windy night."

You can sleep through the night, if inside your skies are blue.
Takin' care of business before business takes care of you.
No matter what the forecast, if prepared there is no plight
While others stay awake and stir, you can sleep on a windy night.
—Dan Clark

There is no better way to describe what I learned from the soldiers I interviewed in Iraq and Afghanistan than to say that they can sleep on a windy night. I asked the troops what happens when they come under attack and what they think and do when the bullets and rockets start flying. Each one looked me in the eye and confidently answered, "We trust our training. If each of us—the soldier on the left of you, in front, behind, and to the right of you—does exactly what he or she has been trained to think and do, we all have a great chance of making it home alive."

Obviously they were trained in marksmanship, obstacle course, and specific job skills, and they were physically fit to fight. But there was more to their training—something that we could all use in our personal and professional lives to prepare ourselves for life's storms.

I discovered this training and learned about it in detail as I had the honor and privilege to be the keynote speaker at the National Conference on Ethics at the United States Military Academy at West Point in 2005. For two days I heard about ethics from renowned scholars, studied it, and saw it in action as I toured the campus, attended lectures, and interviewed leaders, officers, cadets and two Medal of Honor recipients.

I was taken on a personal tour of the historic West Point grounds and buildings by Commandant General Mike Scaparrotti who presented me with an autographed copy of a small hard cover book called *Bugle Notes 2005–2009*. This book, given to every new incoming freshman "Plebe" with a required order to commit all 320 pages to memory, becomes their philosophic backbone. *Bugle Notes* pretty much covers everything, including General Douglas MacArthur's most famous speech delivered at his acceptance of the famed West Point Thayer Award in 1962. Every American should read this "Duty, Honor, Country" speech and ponder what this belief and conviction would do to strengthen our nation.

Because our soldiers are some of the best and brightest men and woman in America and are clearly the best trained and prepared military in the world, it is critical to share four documents

that give insight into military training and culture. This information greatly affected me while at West Point, and it continues to
positively affect my life each and every day.

THE MISSION OF THE UNITED STATES MILITARY ACADEMY

"To educate, train, and inspire the Corps of Cadets so that
each graduate is a commissioned leader of character committed to the values of Duty, Honor, Country; professional growth
throughout a career as an officer in the United States Army; and
a lifetime of selfless service to the Nation."

THE MISSION OF THE UNITED STATES CORPS OF CADETS

"To develop each cadet into a commissioned leader of character who possess the will to win, personal courage, adaptability,
physical fitness, and mental toughness essential to the profession
of arms, and is inspired to a career of professional excellence in
the United States Army."

THE OATH TAKEN UPON BEING COMMISSIONED IN THE ARMY

"I, (your name), having been appointed an officer in the
Army of the United States, do solemnly swear that I will support and defend the Constitution of the United States against
all enemies, foreign and domestic, that I will bear true faith and
allegiance to the same; that I take this obligation freely, without
any mental reservation or purpose of evasion; and that I will well
and faithfully discharge the duties of the office which I am about
to enter; so help me God."

These three statements clearly outline the expectations of
a West Point education, but what are the behind-the-scenes
thoughts, beliefs, and convictions that continually produce high
performance? The answer lies in a brief analysis of the United
States Military Academy Honor Code and the entire US Army's

Seven Core Values that are the foundation of and the guideposts for character development.

The West Point Honor Code simply states: "A Cadet Will Not Lie, Cheat, Steal, or Tolerate Those Who Do." That's it! Although brief, it gets to the profound point that this is *the* standard to live by and the fountain from which all strength flows. Strict compliance to this code allows cadets to develop an understanding of the importance of integrity as an essential aspect of leadership, to develop a strong desire to maintain an honorable lifestyle, and to achieve a level of ethical and honorable conduct necessary to prepare themselves for the storms that will challenge their integrity throughout this lives.

This all makes sense when you understand the seven core values and the Army's definition of them:

US ARMY CORE VALUES

- *Integrity:* Making decisions and taking action based on our country's shared values.
- *Honor:* Being honest, fair, and just, and demonstrating due regard for the property of others.
- *Respect:* Recognizing the infinite worth and dignity of human life—displaying compassion, consideration, and civility.
- *Duty:* Accepting responsibility for one's actions and doing all that should be done as well as it can be done.
- *Loyalty:* Being faithful, displaying fealty, devotion, and commitment (for the soldier, loyalty means allegiance to the Constitution of the United States of America).
- *Service:* Contribution on behalf of others; dedication to the goals of a group (unit, team, society, etc.), rendering assistance and support without regard to personal profit or gain.
- *Courage:* Bravery, valor, fortitude in spite of risk, fear, doubt—acting in accordance with one's beliefs in the presence of adversity, danger, and criticism.

If living by this code doesn't prepare you for a storm, nothing will. And when you dovetail all of this into the Three Core Values of the US Air Force that I love to discuss, it becomes obvious that these values apply to every aspect of our civilian lives as well. There will be storms, so we must get prepared and stay prepared!

LIFE'S STORMS

Storms are part of life. You have to have a storm in order to have a rainbow. You must have rain to appreciate the sunshine. If you are not failing now and then, you are not pushing yourself hard enough. There is an opposition in all things. Years ago, United Technologies ran this full-page inspirational ad in the *New York Times:*

"You've failed many times, although you may not remember. You fell down the first time you tried to walk. You almost drowned the first time you tried to swim. Did you hit the ball the first time you swung the bat? Heavy hitters, the ones who hit the most home runs, also strike out a lot. Babe Ruth struck out 1,330 times, but he also hit 714 home runs. R. H. Macy failed seven times before his store in New York caught on. English novelist John Creasey received 753 rejection slips before he published 564 books. See! Don't worry about failure. Worry about the chances you miss when you don't even try."

Don't you think it's better to attempt something great and fail than to attempt nothing at all and succeed? Attempting is the formula for success. Most people are so afraid of failure that they are afraid to risk success. Yet the great law of growth is to try, fail, adjust, and try again. How does a bird learn to fly? How does a person become great at anything? The answer is always the same: Through hard work. Through trial and error. Through attempting something great and failing, falling, getting up, and trying again. We must remember that for every seed of adversity in life there is also a seed of success, and we must look for that seed.

FEAR: FALSE EVIDENCE APPEARING REAL

In a scene from the movie *Rocky III,* Rocky is afraid of losing an important fight and is being lectured by his wife. He has already been beaten badly and has lost his heavyweight championship; he is scheduled to again fight the man who beat him and is truly afraid. The following conversation is paraphrased from the movie dialogue.

Adrian: "You've never quit anything before. Why now?"

Rocky: "Because before, in all the other fights, I thought I was something. I thought I was good. I thought I was a champion. Mickey [his former trainer] didn't have to lie to me and make me feel like I was better than I was when I wasn't. The fighters were handpicked. Nothing was real! You see, Mickey was just trying to protect me, but it only made things worse. I've gone three years thinking I was a winner, but I'm not. I'm really a loser! So what if I had the title for so long? I don't believe in myself anymore! And when you don't believe in yourself anymore, you're finished, through—that's it. Now, for the first time in my life, I want to quit. I'm afraid. Adrian, I'm afraid!"

Adrian: "I'm afraid too! But there's nothing wrong with being afraid! You're human, aren't you? You have no right to feel guilty for what happened. You were a champion, and you did what you were expected to do. You did what I and everybody else thought you should do! And now you're trying to tell me these fighters weren't real? Well, I don't believe it! But it doesn't matter what I believe because you're the one who has to carry that fear around inside you. Afraid that everybody is going to take things away! Afraid you're going to be remembered as a coward! That you're not a man anymore! Well, it's not true! But it doesn't matter what I think because you're the one who has to settle it. And you've got to overcome the fear now, or it will bother you for the rest of your life. Look what it's done to you already! No matter how hard it might be, you've got to fight. Apollo [the new trainer] thinks you can do it, and I think you can do it, but you've got to want to do it for the right reasons. Not for me, not for anybody!

Not for the title, for money, or for those who chant your name, but for yourself! For you, and for you alone!"

Rocky: "And if I lose?"

Adrian: "Then you lose! At least you lose with no excuses—with no fear! You lose with your head high, knowing you gave it your very best shot. And no one ever needs to be ashamed of that."

Rocky went on to win and always wins because he keeps swinging. I guess a man is not finished if he is defeated. He is finished only when he leaves the ring!

REAL-LIFE ROCKY

This movie dialogue makes more sense when you know the inspirational story behind the story. Sylvester Stallone ended up at the Muhammad Ali/Chuck Wepner heavyweight fight. Wepner, a battling bruising type of club fighter who had never really made the big time, was now having his shot. But the fight was not regarded as a serious battle. It was called a public joke. He would barely go three rounds, most of the predictions said. The history books will read that he went fifteen rounds and established himself as one of the few men who had ever gone the distance with Muhammad Ali, and he can hold his head up high forever no matter what happens. Stallone later wrote that that night must have meant more to Wepner than any money he could have ever received from fighting because now he had run the complete circle. This is why he had been training for thirty-four years.

At that time Sylvester Stallone was a starving "nobody" actor with a dream to write a screenplay. After that fight his character began to develop. He was going to create Rocky Balboa, a man from the streets, a walking cliché of sorts, the all-American tragedy, a man who didn't have much mentally, but had incredible emotion and patriotism and spirituality and good nature even though nature had not been good to him.

The second ingredient had to be the specific storyline for the movie, which turned out to be Stallone's personal story of his inability to be recognized, looking only for a break to show what he could do. So, Stallone took his own predicament and injected it into the body of Rocky because no one, he felt, would be interested in listening to or watching or reading a story about a down-and-out, struggling actor/writer. This script idea just didn't conjure up waves of empathy to give him a shot at making a movie. But Rocky Balboa was different. He was America's child. He was to the 1970s what Charlie Chaplain's Little Tramp was to the '20s.

What some do not know is that the catch in Stallone's sales pitch to the film production companies was that he came with the script. If they wanted to make the movie, Sylvester would definitely be playing the lead part and star as Rocky. The rest is history—Academy Award for Best Picture, followed by five sequel Rocky movies released in subsequent years with *ROCKY VI* released December 25, 2006, to complete the enormously successful series. In a nutshell, Sylvester Stallone faced his fears and didn't just sit by and let life come to him; he came to life. He conceived, he believed, and because he planned his work and worked his plan, he achieved exactly what he set out to do.

FEARLESS THINKING

Inspiration, motivation, and having "FT" and "PMA"—Fearless Thinking and Positive Mental Attitude—have always been an integral part of overcoming fear. Why? Because you fail so many more times than you succeed that if you are serious about winning, you must ignore the fear and fail your way to success.

A young man decides he wants to become a boxing champion, so he employs a trainer. They meet at the gym, but the trainer excitedly greets him at the door with a pep talk, saying, "Hey, you don't have to work out. Just think positive, and you can beat anybody!" The next week he has his first fight against a huge, well-trained, experienced opponent.

"Ding," the bell rings for round one. Our guy gets pummeled and staggers back to his corner. He asks, "Am I doing any damage?" His trainer excitedly replies, "Whoa, he hasn't even hit you yet. Keep thinking positive; you can win if you just think you can!" Ding. Round two and the big guy starts where he left off, knocking our guy from one side of the ring to the other. Bloody and swollen, our guy crawls back to his corner and again asks if he is doing any damage. His excited trainer again answers, "You're doing great. Just keep thinking positive. He hasn't even hit you yet." To this our guy replies, "Okay, but could you keep an eye on the referee 'cause somebody out there is beating the crap out of me!"

Of course I wholeheartedly acknowledge our constant need for inspiration, motivation, and positive thinking. But nothing can replace hard work and sacrifice.

FAILURE IS NOT AN OPTION

A young girl from Romania won five medals as a gymnast in the 1976 Olympic Games: three gold medals, one silver medal, and one bronze medal. Her name was Nadia Comaneci. (I take pride in calling her and her husband, US gymnastics Olympic champion Bart Conner, friends). But winning the medals is not the amazing part of Nadia's story. The amazing part is that she received seven perfect scores—a perfect ten points out of ten points possible. It was the first time in Olympic history that any gymnast had ever received a perfect score, let alone the seven that Nadia received. Think about it. She was only fifteen years old, and she was the greatest gymnast in the world!

Now I have a question. Was Nadia Comaneci always perfect? Could she always get a perfect score, or do you think she had to work for it? How many times do you think she fell before she mastered her amazing and difficult routine? Let me answer this with another story.

UNIVERSITY OF UTAH

In 1980 the University of Utah women's gymnastics team won the national championship. Because of my continued involvement at the U, I had several opportunities to watch the team work out.

One particular day I'd been there a few minutes when I noticed a girl working on a certain exotic acrobatic move on the uneven parallel bars. The move consisted of her swinging around on the upper bar twice to gain momentum, letting go of the bar, spreading her legs in a Chinese split position to avoid the lower bar, grabbing the lower bar as she flew through the air, swinging around the lower bar, letting go again, and grabbing the upper bar again to continue with her routine.

It was a difficult move to learn, and she was having an awful time figuring out how to do it! For more than an hour she tried time and time again to master it. I watched as she climbed up on the bar, started twirling around, let go, spread her legs, reached up to grab the lower bar, and missed. She flew right past it and crashed! Her coach ran over, helped her up, encouraged her to try it again, and helped her climb back up on the bars. Again she twirled to pick up speed, let go of the upper bar, spread her legs, flew through the air, grabbed for the lower bar, missed it, and crashed to the floor again. After eight crashes, this girl was sobbing with pain and limping around. But this didn't stop her. I watched her climb up on the bar thirteen times and suffer thirteen brutal crashes. But on her fourteenth try, she finally got it right.

Can you imagine the pain she must have felt? And this was just to learn one of the many moves in her total routine! What about all the crashes I hadn't seen that she must have had as she tried to learn her other moves?

But her efforts paid off. She won on the uneven parallel bars in the national championships. Her practice, hard work, and determination paid off.

So was Nadia Comaneci always perfect? No more than the University of Utah gymnast who was named best in the nation. Both girls had to work countless hours, persevere, and endure pain and agony until they had pushed themselves to the limit. From a very young age, they had spent countless hours striving to become the best they could possibly be. What if that Utah gymnast had quit after her thirteenth crash, not knowing that in just one more try, she would be successful? How many of us would have rationalized that thirteen tries was more than enough? How many of us would have said, "I did my best and surely no one can expect me to do anymore!" We never know when success will be just one more try away.

Yes, hard work pays off, but I must bring us back to the title of this chapter—Preparing for a Storm—by sharing one of my favorite experiences that a young mother told me.

ATTITUDE IS EVERYTHING

What follows is in her words:

When my son Spencer was in the first grade, he was having speech trouble with his Rs. We thought it was cute until one day Spencer came home with tears in his eyes. I asked what was wrong, and he softly said, "The kids at school ah making fun of me. They say I can't say my ah's vewee good."

"What should we do about it?" I asked.

"The nuse lady said my attitude is evweething. All I have to do is just pwactice."

Everyday before and after school he stood in front of the mirror and worked and worked until two weeks later, Spencer could say his Rs perfectly. In the third grade he entered competitive sports. He was ready for the ordeal—I wasn't. I thought he still looked newly hatched and terribly vulnerable. "Today I have to stay after school again and practice track," he announced one day. "Why don't you come watch me?"

Of course I went. I watched, and my heart ached because he was trying so hard with such discouraging results. From birth, one leg was three inches shorter than his other, and he had great difficulty running. Consequently, he was a high jumper, who, with one strong leg, flung himself through the air, often landing on the bar. Although he became scratched and battered from his fifteen attempts, he relentlessly pursued his goal.

"Haven't you had enough?" I asked in a feeble attempt to protect him from further failure. With tears in his eyes, he softly answered, "The kids make fun of me and say I'm not good at track, but the coach said I can't quit; it's a league rule."

On the next try he cleared the bar.

By the end of track season, I thought he had had enough last-place finishes to last a lifetime. To the contrary, he excitedly proposed, "I think I'll try out for the Little League baseball team. Maybe I'm good at baseball." He wasn't. He couldn't run, and couldn't see the ball. He wore thick Coke-bottle glasses. Each evening left him exhausted and tired, but he never complained about what he couldn't do, and he always had a smile.

"I missed every fly that came my way," he said one night.

"That's too bad," I sympathized. I put a comforting hand on his shoulder and noticed several bruises on his chest.

"What are these spots?" I asked.

He looked down. "Oh those. That's where the ball hit me."

"My goodness! Shouldn't you duck when you're about to get hit?"

His eyes widened. "Mom, I wasn't supposed to get hit."

"Why didn't you catch it?" I persisted.

Spencer's countenance changed, and his head dropped. "That's what I was trying to do."

That night I cried myself to sleep wondering if and when he would ever really succeed. The next day when I picked him up from practice, he had his new uniform. He ran to the car with the blue and gold jersey slung over his shoulder and a smile that lit up his face like a Christmas tree.

"I got a uniform," he announced. "There were only twelve of them. Most guys did not get one. This was the last uniform, and the coach gave it to me. He said I'd earned it."

"Way to go," I said. It was wonderful to see him so happy.

The bench-warming period began after that, and although he never missed a practice or a game, I lost interest. Rationalizing that I had something better to do than just sit on a hard bleacher and watch my son sit there, I stopped going. Spencer pleaded for me to cancel my Friday evening date and come to his final game. I arrived late but still in time to see him play. I guess his persistence had finally gotten to the coach, and he put Spencer in. In the sixth inning, which was the second-to-the-last inning, the ball was hit his way. Spencer hobbled as fast as he could but missed it. Three more times he missed it, letting the other team catch up. Then when it was his turn to bat, he struck out.

Each mistake was announced over the loud speaker. I was mortified and embarrassed, but somehow Spencer was not. After his poor performance, I thought for sure Spencer would be pulled from the game. It was close, and they needed a victory to win the championship. To everyone's surprise, the coach yelled to the end of the bench, "Williams, you're back in."

As Spencer walked past the bleachers, he looked up at me and the other parents and with his patented positive attitude and reassured cautioned, said, "Whoa, Mom, we are only ahead by one run, and I don't know if even I can hold them off with only one inning to play!"

We laughed; he was dead serious! No one seemed to worry, though, because this time Spencer was put in right field where no balls had been hit all game long.

There were two quick hits, and the winning run now stood on first base. Two quick outs then followed. The third hit came Spencer's way. I saw the coach wince and cover his eyes. The ball sailed right into Spencer's glove. We stood to cheer, but he had collided with another player. He lay motionless. The other player got up and screamed that Spencer's nose was gushing blood.

"I think he's dead!" he shouted. "You'd better come quick."

With the apparent winning run crossing home plate, and the ballpark hushed in concerned silence, the coach ran out of the dugout to administer first aid. Suddenly, Spencer raised his hand in the air. The ball had stayed in his glove. The umpire yelled, "You're out!"

Our bleachers erupted into a long, cheering standing ovation. Spencer's team had won the game! The coach couldn't believe it. No one could. With tears in his eyes, the coach proudly started to clap. Then, in a spontaneous eruption of sportsmanship, the other team started to clap. Although they had just lost the game, one by one the opposing team members stood. Within a minute, the other fans, the two umpires, the other team's coaches, and every player on both teams were on their feet cheering for this true eight-year-old hero.

My Spencer is now thirteen years old. It has been five years since that amazing day, and I've never missed another one of his extra-curricular activities. In fact, I've stopped procrastinating, changed my previous life perception from half empty to half full, stopped whining about my job layoff, got more education and training, which landed me more fulfilling employment in a new job, and have never missed another day of work or a day at the gym since then. How could I when I now know that attitude is everything!

HEAVY WEIGHT FIGHTS

Not only do boxers have storms, but they also create them. They are always looking for their next fight. Because I was an amateur boxing camp and am still a boxing fan, I've always been curious why an undefeated heavy-weight champion of the world gets knocked out and is defeated by a much weaker opponent. The reason is complacency.

The champ thinks he is defending his title and loses his competitive advantage. He fails to realize the difference between playing to win and playing not to lose. He has started thinking of himself as *the* competition and has lot his "eye of the tiger" fighting heart, burning desire, and focused work ethic that won him the championship in the first place.

To avoid complacency, the champ must realize that from now on, once the fight begins, he no longer holds the championship title. He has put it up for grabs and must fight and swing and get up every time he is knocked down. In every new match and so-called title defense, he must fight to win the—not *his* but *the*—championship back! No matter how tough, strong, or prepared he has been in his previous fights, he must be prepared with each new storm.

In every sense of the analogy, it's the old bank account example where we must make deposits while things go smoothly, running in the black when the weather is good so that we have enough to withdraw when the weather deteriorates and we must run in the red until we can recover. The key to Noah's survival and triumph over his devastating storm was that he didn't get complacent and forget about his disciplined commitments to walk on higher ground; nor did he ignore the warning signs. In fact, had everyone else heeded the warnings and prepared, more then eight people would have survived.

PRIOR PERSONAL PREP PREVENTS POOR PERFORMANCE

We should act on the signs that a storm is brewing. But this is not enough. Our goal in any situation should never be to just survive. It should always be to thrive. This is why I am a fan of the Boy Scouts of America. Their motto is: "Be Prepared;" the Scout Slogan encourages: "Do a Good Turn Daily;" The Scout Law States: "I am trustworthy, loyal, helpful, friendly, courteous, kind, obedient, cheerful, thrifty, brave, clean and reverent;" the four Bs of their Outdoor Code that should be used to teach every child the importance of taking care of the environment are: "Be clean in my outdoor manners, Be careful with fire, Be considerate, and Be conservation minded. The focus all of their merit badge advancement programs and achieving their highest Eagle Scout Award is captured in the Scout Oath and Promise: "On my honor I will do my best to do my duty to God and my country and to obey the scout law; to help other people at all times; to keep myself physically strong, mentally awake, and morally straight."

When life's storms come, and they definitely will come, it is survival of the fittest and thriving of the strongest—not from without, but from within. When the time comes for us to stick up for our values and beliefs and go against popular peer pressure opinion, our personal mottos, laws, and oaths that are governed by character that get us through the storm. Our inner strength will determine whether we react or respond, whether we make mistakes or learn lessons, and whether we weather our storms or are destroyed by them.

Fundamental 11

WRITE WHAT'S MOST IMPORTANT

I think this is the most extraordinary collection of talent and human knowledge that has ever been gathered together at the White House, with the possible exception of when Thomas Jefferson dined alone.
—Address given by President John F. Kennedy
at a White House dinner honoring Nobel Prize winners

Given the privilege of the platform and the power of the pen, what would you be saying, writing, or singing at this moment in your life? Garth Brooks sang, "I could have missed the pain, but then I would have missed the dance." Are you continually tweaking and improving or only hoping to be happy and successful? How would you document the world and your role in it? Paul McCartney wrote, "Yesterday. All my troubles seemed so far away . . . oh I believe in yesterday." John Lennon wrote, "Imagine all the people living for today . . . nothing to kill or die for . . . living life in peace—You may say I'm a dreamer, but I'm not the only one—I hope someday you'll join us, and the world will be as one." Together Paul and John sang, "Help. I need somebody. Help. Not just anybody. Help!" Mick Jagger reminded us, "You can't always get what you want." And when the talented teenage recording artist McCall Clark wanted to inspire her eight-year-old Make-a-Wish Foundation friend Saydees to continue battling leukemia, she wrote, "I wanna cry and not hold back, throw away the fears and laugh, I wanna love and forgive, I wanna live—Be the friend in someone's life, that makes everything alright, every moment is a gift that I wanna live."

Would your song be called "Tsunami of Tears: SOS, May Day, Call 911, The Sky Is Falling, The World Is Wounded, Who Will Sooth My Fears?" Many people thought the world was coming to an end on January 1, 2000. The Y2K scare and accompanying uneasiness permeated the globe. Personally, I'm glad the fanatical religionists were mistaken and the world did not end. Armageddon was put off until another day. However, it seems things are in a more rapid decline since January 2000.

Enron, WorldCom, and the Balco Olympic/professional baseball steroid scandals are only three of the thousands of stories in which character was neglected in the pursuit of fame, fortune, and perfection. A college basketball player is up on a rape charge, has burned down the block of a rival gang member, and is suspended for choking his coach, and an NBA owner still asks, "But how fast is he? How high can he jump? Can he really shoot the three?" Greedy American corporations pay big money to thug athletes because of the big bucks their endorsements generate. Even after the terrorists attacked on September 11, we still have American companies lowering their standards doing business and building the economy in terrorist-sponsoring countries like Iran.

Don Henley wrote, "Desperado, why don't you come to your senses, This is the end of the innocence," and "There's a whole in the world tonight—don't let there be a whole in the world tomorrow." My dear friend Monty Powell wrote "Tonight I'm Gonna Cry" and "Who Wouldn't Want to Be Me" for Keith Urban; fellow football player and friend Mike Reid wrote, "I can't make you love me anymore" for Bonnie Raitt; mutual friend Chuck Cannon wrote, "How do you like me now?" and "American Soldier" for Toby Keith; my associate Larry Henly wrote, "You are the wind beneath my wings;" and colleague Tim Nichols wrote "Live Like You Were Dying" sung by Tim McGraw. What would you write?

Most bestsellers are *Get Rich in a Minute* and *Lose Thirty Pounds in Thirty Minutes: Celebrity Diet*—books that sell millions, not because the authors know how to get rich or lose weight, but because they know how to sell books. TV shows depend heavily on makeover fantasy and sudden reconstruction of outside appearances of houses, cars, and motorcycles and extreme changes in clothing and hairstyles, and live broadcasting of cosmetic surgery! Madness, it is. Total insanity! Will it ever stop? Slow down? What are we to do?

WHAT WOULD YOU IMPROVE?

I'm losing hair in the front of the top of my head and growing it in my ears, nose, and on my back in places I didn't think hair could grow. My only hope is that the hair in my right ear will grow long enough that I can comb it up over the top of my head!

At my twenty-year high school reunion, I realized that students used to laugh at me because I was different, and now I laugh at them because they are the same. I would change very little. However, improving on absolutely everything is my life-long ambition. If we are honest with each other, we will admit that on the outside everyone tries to portray the perfect, flawless, got-it-all-together image of someone who is saving the world and changing everyone in it. But until we subscribe to Gandhi's words—"We must be the change we seek in the world"—we will at some point in our lives put others down as we try to make ourselves feel better about who we are. When we are stuck and going nowhere, putting others down makes us feel that we are moving and progressing when we are not.

Ignoring the importance of improving ourselves and doing nothing are the worst things we can do. In a free country with free elections, bad politicians are elected by good citizens who don't vote. We must get involved and stay involved by taking inventory of what we can and cannot change.

WHAT CAN WE CHANGE?

As mentioned earlier, we cannot put our confidence in and draw stability or comfort from the earth, because it changes. We have no say in the changing seasons, but we can learn life lessons from the cycle of nature. We cannot control the beautiful, tranquil Caribbean when it changes into hurricane season or melancholy streams that change into flash-flooding rivers or Indian Ocean earthquakes that change waves into deadly tsunamis.

Neither can we control people who think they can change others. And we can't change lovers and significant others who believe they will change their partners after they get married. Yet seminars and workshops across the globe are crammed full of people sent by companies or loved ones—paying huge tuition—who think that with enough time and money they can turn a person into something and someone they are not.

The thought is ludicrous. To attempt it is reckless. Remember my college roommate? He said, "You shouldn't try to teach a pig to sing. It's a waste of your time, and it annoys the pig." However, we can change expectations and inspire motivation. We can raise the bar and expect class.

SYSTEM VS. INDIVIDUALS

It is important to realize that oftentimes it is the system that is flawed or broken, not so much the individual. It is human nature to push the envelope and exploit the system. People—employees and players—will get away with what we let them get away with. Contrast your organization with the following comparison between professional golf and other professional sports made by Bob Gempleler:

- Golfers don't get per diem and two seats on a charter flight when they travel between tournaments.
- Golfers don't hold out for more money or demand new contracts because of another player's deal.
- Golfers don't demand that taxpayers pay for the courses on which they play.
- When golfers make a mistake, nobody is there to cover for them or back them up.
- The PGA Tour raises more money for charity in one year than the National Football League does in two.

- In golf you cannot fail 70 percent of the time and make $9 million a season like the best baseball hitters (.300 batting average).

In their prime, Greg Norman, Arnold Palmer, and other stars would shake your hand and say they were happy to meet you. In his prime, Jose Canseco wore T-shirts that read "Leave Me Alone."

At a golf tournament (unlike at taxpayer-funded sports stadiums and arenas), you won't hear a steady stream of four-letter words and nasty name calling while you're hoping that no one spills beer on you.

We must never forget that the system—team expectation, corporate culture, family organization—must first be right if we are to grow, develop, nurture, attract, and keep the right individuals. Every human being is born with and eternally endowed with the character traits and attributes of our Creator, and all of us are tempered and sculpted daily by "survival of the fittest" hard knocks into the masterpiece we were born to be. We are more like Michelangelo's raw marble blocks—inherently solid, rough, steadfast, never changing in molecular makeup and substance, and able to withstand stormy winds and rains. Yet we're grindable, chipable, carvable, and polishable—thus able to become more of what we already are inside.

Oh, the breathtaking masterpiece marble statues of Michelangelo! Likewise, it is from our inherent, rock solid original strengths and talents that we become more of who and what we already are!

WHAT DO YOU KNOW?

Now that you know thinking isn't necessarily knowing, what do you know? How long have you known it? From whom did you learn it? Is what you've been taught fact or opinion? Do you know enough to be successful right now? Have you sorted and sifted through what you know? According to *Webster's Dictionary*, a fact is "truth; a piece of information presented as having objective reality; actual existence; undisputable knowledge."

There comes a time in every one of our lives when we must face the facts, conduct a thorough self-audit, look ourselves in the mirror, and internally excavate who we really are, what we really know, and what we are going to do about it for the rest of our lives. You see, the rest of *Webster's Dictionary* definition of fact states, "A thing done; doing; an event and actual occurrence; evidence through performance." The fact is, we don't learn to know, we learn to do. It doesn't do us any good to know how to read if we never read.

Many books have been written about what authors think and believe, but we all know we should not believe everything we think. This book is the twentieth book I have written. It has taken me ten years to complete it. It is less about what I think or believe and more about what I know to be true, where I learned it, and the experiences that taught me time-tested truths. Notice that all the answers are in the box.

I Know

- Too many powerful people leading major organizations and even teaching in prestigious educational institutions know the price of everything and the value of nothing; they don't know what they are talking about and make us feel that it's our fault. The scary thing is, they don't know that they don't know.
- We must see who we are and say who we are before we can be who we are.
- It's harder to find right answers to the wrong questions than to ask the right questions.
- Success in life is not determined by our abilities; it is determined by our choices. Choices are made based on correct knowledge (truth), correct attitude (what, when, and why we act on knowledge), correct perspective (how knowledge and attitude interface to help us make sense of each situation we encounter), and unquenchable curiosity (relentless questioning

of "if" and then "what," with a cause-and-effect analysis and drive to seek out the best available data to unveil the grandest possibilities).

- Success is never final. Charles H. Duell, commissioner of the US Office of Patents, said, "Everything that can be invented has been invented." That was 1899! In 1962, a Decca Recording Company executive rejected the Beatles, stating, "I don't like their sound, and guitar music is on the way out."

- Whatever is sufficient to get us to this point is insufficient to get us further.

- Computer memory is getting so powerful that it could eventually hold grudges! In our high-tech world we must seek more truth and then apply it with high touch. High tech is the hardware, mainframe, hard drive, letter-of-the-law side of success where the answers are 100 percent accurate but totally useless. High touch is the software, spirit-of-the-law, intangible qualities side of success where the emotional application of the high-tech knowledge creates wisdom, empathy, compassion, urgency, and action.

- Common sense is no longer common. Neither is common courtesy or common knowledge.

- What we have been in the past does not make us who we are as much as what we hope to become in the future. No matter what our past has been, we have a spotless future.

- The things we hate to hear the most are usually the things we need to hear the most.

- Our initial success in life is about saying "yes," but significance and balance are usually about saying "no."

- The main thing is to make the main thing the right thing. Time management and prioritizing make the difference and create the "W-I-N" definition of What's Important Now.

- There is no such thing as a financial crisis, only an idea crisis. Ideas create income.

I Know

- Competition is good, healthy, and productive; comparison is destructive. Knowing the difference between competition and comparison is paramount. Comparing brings arrogance, disappointment, and discouragement—and all three are bad.
- Competition can bring disappointment, but that's okay—you learn more from failure than success. Success and failure mean nothing by themselves. The meaning of both emerges only in comparison to something or someone else, and this is bad.
- You can become a champion only when losing hurts worse than winning feels good.
- There is a difference between depression and disappointment—between the person and the performance. Failure is an event, not a person.

I Know Practical Things Teenagers Need to Know:
He's teaching her arithmetic;
He said it was his mission.
He kissed her once, he kissed her twice, and said,
"Now that's addition."

And as he added smack by smack
In silent satisfaction,
She sweetly gave the kisses back and said,
"Now that's subtraction."

Then he kissed her, she kissed him,
Without an explanation,
Then both together smiled and said,
"That's multiplication."

Then Dad appeared upon the scene
And made a quick decision.
He kicked that kid three blocks away and said,
"That's long division!"

And Yes, I Know

- Every "professional" speaker on the planet has written his own book. Although I'm a major contributing author to the *Chicken Soup for the Soul* series, co-author of *Chicken Soup for the College Soul*, author of *Puppies for Sale* and *Little Souls—Best Night Out with Dad*, and although I've written twenty other books on leadership, customer service, inspiration, teaching, poetry, comedy, and public speaking, this is my definitive "How to succeed in business, by being brilliant at the basics, leadership from the inside out, personal development—you can become more of who you already are because the answers really are in the box" book.

I acknowledge that it's easier to act your way into positive thinking than to think your way into positive action; that in life's rugged pull, you can't hit the bull's-eye by shooting the bull. But I also acknowledge the power of inspirational words and stories that emotionally stimulate us to take action. *This* is the sole purpose of this book.

Inspiration vs. Motivation

Inspiration is nothing more than "possibility thinking." To inspire is to have dreams for sale, to keep hope alive, to outwardly express faith to help others see what they cannot see, and to openly suggest that the best is yet to be. A nurse shared the following true story with me.

John and Bill became acquainted during their care at the Huntsman Cancer Institute in Salt Lake City. Separated by only a curtain, they both shared the same treatment room one day during a unique chemotherapy treatment. John had been in the hospital for a while and was so sick that he was stuck flat on his back. From several surgeries, and because of the way he was hooked up to machines, once John was taken to a private room, he would most likely not be moved for a month.

The two men never saw each other, but they became instant friends as they talked and even laughed through their painful ordeal. As the three hours of intravenous treatment ended, they said their good-byes, but not before Bill promised to drop by John's room in the morning to visit.

Sure enough, the following day an orderly picked Bill up and wheeled him from his room to John's room. John was flat on his back and could not see Bill come in. Bill was not allowed to get close to John's bed, so he entered and immediately took up a position by the window. "Hey, John," Bill greeted. "How ya feeling? Man, it's a beautiful day. I'm sitting here at your window in my wheelchair, and my oh my, it is gorgeous."

John replied, "Hey, buddy. Thanks for coming. Tell me what you see, my friend."

"Oh my gosh, John, the flowers are red and white and look like a flag. The grass is lime green with perfectly cut, eighteen-inch-high hedges serving as an elegant border to the sidewalk for as far as I can see. There are two hummingbirds hovering by the window seal and a big white cat lurking on the fence. Someday when we can open the window, or better still, get out of here, you will again hear the cheerful chirping of the three robins in the tree, and I will take you fishing on a breathtaking blue cloudless sky day just like today!"

For thirty minutes John got excited and then thanked Bill for sharing the outside world with him. "Being confined in here really gets depressing, and though I can't go to the world, you have brought the world to me. Thank you, thank you, my new friend."

As Bill was wheeled out of the room, again not being allowed to get close enough for eye contact, the two men exchanged their love and support.

"Will I see you tomorrow?" John pleaded.

"You can count on it, old buddy."

The next day Bill was wheeled in again by the orderly and parked by the window in John's room. They exchanged pleasantries and Bill spoke up. "Holy cow, John. You should see the fancy cars parked in the parking lot. These doctors are driving some fine rides. No wonder they wear surgical masks. They charge so much they don't want us to see who they really are!"

They laughed and laughed! Bill continued. "There's a stereotypical red Ferrari. Oh, and look over there at that black Porsche and lavender Corvette. I guess if you've got a Corvette you think you are so much of a stud that you can actually drive a 'foo-foo' colored car!" They both laughed again.

"Wow, with the mist from the lawn sprinklers, I can actually see a rainbow," Bill continued. "Just like us, buddy. You've got to have a storm in order to have a rainbow. When we weather this cancer storm and get out of here, with all your money you can buy me a Lamborghini, and we'll go pick up some babes! Money matters when you're bald and ugly like me."

They both laughed again, and after the usual thirty-minute visit, Bill was wheeled back to his room without John seeing him. This visiting went on for seven days straight. Unbeknownst to John, Bill was taken in for surgery on the eighth day. John waited all day and into the night, but Bill did not come. The next morning an oncologist and a nurse who had never treated John before came to administer tests. John spoke up, "Doc, do you happen to know my friend Bill Johnson?" The doctor and the nurse both cringed and said, "Friend? How do you know Mr. Johnson?" John explained how they had met and how, for the past week, Bill had been wheeled into his room every morning and had sat by the window, describing in detail what he saw as he lovingly opened up the outside world to John.

The nurse gently took John by the hand and said, "I'm sorry, John. Yesterday, Bill had his long-awaited operation, and the surgery didn't go as well as we had hoped. We did all we could do. Bill passed away in the evening with his family around him. We didn't know you were such good friends, or someone would have told you."

John started to cry. "I've been confined on my back in this prison-like predicament for so long I had lost all hope and desire to fight my cancer and get better. Then Bill came along. Every day he came to my room and helped me see what I could not. He painted beautiful word pictures full of colors, sounds, and dreams. He allowed me to see a brighter day through his eyes. Oh, how I will miss him sitting at my window describing a world that made me look forward to getting better."

The nurse and the doctor again looked at each other as the nurse quietly spoke. "Isn't that interesting, John. Your friend Bill was totally blind."

INSPIRATIONAL QUALIFICATIONS

There is a huge difference between inspiration and motivation. Inspiration affects attitude—the way we think and the lens through which we see life. Motivation affects behavior—the way we act. Therefore, no one can really motivate another. The only thing we can ever hope to do is paint a bigger, brighter picture to inspire one another to want to motivate ourselves. Most of the time, peak performance—taking ourselves to the next level, stretching and becoming everything we were born to be—is inspired from without until we see it, want it, buy into it, and own it to the degree that it comes from within. Let me reiterate: What do you know that is true? From whom did you learn it? What qualifies someone to be inspirational?

It has been said, "There are no heroes—only ordinary men and women caught in extraordinary circumstance who place service before self."

It has also been said that you can't lead where you won't go, and you can't teach what you don't know. I agree, and therefore I don't necessarily respect and follow someone just because he practices what he preaches. Inspiring people preach only what they practice. Inspiration implies that you know something and do something with what you know. My mother used to joke that a male gynecologist is like an auto mechanic who never owned or drove a car! To be an effective manager requires character. To be an effective leader requires credibility. To be inspirational in another person's life requires both character *and* credibility.

It's motivating to see a person beat the odds when placed in a situation that requires great fortitude and action. It's inspiring to read of a prisoner of war who survives to write about how he handled torture and made it through his ordeal. I know a handful of heroes. Two are real heroes who, through their character and credibility, inspire all who know them. They are Hal Hornburg, a retired US Air Force four-star general, and my dear father, S. Wayne Clark.

INSPIRING HEROES

Webster's Dictionary defines a hero as "a mythological or legendary figure often of divine descent endowed with great strength or ability; an illustrious warrior; a man or woman admired for achievements and noble qualities; one that shows superior courage; the central figure in an event, period, or movement who is the object of extreme devotion; someone's idol; a role model leading by example, inspiring with character, facing all fear, self sacrificing and exhibiting or marked by daring."

General Hornburg is a great American, former command fighter pilot, influential world leader, multiple war hero, devoted husband, father, grandfather, musician, athlete, and trusted friend. He knows and inspires people through his deeds and his words:

- "People first, mission always."
- "Leadership is an analog job in a digital world."
- "The purpose of a leader is to grow more leaders."
- "Leadership at the lowest level is about presence, programs, and people; leadership at the highest level is about passion, principles, and people."
- "We rise higher and see further standing not only

on the strong shoulders of those who have gone before us but also on the shoulders of those who are currently under our command, supporting us and following our lead."

- "A celebrity is a big name—a hero is a big man."
- "It's better to wear out than to rust out."
- "Quality of life is more than new furniture."
- "You recruit the individual, but you must retain the family."
- "We enter the armed forces to serve our country, but we fight for our teammates, for each other, for our buddies fighting beside us."

General Hornburg knows and reminds us that *transformation* is an inside-out job—that you really can take an eighteen-year-old who barely graduated from high school and has been a cocky, undisciplined Attention Deficit Disorder-labeled student, put him through a six-week Basic Cadet Training boot camp course at Lacklin Air Force Base in San Antonio, Texas, and turn him into a respectful, disciplined, patriotic young man.

All the Air Force did was give him responsibility, purpose, self-respect, high expectation, extraordinary trust, and an opportunity to be a part of something larger and more important than himself. Then, through training and a couple years of experience, he is put in charge of a $50 million jet—maintaining it or fixing it or keeping it combat ready or flying it. General Hornburg knows that what the Air Force does with 37,000 recruits each year is unveil to them what is already inside of them.

"You can if you think you can" is more of a powerful transformational mantra than anyone can imagine. General Hornburg leaves an inspirational legacy that will always be remembered: "In any endeavor, people matter most—we are in the people-building business!"

INSPIRATIONAL FATHER

My dad, S. Wayne Clark, clearly my superhero, was a legislator, pilot, US Air Force officer, cotton farmer, silver miner, rancher, entrepreneur (who started his own insurance company), owner of two large cemeteries/mortuaries, and creator of a successful financial corporation. He still made time for church and family, and he always did, and still does, inspire me with his actions and wisdom:

- "When everybody thinks alike, nobody thinks very much."
- "Growth is good, but growth without good growth is no growth."
- "Giving half effort doesn't get you half results—it gets you no results."
- "Unless you try something beyond what you have mastered, you will never grow."
- "It's not how much you make, but how much you spend—nickels make dollars."
- "We get what we inspect, not what we expect."
- "Knowledge is awareness of the fact that fire will burn—wisdom is remembrance."
- "Remember who you are; any male can be a father, but it takes a special man to be a dad."
- "Real success, self-fulfillment, and peace of mind can only come through living on purpose with someone to love, something to do, and someplace to go in order to feel wanted, important, loved, and capable."
- "Clear conscience with pure joy comes only when we choose to fill our minds with truth, fill our hearts with love, and fill our lives with service."
- "What you are today is the result of what you have thought up to this moment. What you will be tomorrow depends upon the thoughts you think from now on."

- "Always have family prayer—the family that prays together stays together."
- "It's not where you serve but how you serve that matters."
- "Pay a full 10 percent tithe, seek for the Spirit, and stay true to you!"

IMPLEMENTED KNOWLEDGE

I love, admire, and respect these two men not just because of what they know but also because they live what they know. Knowledge and action are inseparable. Character and credibility make them inspirational, and herein lies the secret to their success.

Obviously knowledge comes from outside in, but its sole function is to allow us to exploit the God-given talents we were born with and to become more of who we already are. Knowledge doesn't change or give birth to talent anymore than a sow can give birth to a thoroughbred racehorse. Nationwide Insurance Company's motto, "Service So Good That It Sells," sounds good and is important information, but unless we implement and provide that kind of service and realize that customer service is not a department but rather a way of life, the knowledge goes unused as if we never knew it. Nationwide is one of my clients and they know, do, and follow through.

When four brutal hurricanes ravaged Florida in 2004, Nationwide took a 1.2 billion dollar hit. Yet they stepped it up and sent more than 1,200 people to Florida, processed more than 97,000 claims within sixty days of each disaster, and showed up in eighteen-wheel trucks and motor homes filled with water, food, hope, comfort, and a plan to help victims rebuild their lives.

To conclude this chapter, I offer a simple but effective "implementation of knowledge" tool that encourages, teaches, and assists individuals and organizations to both identify true knowledge and to take action on it. I got it from Dennis De Paulo, a buddy in Buffalo, New York, who owns the finest restaurant in the city. I've used this tool many times. It is perfect for small organizations as well as for Fortune 500 companies that desire to evaluate themselves, proactively improve themselves, and better execute with their external customers. I call it "PPI"—personal progress interview. It is a short, six-point crash course in how to mentally and emotionally prepare to be a hero in business, recreation, and family living.

PERSONAL PROGRESS INTERVIEW

1. What is your personal unique ability or characteristic that sets you apart from everyone else? What is your organization's unique ability?
2. What are your personal strengths that make you successful? What are your organization's strengths that make it successful?
3. What are the opportunities that you can pursue right now and for the next ninety days? What are the opportunities your organization can pursue for the next ninety days?
4. What are the immediate, urgent, short-term, and long-term challenges that you face in achieving your personal goals? What are the threats and obstacles to achieving your organization's goals?
5. When will you know you are successful—personally and professionally? When will your organization be considered successful and great?
6. Who have you inspired today? What are you doing to make everybody else around you better and, when they leave you, say, "I like me best when I'm with you, I want to see you again"?

I realize the power of inspirational words. In the headquarters office of Chicken Soup Enterprises, we have more than 1,200 letters from teenagers who say they were going to kill themselves but decided not to commit suicide because they read one of our short three-page inspirational stories. Both survival and success come when we experience emotion in the heart, a lump in the throat, and a tear in the eye. Inspiration outlasts the meeting and the reading with an impact that moves us long after the convention is over and the reading light clicks off. Improving and becoming more of who we already are is inspiring—to ourselves and to others—and that's what I write and why I write it!

I penned the following lyrics to illustrate these points.

Language of the Heart
There's a secret language only lovers know,
Following their hearts to places heads can never go.
Without a word their lips and hands and want-me-eyes reveal
Like dancing partners sensing where to go, they move by feel.

Yes, the eye's the window to the soul.
Lovers look inside and see that passion makes them whole.
Lustfully they fantasize about how love should be
And then find a soul mate seeking self-fulfilling prophecy.

Language of the heart is never said or written down,
Words can't capture what we mean, the silence makes the sound.
Spirit talks to spirit through emotion sets apart,
The language only lovers know, the language of the heart.
There's a secret language only lovers know
Feeling, self-revealing, lying low, and going slow.
Hearing, tasting, smelling, touching, seeing senses flow.
Body talk connecting, only honesty can show.
A squeezing one, two, three says I love you.
A nod and sultry smile says I am thinking about you too.
Touching toes beneath the table's better than dessert,
And without public affection is the way real lovers flirt.

A tender touch says more than words can say.
A kiss heals hurt and sends the pain away.
Holding me, like you'll never let me go
Is the reason that I know.

Fundamental 12

IT'S WHAT YOU DO WHEN NO
ONE IS AROUND

If you find life is empty, try putting something into it. Kindness is the language the deaf can hear and the blind can see. You cannot do a kindness too soon because you never know how soon it will be too late.
—Emerson

Native Americans say, "All the answers are in the forest." They are. I know it! Look around. The answers and cures for cancer and AIDS are already on earth and among us. We need only look around in the shadows, behind the bushes, at the tops of the trees, out on the limbs, in the streams, under every rock, and first and foremost inside ourselves. Those who are proactively looking for truth will find it, and the truth will make them free, healthy, and happy. The way the natural universal laws of the harvest are set up in society dictates that each of us must take initiative and responsibility for our individual and team success.

Do you know anyone who is living a lie? Expecting a free lunch, disgruntled because at birth his umbilical cord that had been freely giving him everything he wanted was cut off, and instead of working, he is spending the rest of his life trying to find another place to plug it back in?

Most people I know expect life to flow smoothly, featuring an unbroken chain of green lights with empty parking places in front of their destination, which has everything on sale. And when life is not a flawless, utopian bliss, they blame their disappointment on the world, the stars, fate, and everything and everybody other than themselves.

For some reason, they believe the world owes them something, and, consequently, they believe that all answers, success, and happiness come from some external source. They see life as complicated. When "spell check" isn't perfectly reliable, they lose faith and experience what psychologists call "unintended consequences"—thinking that there is only one option. Therefore, they never look at both sides of every issue with the big picture in view, accepting failure on their first attempt.

The only way we can snap out of blaming others, blaming the weather, and blaming the stars is to start taking charge of our dreams, emotions, opportunities, and consequences. We must learn to rely on ourselves. Sunshine is delicious, rain is refreshing, wind is cleansing, and snow is exhilarating. There is no such thing as bad weather—only different kinds of good weather. In no direction that we turn do we find ease or comfort, unless we decide it to be so. Like the weather, success and failure, and ranking good, great, and best are all relevant, depending on what you compare them to, especially when it comes to ourselves. Remember what the Roosevelts taught us: "No one can make you feel inferior without your own consent. The only thing we have to fear is fear itself." If we are honest and if we have the will to win, others can stop us temporarily, but only we—you and I—can stop ourselves permanently.

Continuous Improvement Must Become Rapid Growth

In order for change to be meaningful and lasting, it must be controlled and calculated within ourselves. We can always find a frontier where there is an open mind and a willing hand. The past, the present, and the future are today. All point to lead us to another current today! If we worry about what might be and wonder what might have been, we will ignore and miss what is. Yes, we must learn from the past and plan for the future, but nothing changes until we let go and fully live today! Right now—this moment—is changing, and so must we if we are to survive and thrive.

Although we previously introduced the popular phrase "continuous improvement," let's take ourselves and our organizational performance to the highest, ultimate level with the newest productivity truth. After focusing vast amounts of resources and energy on the best program available at the time, a top executive at Wal-Mart suddenly realized that continuous improvement meant slow death. And as Wal-Mart is famous for, he immediately changed from best to right. In our day and age, he discovered he needed *rapid growth*. Rapid growth is the bottom-line secret to Wal-Mart's continuous success.

RAPID GROWTH

Here are two obvious examples: 1) A bank-teller transaction that takes several minutes versus a twenty-one second ATM transaction; 2) Dog owner: "Where's your pet food?" Supermarket employee: "Aisle 9 or 10. I'm not sure." Compare that with the Pet Smart employee: "Ooh, look at your precious baby. What kind of dog? Maltese? Boy or girl? May I hold her? May I suggest this bow for her hair? This for her coat to keep it shiny?"

No wonder purchases of pet food in the supermarket dropped from 95 percent to 41 percent during a ten-year period. In both the bank and Pet Smart scenarios, the answers to success are already inside us. Circumstances require us to keep up with the changing times and stay ahead of the competition but not to change who we are, what we are, and why we are. Herein lies the secret to realizing authentic significant happiness and achieving lasting success.

Inside-out means taking personal responsibility for our attitude and behavior, realizing that we can lie to others and fake out the world, but we cannot lie to ourselves. Inside-out is knowing ourselves and being ourselves 100 percent of the time, especially when no one else is around. Two bizarre experiences reveal that who we *really* are is found and developed from the inside out.

ARE YOU REALLY FIRST CLASS?

I was flying cross-country on a Boeing 757 jet, sitting in first class. I always fly first class—not because I pay for the ticket, but because I fly more than two hundred thousand miles per year on Delta Airlines and am a "Platinum Medallion" (four-million miler) who automatically gets upgraded. There are twenty-four seats in first class, and I was sitting in my usual window seat.

After about two hours into the flight and five diet Cokes, I got up to use the lavatory. When I walked in and locked the door, I immediately noticed that the tiny bathroom was totally trashed. There was water everywhere, soapy slime dripping down the mirror, used paper towels on the floor, and crap on the seat. Then it hit me. The next person who comes in will immediately think I did all of this! So I started to clean it. With one hand holding my nose and doing everything I could not to throw up, I wiped the mirror and the seat, cleaned up the trash, and mopped up the floor. It was clearly one of the most appalling experiences of my life.

When I had relieved my bladder, I emerged from the lavatory and stood in front of the entire first-class section until I got eye contact with every person sitting in front of me. I was raised to be a gentleman, so I didn't say anything. But I wanted so badly to yell, "Okay, which one of you low-budget loser bums did this?" As I sat down, I realized you cannot buy class. Sitting in first class doesn't make you first class! You can lie to others and fake out the world, but you cannot lie to yourself. It truly is what we do when no one is around that defines who we *really* are.

ELEVATOR GAS

On a more humorous but equally disgusting note, when we landed I checked into my hotel and went to bed. The next morning I boarded the elevator on the twentieth floor to go downstairs to the ballroom to speak to 3,500 hundred people attending the general session of a convention. I was on the elevator alone until it stopped on the fifteenth floor. On walked a large man dressed in an expensive suit. As soon as the doors shut, he passed gas in a long, loud, offensive way. I couldn't believe it! He looked sophisticated on the outside, but he lacked couth on the inside!

Then, wouldn't you know it? He got off on the very next floor, leaving just as it started to smell. My eyes were watering and my saliva dried up. I've hit skunks on the road that smelled better. Then, "ding," the elevator doors opened on the tenth floor, and eight people with conference name tags hanging around their necks got on. They were going to be in my audience, and every one of them was staring at me in disgust, thinking I was the skunk.

I wanted to explain and tell them what had happened, but I couldn't. In this case, it's more truth than humor that rank character can linger a long time. There's something to be said about leaving a positive legacy and taking pride in how we will be remembered after we are gone.

FOOLING YOURSELF?

William James said, "I have often thought that the best way to define a man's character would be to seek out the particular mental or moral attitude in which, when it came upon him, he felt himself most deeply and intensely active and alive. At such moments there is a voice inside which speaks and says, "'This is the real me!'"

So is the "real me" what you know and how much you know? No! Some people try to get us to believe what they think instead of what really is. With all due respect, academic credentials do not necessarily translate into truth. We should not confuse head knowledge with truth and wisdom. Academicians are often guilty of trying to explain away the simplicity of living and the reality of absolutes. And the so-called results they publish are devastating. We must always remember that no one should ever believe everything they think. Our old beliefs (wives tales, traditions of our forefathers, and so forth) aren't necessarily the truth.

It is important to look ourselves in the mirror every day and realize we can fool others, but we cannot fool ourselves. We often go through the motions, striving to be popular for the moment instead of respected for a lifetime. But at the end of every popular fad, the rules have not changed. Yet wrenching restructurings and radical change programs are being implemented in our corporations and organizations as if there were no tomorrow. Historically outside-in programs for change have not worked because they last only until the new leader with his new program replaces the old one. One major telephone company I've worked with has had four different vice presidents in five months, each touting his own unique, outside-in system of success. The results? Nothing has really changed. It's like the out-of-shape, overweight guy who can't change his results by exercising and going on a diet. Diet is not the answer; lifestyle change is. What's needed is new thinking.

OLD SCHOOL HUSTLE

We've already discussed achieving results, and anybody can do that. Achieving *desired* results is the key. As we will discuss at the end of this book, you can't coach results; you can only coach behavior. Behavior is created by mental state, which is determined by internal belief. You can't coach belief either; belief is the *effort* part of being an athlete. It's the personal, private commitment part that proves it doesn't matter how tall or short we are, whether we are male or female, how much we weigh, or if we're fast or slow. *Everyone* of us can hustle! Hustling is maximizing behavior, which oftentimes accelerates achieving desired results.

I've interviewed hundreds of championship-winning coaches and hundreds of successful, wealthy corporate CEOs, and the one thing they all have in common is an extreme and intense sense of hustle. In sports, hustle is old-school thinking. Off the athletic field and floor and into the corporate arena it is *new thinking*. We call it *urgency*.

NEW SCHOOL URGENCY

I was flying from Dallas, Texas, to Salt Lake City—approximately a two-hour and fifteen-minute flight. As I boarded and settled into my seat, I noticed a gentleman sitting next to me reading a newspaper account of the United jetliner that crashed in Iowa in 1989, killing hundreds of passengers. I couldn't help but look over his shoulder and read that the cause was failure in the hydraulic system. The pilots lost their ability to steer the aircraft.

I fell asleep at takeoff, only to be awakened about thirty minutes later by the pilot's voice speaking over the PA system. He said,

"I'm sure you've noticed that we are lumbering in the sky about seven thousand feet above the ground still on the outskirts of Dallas. We have lost the hydraulic steering system on the aircraft. We will remain airborne for another hour and a half to burn off excess fuel. Then we will attempt an emergency landing."

From my window seat, I looked down at the ground thinking, *this could be it!* I always thought that I would die of old age on a golf course! But no. I was going down in a plane crash and only had a couple of hours to live.

I reached for the "airphone" in the seat in front of me, entered my credit card, and dialed the first telephone number I thought of. What about you? If you knew you were going to be involved in a fatal automobile accident in the next two hours, whom would you call? What would you say? And how would you be remembered? As a positive influence who left your family, friends, job, and world in better shape than you found them? Or as a negative pessimist who dragged others down and made your associates miserable and nonproductive?

I phoned my mother first. I love my mother. As I was growing up, she always kept me on my toes with wonderful wisdom like, "Don't climb up that tree. If you fall down and break both your legs, don't come running to me!" So I prepared myself. This time she was the concerned financial counselor:

"Danny, is that you? You sound a long ways away."

"Yes, mother dear," I said. "I'm on an airplane."

"Isn't that expensive?" she asked.

"Yes, Mom, a few dollars a minute," I said.

"I'm ashamed of you. Who do you think you are, throwing money away like that? This is irresponsible. You hang up right now and phone me when you land."

"No, wait, wait, I need to talk now."

I couldn't tell her I was going to crash because she would have probably interrupted with another mom-ism like, "Do you have on clean underwear?" I didn't share the plane's predicament, but I did say I had been thinking and feeling many things for quite some time and decided not to procrastinate saying them any longer. I thanked her for going without a new dress so I could have the best football cleats and for postponing family vacations so I could stay home to play on an all-star baseball team—simple things that she thought went unnoticed all those years. I told my mom I loved her and needed her. She started crying, saying, "I love you too," and we hung up.

I then phoned my wife and had an extremely intimate conversation—a playful, flirtatious, sensitive interaction similar to the good old days, expressing love, need, respect, and support. I have a four-million-dollar life insurance policy and for what, sometimes I do not know. When I die I want it to be a real tragedy! I definitely wasn't going to tell my wife that I might crash, or she might have already been headed to the mall! I could see her at my funeral, crying, "I'd give ten thousand of the millions just to have him back!"

I then phoned my older brother and told him I loved and needed him. He was obviously knocked off guard, thinking I must have hit my head and started kidding me, "No, you're not in my will and no, you can't have my boat and cabin." We laughed and he confessed, "I love you too, man!"

I then phoned my sister, my younger brother, and a couple of my dearest friends, engaging all of them in similar intimate conversations.

Obviously we didn't crash, and that was cool until I got the phone bill! But because I learned a most profound lesson in urgency, this experience became another one of my Significant Emotional Experiences that transformed my life forever.

WHY HUSTLE?

With a desire to hustle and a feeling of urgency, our performance increases. Not because it is expected by others, but because it is demanded by ourselves. Hustle and urgency can only be generated from inside out. As I mentioned, no one can coach the amount of effort someone gives. It is an attitudinal thing spawned by simple why questions: Do I want to go out of my way to exceed customer expectations? Do I want to stay married? Do I want to be classy?

Once we answer in the affirmative, the rest is education. Love is an action verb, and therefore we work to make marriage work, for better or worse; we say please and thank you and open doors and do the right thing when no one is around. Henry Ward Beecher wrote: "Hold yourself responsible for a higher standard than anybody else expects of you. Never excuse yourself. Never pity yourself. Be a hard master to yourself, and be lenient to everybody else."

In concert with this line of thinking, why is it so difficult to understand that buying new clubs doesn't fix a golfer's swing? Wearing boots and a big hat doesn't make a man a cowboy. It's not the size, shape, or color of the balloon that makes it rise. It's what's on the inside, out-of-sight side that makes it rise and fly.

Who can imagine the magnificent butterfly stretching forth its wings before it emerges from the tiny cocoon? Who can imagine the wonderful, cuddly chick that gets tired of being confined in a small, stifling shell before it breaks its way to freedom? Who can imagine the tiny baby coming from the birth canal after nine months of grueling pregnancy and nine hours of labor? Or better still, who can imagine the successful, educated adult with limitless potential for greatness upon seeing the helpless, innocent newborn through the nursery window?

As we ponder these possibilities, let us realize that there are no so-called quick overnight successes. There was an out-of-sight inside incubation process of growth, nurturing, stabilizing, and strengthening. There was a certain set of natural laws followed with unchanging rules obeyed. Everything that is real, important, and lasting comes into existence, grows, changes, and just plain *is* from the inside out—especially the ever-elusive critical goal and desire called *balance*.

Life is simple and success is simple—not easy and maybe hard, but simple. Balancing a ball or broomstick may be difficult at first, but with practice it can be done because the physics and technique are simple! We need only learn the rules, understand that the rules won't change in the middle of the game, ask the right questions, acquire knowledge, find and accept inspiration, challenge the status quo, and, with a sense of urgency, become more of who we already are. This is how we take ourselves, our organizations, our families, our communities, and our teams to the next level—one person, one moment at a time, inspiring another and another as those persons, in turn, lead and inspire others.

BALANCE WHEEL

The best visual illustration of balance is a wheel. I've driven a car at high speed that had its steering out of alignment. Its wheels started to shimmy and shake. I've had a flat tire going around a corner and lost control. When I bent the rim on the front wheel of my motorcycle, I was immobilized. Unless the wheel is perfectly round, the ride is unsafe, uncomfortable, and eventually impossible. At best, it's a hay ride.

BALANCE WHEEL

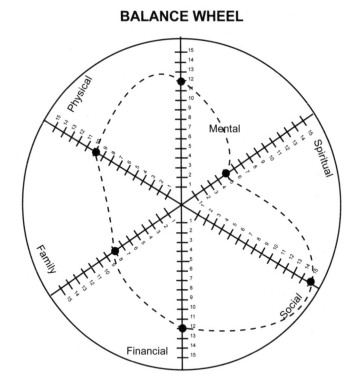

From 1 to 15 (15 being the highest level of performance), grade your commitment in each of the six areas of life. For example:

- Physical: 10
- Mental: 12
- Spiritual: 5
- Social: 15
- Financial: 12
- Family: 8

Your balance graph will look like the dotted line drawn within the Balance Wheel. Obviously, the response to this test is to maintain and improve on your highest categories—in this example, Mental, Social, and Financial—and more important, work hard to develop and strengthen the weak categories of Spiritual, Family, and Physical. Only when each of the six categories in the Balance Wheel reflects the same commitment level of time, resources, and talent can we achieve balance and enjoy a smooth ride through life.

We *can* achieve balance in our lives. Perhaps doing so is hard, but as promised, it is relatively simple. Let me briefly bring you up to speed on a much quoted theory and then share my version. Maslow's Hierarchy of Needs is a theory in psychology that Abraham Maslow proposed in his 1943 paper "A Theory of Human Motivation." His theory contends that as humans meet "basic needs" they seek to satisfy successively "higher needs" that occupy a set hierarchy. Maslow's theory is often referred to as a pyramid consisting of five levels: the four lower levels are grouped together as *Deficiency* needs associated with physiological needs: Body Wellness/Comfort, Safety/Security, Love/Belonging, and Self Respect/Esteem; while the top level is termed *Growth* needs associated with psychological needs Maslow calls Self-Actualization. While deficiency needs must be met, growth needs are continually shaping behavior. The basic concept is that the higher needs in this hierarchy only come into focus once all the needs that are lower down in the pyramid are mainly or entirely satisfied. Growth forces create upward movement in the hierarchy, whereas regressive forces push the peak performance needs further down.

As mentioned, Maslow's highest level is Self-Actualization which means: "the instinctual need of humans to make the most of their unique abilities and to strive to be the best they can be—the intrinsic growth of what is already in the organism." In other words, not to change, but to become more of who we already are!

With all due respect to Maslow, I have experienced a similar but different set of needs in my personal and professional lives, which resulted in the creation of my own Hierarchy of Needs illustrated in the forthcoming diagram. Because it is easier to identify a program than it is to implement a process, I offer five attributes that will assist us in the application of both Maslow's needs and the modified version I present. So far in my personal experience, I have found that everything anyone would ever want to be begins and ends with being:

- Meek—patient; enduring without resentment; teachable.
- Patient—bearing pains or trials calmly and without complaint; steadfast despite opposition, difficulty or adversity; not hasty or impetuous.
- Submissive—surrendering to the authority or control of another; the condition of being humble; to yield oneself to the will of a higher power source.
- Loving—having strong affection for another arising out of kinship and personal ties; affection based on admiration, benevolence, and common interests; unselfish devotion and loyal concern for the good of another.
- Charitable—serving and doing something for a total stranger who can't do anything for you in return, knowing you won't get any credit.

Comprehending our true needs provides the motivation to endure to the end of the balancing process and always do the right thing simply because it's the right thing to do, especially when no one is around. Your assignment is to familiarize yourself with this pyramid. Ponder how each of the five attributes makes possible the achievement of each need and how they drive you up the pyramid to satisfy the next higher need until you begin self-actualizing through self-expression.

HIERARCHY PYRAMID OF NEEDS

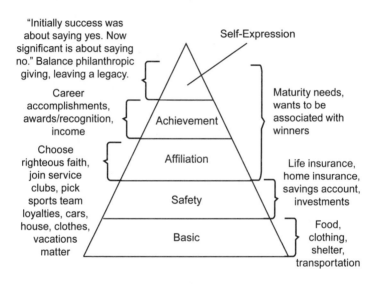

"Initially success was about saying yes. Now significant is about saying no." Balance philanthropic giving, leaving a legacy.

Career accomplishments, awards/recognition, income

Choose righteous faith, join service clubs, pick sports team loyalties, cars, house, clothes, vacations matter

Self-Expression

Achievement

Affiliation

Safety

Basic

Maturity needs, wants to be associated with winners

Life insurance, home insurance, savings account, investments

Food, clothing, shelter, transportation

Fundamental 13

BE AN INSPIRATIONAL EXAMPLE, NOT A HORRIBLE WARNING

The deadliest enemies of nations are not their foreign foes; they always dwell within their borders. And from these internal enemies civilization is always in need of being saved. The nation blessed above all nations is she in whom the civic genius of the people does the saving day-by-day, by acts without external picturesqueness; by speaking, writing, voting reasonably; by smiting corruption swiftly; by good temper between parties; by the people knowing true men when they see them, and preferring them as leaders to rabid partisans or empty quacks.

—William James

In my book on the art and science of public speaking titled *The Privilege of the Platform*, I point out that every audience member, regardless of occupation, wants to know three things from the speaker or instructor: 1) Why should I listen to you? Have you done it? Are you currently doing it? Don't just practice what you preach; preach only what you practice. This establishes expected and needed *credibility*. 2) Can I do it too? With my talent, ability, and shortcomings, can I do what you have done? This gives *hope*. 3) How do I do it? What is the specific plan and process I must follow to get my desired results? This is the challenge to take *action*. All three of these questions must be answered in order, to inspire anyone to become more of who they already are.

Inspiration obviously comes into our lives from every direction: preachers, public speakers, stories, books and songs. As a country songwriter, I might be remembered for "Had I Shot You When I Met You I'd Be Out of Jail By Now," "I've Got You on My Conscience, but at Least You're off My Back," "How Can I Miss You if You Won't Go Away," "I'm So Miserable without You, It's Like Having You Here," and my all-time favorite, "My Wife Ran off With My Best Friend and I'm Going to Miss Him Dearly." Even my golf song is even inspirational: "How You Found Your Nike on the Fairway, When You Hit a Top Flight off the Tee."

On a serious note, have you ever thought about how you will be remembered, what your legacy will be? Have you ever quit something and later realized that pain is temporary but quitting lasts forever? Do you feel obligated to now teach others what you've learned? What will they say at your funeral? Did you make everybody else on your team better? Will you and your life be an inspiration to others after you're gone?

Mother Teresa wrote, "Loneliness and the feeling of being unwanted is the most terrible poverty. We can do no great things—only small things with great love. I am a little pencil in the hand of a writing God who is sending a love letter to the world."

I was asked once to name three influential, inspirational figures in the history of the world and explain how and why they are at the top of my list. Who would your top three be? Why? And what would you ask them if you could spend some personal one-on-one time interviewing them?

The list of names that repeats itself most when I conduct this exercise in my seminars consists of Abraham, Moses, Isaiah, Noah, David, Jesus, Muhammad, Gandhi, Christopher Columbus, Abraham Lincoln, Winston Churchill, Malcolm X, and Martin Luther King Jr. I've been inspired by some incredible individuals with whom I have shared the program, interviewed, and/or had dinner with, including my dad, Doc Sansom, Congressional Medal of Honor winners General Foley and Colonel Jacobs, POWs Coffee and McCain, Michael Jordan, Cal Ripken Jr., Yogi Berra, Arnold Palmer, Jack Nicholas, Phil Mickelson, Bo Jackson, Emmitt Smith, the Righteous Brothers, Willie Nelson, Garth Brooks, Keith Urban, Natalie Cole,

Amy Grant, Walter Cronkite, astronaut Buzz Aldrin, Colin Powell, Henry Kissinger, Rudy Giuliani, President George Bush, Charlton Heston, and Bill Marriott. I was also the house guest of Larry King, Wayne Gretzky, and Muhammad Ali. As you contemplate the contribution that each of these extraordinary human beings has made to the professions and to the society as a whole, you will realize the truth about inspiration.

"Most inspirational" is based on credible knowledge, experience, superior performance, and expertise. On a team, it's making everybody's family feel wanted, important, loved, capable, and that they matter to you and the organization. It's raising the emotional attitude bar for everybody around you through emotional words and passionate, productive, positive example. It's taking yourself with a grain of salt and inviting people to laugh with you. I hired a caddie to carry my bag at Pebble Beach. I was playing horribly and commented, "Man, this is a tough course." The caddie replied, "With all due respect, Mr. Clark, you haven't been on it for over an hour." The foursome bent over with laughter.

As you know, I played football for thirteen years from ages ten to twenty-two, when I suffered a debilitating injury. To recover and become fully rehabilitated, I needed inspiration, not sympathy. I needed tough love and a kick in the butt, not empathy. But wouldn't you know it, all anybody ever said was, "I know what you're going through." I used to think, "No you don't. How could you? Let me rip your dominant arm off and leave your right side numb for over a year and see how it feels to have your heart broken and lose your dream, your identity, your relationships, and your chosen career."

Because of my past this is an inspirational, self-help, organizational development book because we don't need any more habits, twelve-step programs, or processes and procedures. Enough is enough already! We need to get out of the planning stage and into the go stage and start dreaming out loud while we are awake! We need to start hanging out with winners and commit to being one.

WINNING BY ASSOCIATION

An intriguing side of winning that permeates the minds of sports fans everywhere is the belief that we win by association. As you recall, I made the observation earlier that when you put a hard-to-catch horse in the same field with an easy-to-catch horse, you usually end up with two hard-to-catch horses, and that sick children make healthy children sick. Winning by association is a true principle of success. But, can we feel a sense of accomplishment through simple affiliation even when we don't do anything to contribute to the win?

Yes, and this is a major source of inspiration in our world, especially for the big, lazy, beer-gutted, burping couch potato who needs to feel successful when all he does is sit in front of the TV ordering his wife and kids to bring him more chips and Bud while he watches games all day and night. He believes he is a winner—a champion by association. To some degree we all do.

All things being equal, you root for your own town, your own sex, your own culture, your own team. And what you want to prove is that *you* are better than the other person. Whomever you root for represents you, and when he wins or they win, *you* win.

An experiment conducted by students on the campuses of Michigan, Louisiana State, Pittsburgh, Arizona State, Southern Cal, and Ohio State showed that hundreds more students and fans would wear their school's shirt if their football team had won its game the previous Saturday. What's more, the larger the margin of victory, the more such shirts appeared. It wasn't a close, hard-fought game that caused students to dress themselves in success and victory. Instead, it was a clear expression of in-your-face superiority.

Does this principle apply to our jobs? Of course it does. From a leader's perspective, this is Inspiration 101. Find out what excites your people, collectively and especially as individuals, and connect with them in this event, at its location off-task-time. Once you validate to your people that you also know winning can be through association, and that pride, support, uninhibited expressions of emotions and loyal allegiance are ignited through believing in something larger than ourselves, it's only a matter of changing the events and circumstances from sports to work, from a school or team game to your company's game of work. Because we win through association (we really are judged by the company we keep), right leaders attract right people by affiliating with right charity causes that ignite the same emotions they feel when their team wins. Remember the difference between leadership and authority boils down to our ability to inspire.

CRUISE, PITT, RICHARDS, OZZY

Inspiration is a two-edged sword. On one hand we have Tom Cruise and Brad Pitt, who are examples of success. They are smart, talented, healthy, chiseled, handsome hunks with stomach muscled "six-packs!" They inspire us to take ourselves to the next level because they did. Through their examples we know that with enough hard work, we too can get in shape and find our unique talents and niche in life.

On the other hand, guitarists Keith Richards of the Rolling Stones and rocker Ozzy Osborne inspire us as well to . . . let's just say if you can't be a good example, you can still be a horrible warning! To them, a "six-pack" is not enough. There are twenty-four beers in a cold case and twenty-four hours in a day. Coincidence? They don't think so! And if you snort Ajax cleanser, drink dragster fuel, and bite the heads off of bats, you too can look like them!

As we already established, inspiration doesn't come when we learn from our own mistakes. That's wasting precious life and time we can never relive or get back. Inspiration comes when we learn from *other* people's mistakes.

I know ten people whose dads or moms were alcoholics, and because of their bad example, their children never touched a drink. Regardless if our inspiration comes through a good example or from a horrible warning, inspiration is inspiration, and we all need it in our lives to become everything we were born to be—more of who we already are.

When I was eight years old, I nearly cut my thumb off with a knife, severing tendons in a serious, deep wound and creating a bloody, gushing mess. I ran home, and my sweet mother tried her best to stop the bleeding. To no avail and with my dad at work with our only car, my mom said, "Let's go. We've got to walk a few blocks to the hospital." While we were walking, Mom was holding a cold, wet rag tightly around my thumb.

After five minutes I looked up at her and saw her crying. I joked, "Mom, I'm the one injured. Why are you crying?" She said, "I wish I could fix your thumb, but all I can do is hold your hand and cry." I wrote the following inspirational story as a result of this experience. I've already published it as a song.

The Broken Doll

As a young girl was leaving for school, her mother reminded her to come straight home when her last class ended. That afternoon, thirty minutes late, the girl finally walked through the front door. Her mother scolded her, "Where have you been? I've been worried sick."

With concern on her face, the daughter replied, "I walked home with my friend Sally. She dropped her doll, and it broke all to pieces. It was awful!"

Her mother inquired, "So you're late because you stayed to help her pick up the pieces and put it back together again?"

"Oh no, Mommy," she replied. "I didn't know how to fix the doll. I just stayed to help her cry!"

Puppies for Sale

In 1967, when I was in the eighth grade and thirteen years old, I wrote the following story for an essay speech contest. My family and I are proud of it and told it for many years until I published it on a holiday greeting card and then in my first book in 1982. It was made into a film by Ron Krauss at Paramount

Studios, starring the late Jack Lemmon and featuring a musical score by Elmer Bernstein.

A store owner was tacking a sign above his door that read "Puppies for Sale." Signs like that have a way of attracting small children, and sure enough, a little boy appeared under the store's sign. "How much are you going to sell the puppies for?" he asked.

The store owner replied, "Anywhere from $30 to $50."

The little boy reached in his pocket and pulled out some change. "I have $2.37," he said. "Can I please look at them?"

The store owner smiled and whistled, and out of the kennel came Lady, who ran down the aisle of the store, followed by five teeny, tiny balls of fur. One puppy was lagging considerably behind. Immediately the little boy singled out the lagging, limping puppy and asked, "What's wrong with that little dog?"

The store owner explained that the veterinarian had examined the little puppy and had discovered that it didn't have a hip socket. It would always limp. It would always be lame. The little boy became excited. "That is the little puppy I want to buy."

The store owner said, "No, you don't want to buy that little dog. If you really want him, I'll just give him to you."

The little boy got upset. He looked straight into the store owner's eyes, pointed his finger, and said, "I don't want you to just give him to me. That little dog is worth every bit as much as all the other dogs, and I'll pay full price. In fact, I'll give you $2.37 now, and 50 cents a month until I have paid for him."

The store owner countered, "You really don't want to buy this little dog. He is never going to be able to run and jump and play with you like the other puppies."

To this, the little boy reached down and rolled up his pant leg to reveal a badly twisted, crippled left leg supported by a big metal brace. He looked up at the store owner and softly replied, "Well, I don't run so well myself, and the little puppy will need someone who understands!"

ALLIE SCHNEIDER

Allie Schneider is a dear friend of mine. I've known her parents for more than twenty-five years, and their unconditional love and example of inner strength and personal courage are examples to all who know them. I remember when Allie was born. She has been given wonderful opportunities and is positive and inspirational because of her parents and supportive siblings. I love to share the speaker's platform with Allie because she has an amazing ability to inspire and electrify any crowd. She walks out on stage, smiles her big, beautiful smile, and at under five feet tall sweetly announces, "Hi, I'm Allie Schneider. I'm twenty-one years old, and I had a dream to play professional basketball. But as you can see, I'm a little different than you. I'm short!"

As the audience laughs, Allie continues, "Actually, I have a disability called spina bifida. Technically, spina bifida is a neuro-tube defect, which means my spine didn't fully develop at birth. Because of this defect I'm unable to use or even feel my legs. I have walked with crutches my entire life. I give you this explanation because I'm here to talk to you about challenges. We all have challenges in our lives—some big and some small. Take a second and look around at your friends. They have challenges, but you might not know it because they keep them inside. With me it is obvious what my challenge is because you can see it, and in a way that makes it a little easier for me to handle it. When I was born the doctor told my parents that because of my disability I would never walk, and I wouldn't be able to do much.

"As you can see, I was able to prove the doctor wrong. With my braces and crutches I walk; I just do it differently than the rest of you. There are many other things that I can do and that I love to do that you might not expect. I waterski, horseback ride, play tennis, swim, drive a car, and scuba dive. I even drive a bobsled. Now I don't tell you this to brag, but to show you that you can do anything you put your mind to. As my wise friend says, 'No matter what, don't let what you cannot do interfere with what you can do!'"

Allie continues her speech: "Swimming is something I have done the longest and have enjoyed the most. When I was seven years old I was on a summer league swim team, and when I would race I would be racing against able-bodied kids. I never won a single race, but at that time I didn't realize it. When I would finish my race, I would be the only one in the pool, so it made me think that I had won the race. Even though I never won, I still felt like a winner because every time I got out of the pool, I knew that I had done the best I possibly could, and that was enough for me.

"I had finished my race at one particular meet, and as my parents were helping me out of the water, I saw NBA basketball star Utah Jazz forward Karl Malone cheering for me. Now that is a real role reversal! I love him and have cheered for him for years! Being on a swim team also gave me the opportunity to be in an award-winning television commercial.

"A man named Michael Dunn saw me in one of those races and wondered why I was going so slow. When he saw my parents help me out of the water at the end of the race and realized that I couldn't use my legs, he approached my parents and me about the TV spot.

"One week later, the three of us were flown to Los Angeles. When my parents and I arrived in LA, we went straight to the director's house, where I hopped into his freezing pool and showed him what I could do with my swimming skills. Two weeks after that we flew back to LA to film the commercial. The commercial only took one day to film, and throughout the day parents of the other children who were in the commercial would ask my parents if I was an actress and how I got the lead role, not realizing that the commercial was about me. The theme of the commercial was 'Whatever you do in life, just do your best.' I have incorporated this saying into my life, and whenever I feel frustrated or discouraged, I remember it. It's amazing to me how simple but profound words and positive encouragement can help us work through whatever obstacle we are facing at the moment. This commercial even won an Emmy in 1993! It holds a very special place in my heart, and I will always remember this experience and the wonderful Michael Dunn.

"I continued swimming competitively all four years of high school, where I won four varsity letters and qualified for the regional meet every year. Now that I am in college, I don't swim nearly as much as I used to, but it's okay. I have turned my devotion to something different—bobsledding!

"When I was five years old, I learned how to snow ski through a program called the National Ability Center—first standing up and then sitting down on a sit ski. However, when I turned sixteen I quit skiing because I never quite felt in control. Then a wonderful woman named Meeche White, chairwoman of the National Ability Center, called me on the phone one day and asked me if I would be interested in riding in a bobsled. After my first try I was hooked and have been doing it ever since. One day my team and I hope to compete in the Paralympics."

Allie's conclusion of her heartfelt speech always brings tears to my eyes and a deeper appreciation for my health and positive attitude. She says, "In no way am I trying to tell you that having a disability is easy. It's not! It can be very discouraging and difficult. But just because you have a challenge like a physical disability doesn't mean you can't accomplish your goals and dreams.

"Again, don't let what you cannot do interfere with what you can do. If you have a goal or dream, go after it. It doesn't mean you can do it alone. You need the love and full support of your friends and family to help you. If it weren't for my family, friends, teachers, and coaches, I wouldn't be the person I am today, nor would I be able to do half the things I absolutely love doing! Yes, I admit that a day doesn't go by that I don't wonder, 'Why me? Why did this physical birth defect happen to me?' However, it did, and there is nothing I can do about it. So I must put a smile on my face and look at it as a challenge to help me become everything I was born to be.

"Please remember two things: It's not what happens to you but what you do with what happens to you that either makes or breaks you; and the theme of my television spot—'Whatever you do in life, just do your best.' If we will, you will inspire me, and I will inspire you!"

Thanks, Allie.

AMERICA—INSPIRATIONAL OR HORRIBLE?

Let me shift gears and turn our attention from individuals who inspire, to a country the entire world looks to for inspiration. That is until lately. On September 12, 2001, the day after the terrorists attacked America, we were the most loved and respected country on earth. As of the Spring 2007 date of this publication, we are the most hated country on the planet. We all can list our opinions and rant about our own political bias on how and why and what has transpired outside of our borders that caused this international outpouring of public despise, but that serves no purpose here. I wish to focus on America from the inside out and remind us about how amazing our country and form of government are and that they're worth saving, fixing, improving, and preserving. After all, if we are expected to inspire the world, we must first be inspiring.

The US is referred to as the United States of America or simply America. Most don't see a difference, but I suggest the United States describes the country, real estate, natural resources, and physical attributes—a group of land masses organized together under one common border. On the other hand, America refers to her ideals and principles, a group of people organized together under one common purpose. While the United States represents justice and the letter of the law, America represents mercy and the spirit of the law.

Never in our nation's history have we needed deeper understanding of American ideals, greater pride in what America stands for, and more character and commitment from our citizens than right now in the twenty-first century. America is still held up as the last ray of hope and the leader of the free world with dreams for sale for those who haven't, can't, and don't know how. Therefore, it is our responsibility as citizens to rise to the occasion and continually strengthen ourselves from the inside out that we may continue to be strong for others.

I beg you to keep reading and evaluating as I go to the edge of controversy and ask two "right," thought-provoking, discussion-stimulating questions and honestly answer them:

1. What is the difference between a "resident" and a "citizen"?
2. What did American citizens learn from September 11, 2001, that should inspire each of us to be positive examples instead of horrible warnings?

RESIDENT VS. CITIZEN

Let me quote two US presidents to soften the blow to illegal aliens. Dwight D. Eisenhower said, "Whatever America hopes to bring to pass in the world must first come to pass in the heart of Americans. Freedom has its life in the hearts, the actions, and in the spirit of men and women so it must be daily earned and refreshed—else, like a flower cut from its life-giving roots, it will wither and die." Abraham Lincoln, way back in 1862, stated what I and hopefully you and every other American believe about our future position in the world: "My dream is of a place and a time where America will once again be seen as the last best hope on earth."

If you agree with these great Americans, let me ask you, are you contributing to or living off the government? Citizens give, residents take. Unless you buy into the full concept of "Constitutional Democracy" which is rule-of-law freedom with responsibility to protect the rights of every single person—unless you buy into a capitalist, free market economic system and especially religious freedom—a separation of church and state and equality for women in religion, politics and society—**living in America does not make you an American.**

The nineteen Muslim hijackers were residents living in our country, buying and eating our wonderful selection of food, taking flying lessons from our extraordinary schools, and partaking of our clean water, clean air, lack of disease, and world class healthcare. These Muslim fundamentalists even partook of our sleazy topless dancer clubs in Las Vegas while they planned their sick attacks on us American "infidels."

Timothy McVeigh was also a resident, claiming to be a citizen with voting rights and guaranteed constitutional rights for a fair trial. But was he? Both of these terrorist plots were carried out from within our own borders by people living in our neighborhoods. I was troubled by and curious about the difference between a resident and a citizen (the differing mindsets and commitment levels) and analyzed them the entire trip. In fact, I still contemplate it to this day. President Lincoln in his ever profound and amazing "Gettysburg Address" did not quote the Constitution as most think. He quoted the Declaration of Independence, which seems to suggest that until we understand, believe, and support the Declaration, we are not guaranteed the rights in the Constitution.

ILLEGAL ALIENS?

On an interesting and more positive note, a friend of mine in New Mexico hired two young men to go into his McDonald's restaurant after hours to clean the bathrooms and make the eating area spit-spot before the customers arrived the next morning. Both of these young men were in America illegally, and neither of them spoke a word of English. But for minimum wage workers, my friend said he had never found anyone who worked harder than these two men. My points? 1) If anyone is worried or ticked off that an illegal alien who can't speak English is going to steal their job, their job must really suck, and their self-esteem must be shaky at best. They need to get more education so they can get the job they dream about instead of just the job that's left over. They need to work harder to become more of who they already are and get a life! 2) These two young illegal aliens of whom I have spoken didn't just sit around content to be what they were. They went to work each night, visualizing what they had the power to become, and taught themselves how to speak and write fluent English. They enrolled in school to learn about business, finance, and how the American free enterprise system works. Both of them now own their own McDonald's franchises and have taken the required steps to become legal United States citizens!

Is Government a Parasite?

Regardless of what any conservative might label it, the government is not a parasite. Bill Hansell, Executive Director Emeritus of the International City/County Management Association, explains that under the surface, government is the "host" for nationhood and community. The parasites are selfishness, ignorance, apathy, and individualism which ignore our interdependence on each other. The parasites are those that live off the government—those who take more than they give. So, the questions are: do you and other people living in America work hard, pay taxes, and contribute to building the life blood "host" organism? If so, you are called by definition a "citizen." Or, are you a parasite just sucking the life blood organism of taxpayers dry, qualifying only to be called a "resident"? Without belaboring the point, living in America doesn't make someone an American. America is a way of life, a set of core values and personal agreements that is an experiment in self-government. The only way America can work, function as a Republic, and thrive in capitalism is if everybody here "buys" into this America, participates in doing his or her part, and gives more than they take. The mindset of a citizen versus resident is similar to owner versus renter. Who takes better care of the property? Who is in it for the long haul? America is so strong and powerful, it will never suffer defeat from any government or army outside of its borders. America can only fall and fail from the inside out. In view of September 11, the old bumper sticker, "America—Love it or leave it" is true! Reasonable thinkers would conclude that you should have to pay the price in order to enjoy the prize. Freedom isn't free. And with it comes responsibility to defend it and live in mutual respect, harmony, and total support to preserve it.

What Did American Citizens Learn from September 11?

US President Abraham Lincoln said, "We find ourselves under the government of a system of political institutions guaranteeing more civil and religious liberty than any of which history and former times tells us. We now find ourselves the legal inheritors of these fundamental blessings. This task, gratitude to our forefathers, justice to ourselves, duty to posterity—all imperatively require us faithfully to perform. How then, shall we perform it? At what point shall we expect the approach of danger?

"Shall we expect some trans-Atlantic military giant to step the ocean and crush us at a blow? Never! All the armies of Europe, Asia and Africa, combined, with all the treasures of the earth in their military chest, with a Bonaparte for a commander, could not, by force, take a drink from the Ohio, or make a track on the Blue Ridge, in a trial of a thousand years.

"At what point, then, is this approach of danger to be expected?

"I answer, if ever it reaches us, it must spring up amongst us. It cannot come from abroad. If destruction be our lot, we must ourselves be its author and finishers. As a nation of freemen, we must live through all time or die by suicide."

President John F. Kennedy Speaks from His Grave

In his inaugural address, President John F. Kennedy passionately and eloquently proclaimed, "We observe today not a victory of party but a celebration of freedom—symbolizing an end as well as a beginning, signifying renewal as well as change. For I have sworn before you and Almighty God the same solemn oath our forebears prescribed nearly a century and three-quarters ago: the belief that the rights of man come not from the generosity of the state but from the hand of God.

"Let every nation know, whether it wishes us well or ill, that we shall pay any price, bear any burden, meet any hardship, support any friend, oppose any foe to assure the survival and the success of liberty.

"Let all our neighbors know that we shall join with them to oppose aggression or subversion anywhere in the Americas. And let every other power know that this hemisphere intends to remain the master of its own house. In your hands, my fellow citizens, will rest the final success or failure of our course. Since this country was founded, each generation of Americans has been summoned to give testimony to its national loyalty. The graves of young Americans who answered the call to service surround the globe.

"Now the trumpet summons us again—not as a call to bear arms, though arms we need; not as a call to battle, though embattled we are—but a call to bear the burden of a long twilight struggle, year in and year out, 'rejoicing in hope, patient in tribulation,' a struggle against the common enemies of man: tyranny, poverty, disease, and war itself.

"In the long history of the world, only a few generations have been granted the role of defending freedom in its hour of maximum danger. I do not shrink from this responsibility—I welcome it. I do not believe that any of us would exchange places with any other people or any other generation. The energy, the faith, the devotion which we bring to this endeavor will light our country and all who serve it—and the glow from that fire can truly light the world.

"And so, my fellow Americans: Ask not what your country can do for you; ask what you can do for your country. My fellow citizens of the world: Ask not what America will do for you, but what together we can do for the freedom of man.

"Finally, whether you are citizens of America or citizens of the world, ask of us here the same high standards of strength and sacrifice which we ask of you. With a good conscience our only sure reward, with history the final judge of our deeds, let us go forth to lead the land we love, asking His blessing and His help, but knowing that here on earth God's work must truly be our own."

WHERE WERE YOU WHEN THE WORLD STOPPED TURNING?

In the Gulf War Desert Storm, some Iraqi soldiers were captured by Coalition troops. They threw their hands up and started screaming in broken English, "Don't shoot us, don't shoot us!" A young twenty-year- old Army Infantryman replied, "What do you mean, don't shoot? We're Americans. We don't shoot our prisoners!"

Alan Jackson asks in his country song, "Where were you when the world stopped turning that September day?" My answer and story of the ride home a few days later was an eye-opening adventure revealing the real heartbeat and honest soul of America.

The day US President W. Bush held the national church service broadcast on TV and radio live from the National Cathedral in Washington, DC, to pay tribute to the 3,000-plus who died, I was in an eighteen-wheeler. Truckers got on the radio and decided during the announced moment of silence they would all pull to the side of the road wherever they were driving and stop in reverence. As we pulled back onto the highway, every trucker communicated over the radio to turn on their headlights and kept them on all day in honor of the dead.

As we continued on our way that same day, I'll never forget the good-old-boy trucker who got on the radio immediately after the service, and in his red-neck, intense but humble, sincere way, spoke out with poor grammar in a slow southern drawl, "I don't mean to offend none of y'all, but somebody's got to pray." I'm here to tell you, he prayed! He talked to the Man above in a way I had never heard, crying, "These sombitches need to be hogtied. Please, Lord, help us find these bastards and with your help we can kill these mangy mutts." Although he was cursing up a storm as he had been across the water in Jersey and had seen the World Trade Center Towers crumble down, I suspect his prayer was heard and answered.

POSITIVE ARRIVAL

The journey on I-70 took us west past the Arch in St. Louis, Missouri, where we saw a long-haired, throwback hippie wearing a tie-dye psychedelic T-shirt. He was holding a giant flag pole and was standing on an overpass proudly waving an American flag with his hippie girlfriend flashing the peace sign. And to contrast this with an experience just days before when I stopped on the road to let someone in and he flashed me a peace sign, while the driver behind me laid on his loud horn and flashed me a half-a-peace sign!

As we drove through the wheat fields of Kansas we saw a farmer driving his tractor working out in his field with a huge American flag draped over the back. We passed cars and other trucks with flags on their antennas, saw flags in store windows, and flags in the front yards of homes for no holiday reason other than we all suddenly realized our freedom was in jeopardy and that freedom is not free.

Everyone was noticeably nicer in gas stations, in restaurants, and on the highway. Strangers were waving at strangers. When I arrived in Salt Lake two and a half days after we left Allentown, I was more proud to be an American than I had ever imagined possible and committed to being more than a mere resident living in America. I was committed to being a citizen with America living in me. Since this experience, whenever I hear the "Star Spangled Banner" played or sung live at a game or gala, I get tears in my eyes and chill bumps over my body. America is just a landmass country. Her people, we citizens, are the ones who can either be an inspirational example or a horrible warning. May our leaders and ourselves always chose the right.

Fundamental 14

STRESS TO SUCCESS

I walk firmer and more secure uphill than down. A smooth sea never made a skillful mariner. All things are difficult before they are easy. Difficulties show what men are.

Have you ever noticed how some people, even "best" players, who practice and practice and become brilliant at the basics still choke come game time? Do you know anyone who has stretched from the inside out and has truly become more of who they already are, and yet when it comes time to perform and show what they can do, they fold under pressure taking a school test, corporate exam, or playing in a big game? Have you wondered why stress even affects some "right" people and seemingly not others?

In the academic world of clinical psychology and the research world of stress and anxiety disorders, we know four things:

1. Some people succeed in pressure-packed, stressful situations while others fail.

2. The same individuals who sometimes succeed fail at other times.

3. The definitive factors in succeeding when competing against others are differences in talent, experience, and ability to control stress.

4. When the external circumstance is the same for everybody competing and involved, it is clear that talent and

experience don't explain differences in performance.

The one and only thing we can control is stress.

As already mentioned, pressure is not something that is naturally there. It's created when you question your own ability. When you know what you can do, there is no question. Pressure is not stress.

The internal impact that stress has on an individual physically and mentally varies greatly among individuals and plays a huge role in performance level. In competition, stress is the only thing that can be controlled to a high degree.

Hard-line research produced the well-known Yerkes-Dobson Law, diagramed below:

Relationship Between Stress and Job Performance

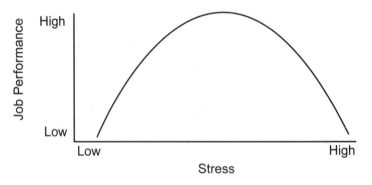

From this diagram it is obvious, and extremely important to remember, that stress and performance are always linked. Stress facilitates performance. Too little stress causes weak performance. However, too much stress is debilitating. Peak performance comes as we seek balance. We must seek the optimal level of stress or arousal.

Surely we are all different in how much stress we can handle. The goal is to push ourselves to our highest degree of intensity so that we may perform at our ultimate capacity and reach our full potential, but how will we know when we have gone past the level of optimal stress?

It's about the simple law of diminishing returns. We can water a tomato plant only so much. At full capacity, when the plant needs no more water, additional watering only diminishes its growth. Once the water level reaches an optimal level, the effectiveness of water quickly diminishes and eventually kills the tomato plant.

So can stress kill you? Certainly. Warning signs of pushing ourselves past the optimal level of stress include heartburn, appetite changes, increase in drug and alcohol use, irritable bowel, increase in urination, itchy skin, nervous habits such as nail biting, insomnia, fatigue, depression, headaches, chest pain, breathlessness, decreased libido, increased blood pressure, increased blood sugar, increased cholesterol, and a decrease in antibodies. Performance-related signs are even more obvious and noticeable, including decreased concentration, resulting in an increase in errors.

So are there some key ways to maximize performance? Absolutely. Here are three ways:

1. Physical management of stress
2. Behavioral management of stress
3. Cognitive management of stress

PHYSICAL MANAGEMENT—DIET

Increase your intake of B-complex and C vitamins, which stress depletes. Vitamin deficiency makes the nervous system more reactive, decreasing your ability to control stress. Eat more cereals, leafy green vegetables, liver, fish, citrus fruits, tomatoes, cabbage, and potatoes. Drink more water. Drink less alcohol, which tends to disturb sleep and dehydrate your body. During pressure-packed, stressful situations, it is also critical to decrease caffeine and nicotine intake. As stimulants, they tend to produce an enhanced stress-like response.

EXERCISE

Increase regularity of exercise during high stress. Exercise burns unhealthy physical byproducts of stress, including increased blood sugar. Exercise improves sleep, provided you exercise three or more hours before attempting to sleep.

REST

It is essential to everybody's physical, mental, and emotional health to take breaks during the day. Get away from your desk; don't eat lunch there. We need a minimum of two ten-minute breaks per day. Relaxation is productive. We need a minimum of thirty minutes per day, especially at the end of the day. Weekends are meant to recharge us from our stressful week. We should decrease activity and increase rest and relaxation. Vacations tend to be stressors. The United States lags greatly in time off offered and taken. We should sleep an average of seven hours per night. We can't make up for lost sleep. In fact, we may need more sleep when we're stressed.

BEHAVIORAL MANAGEMENT

We must make an active effort to solve or manage our problems. This is different from worrying. Strategies include gathering information, planning, making decisions, and acquiring resources.

Championship football coach Lou Holtz said the one common denominator he found in every losing football program was that most of the players whined and complained about everything but never took action to remedy the situation. Now that we have explained the importance of behavior and the difference between saying and doing, what are the results of behavioral management?

There are always three positive outcomes to every positive, calculated behavior modification: focused attention, a sense of mastery and control, and action. Positive emotion acts as a buffer between the individual and the stressor. It helps to replenish resources. It promotes creativity, flexibility in thinking, problem solving, and the processing of important information.

COGNITIVE MANAGEMENT—POSITIVE REAPPRAISAL

We must reframe stressors as challenges. This simple alteration in thinking signals the possibility of mastery or gain and establishes a focus on the value of effort. The positive outcome of this reappraisal is the resolution that stressful encounters can be and should be favorable or successful. The result is a new pride, new skill or resource, and new personal growth. Obviously I have regurgitated some heavy-duty clinical jargon in the last few paragraphs to validate the science of what we are discussing. However, as usual, the practical application of the theory is found in a story.

A rich man had a most precious opal ring. People said the unique opal stone was a "charm," and whoever wore it was made so sweet in character that all loved him. Before the man died, he gave the ring to his only son, and it was passed down from father to son, generation after generation. Finally it came into the possession of a father who had three sons. Perplexed, he had a jeweler make two more identical opal rings to perfectly match the original.

On his deathbed, the father called in each son one at a time, whispered a special blessing, and gave him his sacred ring. When he died, each son pulled out his ring, thinking theirs was the "charmed" one. In anger and jealous disbelief that there were three rings, each cried out that they in fact had the true magic stone. To settle things, they were taken to a wise judge, who after careful examination, admitted he could not tell which ring stone was the "charmed" one. However, he said, they could prove it themselves.

The judge said, "If it is true that the ring gives sweetness to the character of the man who wears it, then we shall all know him by his good life. So go your ways, and be kind, be truthful, be brave, be just in your dealings; and he who does these things will be filled with the magic of love and service and the obvious owner of the best and charmed opal."

GOOD KING ARTHUR

When good King Arthur ruled the land of Britain, he had a throng of knights. Although all were loyal to the king, they were a jealous bunch and constantly stressed, bickered and fought, oftentimes resulting in death as they argued over who should sit nearest to the head of the table. To eliminate all the stress, King Arthur had a solution. He built a round table to seat them, so that all might be equal. They stopped fighting each other, and found identity, strength, and honor in being the famous and feared "Knights of the Round Table." By eliminating the unnecessary stress in their lives, they were able to fight with an energy and unheard of strength for the king.

THE NUMBER ONE CAUSE OF STRESS

In his book, *Seven Habits of Highly Effective People,* Stephen Covey defines the difference between Dependence (You do it for me), Independence (I do it for me), and Interdependence (We do it for us—we will accept help, ideas, and assistance from one another because interdependence is a two-way street). Dependence, obviously, is the most widely misunderstood interactive social element and consequently has emerged as the number one cause of stress in our lives.

DEPENDENCE

Dependence is widely expected in our society because we have been raised to believe the Four Myths of Feeling: 1) I can make you feel good; 2) I can make you feel bad; 3) You can make me feel good; 4) You can make me feel bad. The bottom line is that no one can make us feel any way other than the way we choose to feel. We are in charge and have the power to feel unless we decide to relinquish our power to feel to someone else. Dependence comes when we don't take control of our feelings and attitudes.

In addition to these four myths, dependence is also based on the Four Myths of Action:

The Gene Theory. It's hereditary. You can't do anything about your genetic makeup. You're stuck with a negative personality, bad temper, slow motor skills, and lack of imagination simply because your father's personality is negative. Or, you got it from your mother!

The Cosmic Theory. The universe and the world are the way they are, and you can't do anything about it.

The Astrology Theory. You were born under a specific sign of the Zodiac, on a certain date with specific planets and moons lined up. Therefore this is your assigned personality, and the stars will control your destiny.

The Meant-to-Be Theory. This is the most controversial cause of dependence. To most, "meant-to-be" means you have no free will, choice, or agency to affect the outcome of your life and destiny. You are merely a pawn in God's chess game.

Meant-to-be states: Princess Diana's death in an automobile accident with a drunken chauffeur driver was meant to be. John F. Kennedy Jr. and his wife and sister-in-law crashed and died in a plane crash because his lack of flight training was meant to be. Two teenagers attempt suicide; one dies, one lives because it was meant to be. Why build hospitals or call for an ambulance? It doesn't matter what we do. The situation, circumstances, and outcome are pre-destined and meant to be.

Every person has a predetermined life with a specific expiration date. Therefore God orchestrates two hundred people from thirty-five different states and five foreign countries to all board TWA Flight 800 from New York to Paris on the same day. The plane blows up and kills everybody because it was meant to be.

PREDESTINATION CONTRADICTS UNIVERSAL LAW

I don't know about you, but believing in "meant-to-be" seems to serve only as a scapegoat to eliminate the stress of responsibility to deal with and recover from disappointment, discouragement, and failure. The stronger our belief in "meant-to-be," the weaker our resolve is to endure to the end. "Meant-to-be" minimizes work ethic, dreaming, goal-setting, and reasons to get up when we fall.

I believe that mortal experience is about agency—free will and choice to succeed or fail. Pilots can err, planes can malfunction, air traffic controllers can screw up, the female reproductive system can be traumatized and produce birth defects, but no one said earth life was a guaranteed anything. Remember the hybrid universal law I call *pro-destiny*? Synchronicity only suggests things happen for a reason, but pro-destiny says it is our responsibility to decide what that reason is. Doesn't *synchronicity* suddenly seem even more shallow than before?

DEPENDENCE DESTROYS THE HUMAN SPIRIT

To move from *best* to *right*, perfect the art of execution, and become more of who we already are, we must remember that the Four Myths of Feeling and Action are just that: ludicrous myths of shallow thinkers who are dependent because they aren't willing to ask the deeper questions. Remember our previous discussion. To get a better answer you must ask a better question! To be strong enough to *act on truth*, you must stop blindly going along with the traditions and "old wives tales" of your relatives, leaning on and relying on the conviction and knowledge of another and start doing everything possible to study, ponder, and gain your own testimony of truth!

A major cause of stress is trying to please others and do things for someone else's reasons rather than our own. I'm sure I just slaughtered a few sacred cows of some influential predestination religionists. But we agreed in chapter one that "some things are true whether we believe them or not; everybody is entitled to their own opinion but nobody is entitled to the wrong facts; and we shouldn't believe everything that we think."

I now fully comprehend dependence. It is nonproductive. It appears that dependence actually destroys our human spirit to dream, believe, conceive, achieve, feel exhilaration when we succeed, and feel devastation when we fail. How sad. The real value of something is determined by what we are willing to give up to get it. "Meant-to-be" eliminates choice. Dependence waters down the importance of us setting priorities. This is why Covey says we should move from this "You take care of me/I blame you for my results" dependency into independence, and finally into a total trusting state of interdependence. Independence often brings on too much stress in that we feel alone while stretching. Only through interdependence can we regulate our levels of stress to where we can perform most effectively and efficiently as we share responsibilities and bear one another's burdens.

ARE YOU REALLY STRESSED?

Stressed compared to whom in what circumstances? Pressure is not real—it is based and founded in fear. Fear is False Evidence Appearing Real. Therefore, if you are prepared, you will not fear. Pressure is not stress. Stress is never a problem—only a challenge to be like Christopher Columbus and go beyond your current map to love deeper, laugh longer, think clearer, listen better, and walk on higher ground as you become more of who you already are. If you find yourself stressed, the fastest way to reduce stress is to serve others.

To find yourself, you must first lose yourself. You never know how good you can become until you are stretched, stressed, and tested. Exercise and a hot bath are supposed to help reduce stress, but sometimes we just need to be reminded of challenges and stresses others have faced in order to keep our own circumstances in proper perspective. Allow me to briefly take you off course to pay tribute to some American heroes who were stressed beyond our wildest imagination and yet performed anyway.

IWO JIMA MARINES

Rich Lambert, the director of the Family Support Center at Seymour Johnson Air Force Base in North Carolina, is an incredible and generous human being. He shared with me the following transcript of an impromptu explanation caught on video one night at the Iwo Jima Memorial at Arlington National Cemetery. After my emotional experience with Eddie Wright at

the monument just weeks before, this story deepened my understanding and meant even more.

James Bradley just happened to be in Washington, DC, to
speak at the memorial the following day. He was there this particular evening to say goodnight to his father, who has passed away.
He was just about to leave when he saw two school buses pull up.
Instinctively he felt like talking to the eighth-grade students, parent
chaperones, and teachers. When all had gathered around, he reverently began to speak. Here are his words that night recorded by
someone who had been hired to document the students' trip:

"My name is James Bradley, and I'm from Antigo, Wisconsin. My dad is on that statute, and I just wrote a book called
Flags of Our Fathers, which is number five on the *New York
Times* bestseller list. This memorial is the largest bronze statue
in the world and depicts one of the most famous photographs in
history—that of the six brave soldiers raising the American flag
at the top of a rock hill on the island of Iwo Jima, Japan, during World War II. My book is the story of the six boys you see
behind me. Six boys raised the flag."

FIRST BOY HERO

"The first guy putting the pole in the ground is Harlon Block.
Harlon was an all-state football player. He enlisted in the Marine
Corps with all the senior members of his football team. They
were off to play another type of game. A game called war.

"But it didn't turn out to be a game. Harlon, at the age of
twenty-one, died with his intestines in his hands. I don't say that
to gross you out; I say that because you need to know that most
of the boys in Iwo Jima were seventeen, eighteen, and nineteen
years old."

SECOND BOY HERO

"You see this next guy? That's Rene Gagnon from New
Hampshire. If you took Rene's helmet off at the moment this
photo was taken and looked in the webbing of that helmet, you

would find a photograph—a photograph of his girlfriend. Rene put that in there for protection because he was scared. He was eighteen years old. Boys won the battle of Iwo Jima—boys, not old men."

THIRD BRAVE HERO

"The third guy in this tableau was Sergeant Mike Strank. Mike is my hero. He was the hero of all these guys. They called him the 'old man' because he was so old. He was already twenty-four. When Mike would motivate his boys in training camp, he didn't say, 'Let's go kill some Japanese' or 'Let's die for our country.' He knew he was talking to young boys. Instead he would say, 'You do what I say, and I'll get you home to your mothers.'"

FOURTH EXTRAORDINARY HERO

"The last guy on this side of the statue is Ira Hayes, a Pima Indian from Arizona. Ira Hayes walked off Iwo Jima. He went into the White House with my dad. President Truman told him, 'You're a hero.' He told reporters, 'How can I feel like a hero when 250 of my buddies hit the island with me and only twenty-seven of us walked off alive?' So you take your class at school—250 of you spending a year together having fun, doing everything together. Then all 250 of you hit the beach, but only twenty-seven of your classmates walk off alive. That was Ira Hayes. He had images of horror in his mind. Ira Hayes died dead drunk, face down at the age of thirty-two—ten years after this picture was taken."

FIFTH BOY HERO

"The next guy, going around the statue, is Franklin Sousley, from Hilltop, Kentucky—a fun-lovin' hillbilly boy. His best friend, who is now seventy, told me, 'Yeah, you know, we took two cows up on the porch of the Hilltop General Store. Then we stung wire across the stairs so the cows couldn't get down. Then we fed them Epson salts. Those cows crapped all night.' Yes, he was a fun-lovin' hillbilly boy.

"Franklin died on Iwo Jima at the age of nineteen. When the telegram came to tell his mother that he was dead, it went to the Hilltop General Store. A barefoot boy ran that telegram up to his mother's farm. The neighbors could hear her scream all night and into the morning. The neighbors lived a quarter of a mile away.

"The next guy, as we continue to go around the statue, is my dad, John Bradley, from Antigo, Washington, where I was raised. My dad lived until 1994, but he would never give interviews. When Walter Cronkite's producers or the *New York Times* would call, we were trained as little kids to say, 'No, I'm sorry sir, my dad's not here. He is in Canada fishing. No, there is no phone there, sir. No, we don't know when he is coming back.'

"My dad never fished or even went to Canada. Usually, he was sitting there right at the table eating his Campbell's soup. But we had to tell the press that he was out fishing. He didn't want to talk to the press. You see, my dad didn't see himself as a hero. Everyone thinks these guys are heroes because they are in a photo and a monument. My dad knew better. He was a medic. John Bradley from Wisconsin was a caregiver. In Iwo Jima he probably held over two hundred boys as they died. And when boys died in Iwo Jima, they writhed and screamed in pain.

"When I was a little boy, my third-grade teacher told me that my dad was a hero. When I went home and told my dad that, he looked at me and said, 'I want you always to remember that the heroes of Iwo Jima are the guys who did not come back.'

"So that's the story about six nice young boys. Three died on Iwo Jima, and three came back as national heroes. Overall seven thousand boys died on Iwo Jima in the worst battle in the history of the Marine Corps. My voice is giving out, so I will end here. Thank you for your time."

Suddenly the monument wasn't just a big old piece of metal with a flag sticking out of the top. It came to life with the heartfelt words of a son who did indeed have a father who was a hero!

Do You Still Feel Stressed Out?

In conclusion, before any of us stress and flip out, feeling out-of-control or dependent, or start blaming others in an independent mindset, the old adage is applicable: You must first possess something before you can give it away. You must face enough stress in your own life to stretch and grow and improve. Others have and so can you, and only then can you help others in the interdependent state with their stress.

The power of the mind is immeasurable. Remember, if you think you are depressed, you are depressed. People can think things that create nervousness and false fear, which literally cause a chemical reaction in the body in which excess acids are secreted into the stomach, causing nausea and vomiting. Likewise, we can think ourselves well. When it comes to stress, I'm talking about controlling our thoughts and behaviors and choosing to positively communicate with ourselves and others who think and behave positively. For this reason, I close this discussion with three of my favorite quotes that have always helped me turn my stressful problems into challenges to grow.

The difference between a successful person and an unsuccessful person is that the successful person will do what the unsuccessful person will not do. The successful person does not want to do it either, but he does it anyway.

—Earl Nightingale

Ask not what your country can do for you; ask what you can do for your country.

—President John F. Kennedy

If one advances confidently in the direction of his dreams and endeavors to live the life which he has imagined, he will meet with a success unexpected in common hours.

—Henry David Thoreau

Fundamental 15

CONNECT THROUGH COMMUNICATION

To think justly, we must understand what others mean; to know the value of our thoughts, we must try their effect on other minds. To effectively communicate, we must connect beyond the ears, listen heart to heart, and perfect the art of persuasion.

—William Hazlitt

What is a friend? A single soul dwelling in two bodies.

—Aristotle

Two neighbor women had been feuding for months and finally decided to talk through their differences. They met in their front yards, hugged, and made up. After returning to their homes, one woman noticed her dog in the backyard shaking something in its mouth. Wouldn't you know it? It was her neighbor's rabbit. *Oh no,* she thought. *We finally patch up our friendship, and now my dog kills her rabbit.*

She brought the dead rabbit in to clean it up and used her blow-dryer to fluff up the fur. She then tiptoed over to her neighbor's backyard and secretly put the rabbit in its hutch. Thirty minutes later she heard a blood-curdling scream. She ran out and asked what was wrong. Her frazzled friend answered, "Oh my gosh. Our rabbit died two weeks ago, we buried it in the garden, and now it's back in its cage!"

Communication is obviously more than two people taking

turns talking. The word *commune* means "to connect; to honestly and deeply understand." *Communicate* means "a truthful exchange of information." When we don't honestly communicate, sometimes it is disastrous, oftentimes humorous, always superficial and remembered short-term. When we honestly connect at a deep, emotional heart-to-heart level, it is always effective and memorable. Why? True communication is not just heard, it is felt. People don't want us to merely understand, they want to feel understood. Yes, it's a fine line, but so is the difference between a professional presenter and a professional speaker, a singer and an artist, an average tune and a hit song using the same twelve notes, a good novel and a Pulitzer Prize. Let me illustrate.

When I was recently in Frankfurt, Germany, I saw a television commercial for the international technology company EDS. The commercial was only sixty seconds long, but it moved me enough that still I remember it.

The commercial began by showing three people in wheelchairs who were waiting in line to check into a hotel. The front desk clerk was also in a wheelchair, and the registration counter was built lower than normal to accommodate the eye level of other people in wheelchairs. At the back of the line was a tall, able-bodied man who, upon reaching the counter, had to bend way down to fill out the paperwork.

The next scene was of this same man in his hotel washroom stooping over to shave in the sink and mirror mounted only three feet off the floor. Next, he was squatting way down in the shower because the showerhead was mounted halfway down the wall to accommodate people in wheelchairs. In the next scene, this guy, obviously full sighted, walked into a public library. Every person there, workers and patrons, was blind. Every book and sign was in braille, and the lights were dimmed to near darkness to save electricity. Everyone except this lone full-sighted man was walking around using white canes to navigate, and every bookshelf in this public library was stocked only with books in braille.

In the next scene, this guy walked outside, where lighted street signs regulating pedestrian crosswalks were not flashing "walk/don't walk." Instead, they were mounted on shorter poles and were flashing a green wheelchair or a red wheelchair.

In the final scene of this commercial, a different able-bodied white man was leaving a bustling city street occupied by hundreds of black and brown people, all in wheelchairs, and walking into a busy airport full of only black and brown people in wheelchairs. He went to a rental car counter, built lower to the floor to accommodate a black woman sitting in her wheelchair. The woman was friendly and excited to rent the man a car that only had hand controls.

The words "Accessibility Matters—Everybody Counts" scrolled across the screen as the commercial faded to black. What did I learn? It's no fun to be the odd man out. It's no fun to be in the minority. I must be more empathetic and supportive of everyone who is different than I am. Was this powerful and effective communication? Did it connect two or more parties at a deeper emotional level? Was the information delivered and understood, and the desired results achieved? Certainly!

GENDER DIFFERENCES

Stephen R. Covey says, "Seek first to understand, then to be understood." That's all well and good until reality sets in and practical application is required. A husband and wife come home from work. The husband, trying to be sensitive, supportive, and an equal partner, says, "You seem a little tired. Let me help you do what you're doing." But what she hears him say is, "Honey, you look terrible, and you are incompetent."

A man walks into a room and after a while, his girlfriend smiles and asks, "Notice anything different?" This is a lose/lose situation. If he says "no," he's an insensitive jerk who doesn't pay attention. If he says "yes," he's still an insensitive jerk because he noticed but didn't mention it until she pried it out of him.

What she should have done (and what all of us should do) is not ask a question but rather tell him or show him the specific thing she wanted him to notice. Communication is not communication unless both parties understand 100 percent of what the conversation, including body language, conveys.

In effective, positive communication, we cannot and should not assume anything. Ambiguity, multisyllabic words, or technical/medical terminologies that mean nothing to the other party have no place in effective communication. "Say what you mean—mean what you say" is a simple yet powerful rule of thumb. Being present in the conversation, establishing eye contact, smiling, using the person's name, and genuinely caring about the person is the simple rule of law!

We must perfect the art of effective communication. It is more than verbal. Everyone needs HARR. We all want to be **H**eard, **A**cknowledged, **R**espected, and **R**emembered. And because the first five hundred words in the dictionary have seventeen thousand different meanings in attempting to satisfy these four communication needs, we must simplify our connection.

GENERATIONAL DIFFERENCES

Too many lousy communicators blame their inability to understand and be understood on "Cultural Diversity" and a "Generation Gap." This is absurd. Lousy communicators are simply *lazy* communicators. Anybody, any age, anywhere can connect with anybody else if they want to.

The Search Institute in Minneapolis, Minnesota, which specializes in "healthy communities," has uncovered a list of forty developmental assets that are absolutely necessary in creating healthy, high-esteemed young people. Number one on the list is positive communication. According to their research, every young person needs to receive support and engage in meaningful conversation with six nonparent adults every week.

These six adults, ranging from coaches, teachers, Boys and Girls Club instructors, Big Brother/Big Sister volunteers, Boy Scout Masters, Girl Scout leaders, Camp Fire Girl mentors, and obviously positive role models all convey influence and direction in eight areas of the young person's life: support, empowerment, boundaries and expectations, constructive use of time, commitment to learning, positive values, social competencies, and positive identity. The Search Institute reports that for young people under the age of eighteen, on average they possess a mere eighteen of the forty developmental assets.

THE COMMUNICATION GAP

We talk of a generation gap when in reality we have a communication gap. We adults think we are involved in our young people's lives, but we are not! A classic example took place at a middle school in Georgetown, Texas. The principal called a faculty meeting for the end of the day. Before the mandatory gathering got underway, the principal made a huge banner with the names of every seventh and eighth grade student on it and hung it on the wall of the gymnasium. He then passed out little gold stars and instructed the educators to put a star by the name of each student with whom they had any kind of relationship. Twenty-five percent of the students got most of the stars. Another 25 percent had two or three stars next to their names. Fifty percent of the entire student body had no stars at all! Young people represent 26 percent of our population, yet they represent 100 percent of our future!

How do we solve this horrible trend? We've already discussed the solution. In order to stretch ourselves to personal and professional peak performance, we need to learn to set high expectations. This can only be accomplished through HARR—heart-to-heart communication where both parties authentically feel Heard, Acknowledged, Respected, and Remembered.

The best example of this that I've seen was a short TV public service announcement sponsored by a church advocating better family communication. The mother was talking on the phone in the kitchen when her three-year-old son wandered out the door and down to a busy intersection. As he stood at the curb, his mother suddenly saw him and raced out to save him. Picking him up, she scolded, "How many times do I have to tell you, don't go by the curb!" Frightened and crying, he replied, "Mommy, what's a curb?"

When it comes to communication and getting desired results, people behave based on their interpretation and understanding.

When we listen to the evening news, we don't remember the facts and figures. We remember the interpretation of the facts and figures. We react based on how the news relates to our personal attitude and situation. If twelve people attend a lecture, you can get twelve different interpretations of the same lecture, all based on where each individual is coming from, the person's emotional state, and what the person feels is important at the time. Let me illustrate.

PAY ATTENTION

Jason came from a good family with two loving parents, two brothers, and a sister. They were all successful academically and socially. They lived in a posh neighborhood. Jason had everything a boy could desire. But he was always into some kind of mischief. He wasn't a bad kid who caused trouble, but he always wound up in the thick of bad things.

In first grade, Jason was labeled "special education." School officials tried to keep him out of regular classes. In middle school he was a troublemaker. In high school, although never officially tested, Jason was tagged with having attention deficit disorder. More often than not, his teachers kicked him out of class. His first report card had one C and all Ds.

One Sunday the family was enjoying brunch at the country club when a teacher stopped and said, "Jason is doing so well these days. We're pleased and delighted."

"You must be mixing us up with another family," said the father. "Our Jason is worthless. He is always in trouble, and we just can't figure out why. We are so embarrassed."

As the teacher walked away, the mother remarked, "You know, honey, come to think of it, Jason hasn't been in trouble for a month. He's even been going to school early and staying late. I wonder what's up?"

The second nine-week grading period ended. As usual, Jason's mom and dad expected low grades and unsatisfactory marks in behavior. Instead, he achieved four A's and three Bs and honors in citizenship. His parents were baffled.

"Whom did you sit by to get these grades?" Jason's dad asked.

"I did it all by myself," Jason answered.

Perplexed and still not satisfied, the parents took Jason to school to meet with the principal. He assured them that Jason was doing well.

"We have a new guidance counselor, and she seems to have touched your son in a special way," he said. "His self-esteem is much better, and he's doing great this term. I think you should meet her."

When the trio approached, the woman had her head down. It took her a moment to notice she had visitors. When she did, she leaped to her feet and gestured with her hands.

"What's this?" asked Jason's father indignantly. "Sign language? Why, she can't even hear."

"That's why she's so great," said Jason, jumping between them. "She has taught me how to sign a little bit, but actually she reads lips and understands. She does more than hear, Dad. She listens!"

BUSINESS COMMUNICATION

I was recently part of a department meeting in which a member of each division in a company was asked to give a one-minute description of the organization. All five departments were represented: research and development, operations and engineering, finance, marketing and sales, and labor.

The communication exercise I put them through was a simple request to ponder, write down, and share how they would react to a company invitation to go to Boulder, Colorado. In concert with their unique individual interpretations, the research and development person spent his time asking and answering, "Why?" The person from operations and engineering pulled out a map, prepared to rent a bus and arrange for accommodations, and asked, "How?" The finance person figured the distance, costs of travel and hotel, and asked, "How much?" The marketing and sales person shared the vision and dream of the company, wanted to leave immediately, and asked, "What direction is it?" The person from the labor department questioned whether the company was recklessly squandering money that could be put into the profit-sharing plan, questioned whether the trip was necessary, wondered why they were singled out to go, and wanted assurance that they would be paid for all expenses, including overtime the entire time they were gone.

When communicating to set high expectations, both mutual understanding and empathy are important. We must be sensitive to the other person's needs, responsive to the person's hot buttons, and committed to what, not who, is right! We must be aware of what are called "unintended consequences." We must see the whole picture from both sides of the issue and contemplate all of the possible outcomes.

FAMILY DIALOGUE

To further illustrate, let us review a typical family situation in which a father is discussing curfew with his sixteen-year-old daughter. Because communication is based on individual interpretation and understanding, the role-playing exercise involves putting a piece of paper between them. One side of the paper is painted white; the other side is painted blue. The paper represents the curfew, and each can see only one side and color of the paper.

When the daughter is asked what color she sees, she answers, "White." When the father is asked the same question, he answers, "Blue." Who is right? They both are, depending on what side of the paper they are on and their individual interpretations:

Dad: "I'm right. Your curfew is midnight. What positive thing can a teenager do after midnight that will enhance her life and help her make her dreams come true? I wasn't born yesterday. The sex monster comes out at midnight. Don't argue with me. Break curfew and you'll be grounded!"

Daughter: "Grounded? You are so old-fashioned. Don't you remember what it was like to be a teenager back in the eighteenth century? C'mon. Why do you want me home by midnight? My friends get to stay out till Saturday!"

Dad: "That's it! Don't talk back to me! I brought you into this world. I can take you out of it. You are now grounded for life. You will never date until you are twenty-one years old. Go to your room!"

Daughter: "No! I'm leaving. I'm divorcing you as my parent. I'm running away from home to live with my friends in a loving commune where we can do whatever we want. Good-bye."

Dad: "Good-bye yourself, and don't ever come back until you respect me and do what I say!"

FAILURE TO COMMUNICATE

This exchange reminds me of the old movie *Cool Hand Luke*, starring Paul Newman. Newman plays a man who refuses to conform to the laws that confine him. He is thrown into prison and ends up on a chain gang. Once there, Luke constantly mouths off to the prison guard until the guard finally hits Luke and reprimands him with the classic line: "What we've got here is a failure to communicate."

Whenever challenges arise between people, we seldom ever have a generation gap or a management-labor gap or even a lack-of-respect gap. We usually have a communication gap. In the family scenario, the family was being ripped apart all because of a failure to communicate about a simple curfew. How could this breakup have been avoided? How can we more effectively communicate in business, school, and sports, and jointly decide upon high expectations?

The answer is in the box and is the same dominant guiding principle that has been at the core of this entire book. Put less emphasis on who's right and more emphasis on what's right. We must be willing to come around to one another's side of the issue (the piece of paper) and see the issue (the color) from the other's perspective. This enables us to team up on the same side of the paper so we can see the issue in the same color. It allows us to remove the issue from between us and put it in front of both of us so that together we can find the best solution looking in the same direction. How do we make that happen?

FIXING THE COMMUNICATION

The person in authority (parent, employer, teacher, coach) must make the first move and come around to the other person's side of the paper. The authority figure needs to empathetically walk a mile in the other person's shoes. Then, to complete this process of understanding (reaching mutual respect and support), the authority figure needs to open the lines of communication further by inviting the subordinate (child, employee, student, athlete) to now come over to his side.

As we team up in both instances to discuss issues, an environment is created for allowing dialogue, respecting individuality, accepting consequences of behavior, feeling responsible for individual destiny, and being empowered to do the right thing simply because it's the right thing to do. No argument, only explanation. We must authentically *listen to feel*—listening only to fully understand, not to respond.

Referring back to the family dialogue, the dad comes around to his daughter's side of the paper. He can't believe it, but he must admit that the paper is white just like she said it was. The dad then puts his arms around his daughter, opens his heart and mind, and honestly says, "Daughter, help me see and understand what it is like to be a teenager today from your side of the paper. Why do you have to stay out so late?"

"Oh, Dad, if I come home at midnight before everybody else, everybody will think I'm mama's little lambee pie."

"But what productive things can teenagers do after midnight that will keep you out of trouble and help make your dreams come true?"

"Oh, Dad, don't be silly! It's all because our parties start late."

"Why can't you start your parties earlier?"

"They don't even start the music until late."

"Why can't they start the music earlier?"

"Are you joking me? The guys are so ugly we have to wait until it gets dark before we want to dance with any of them!"

Suddenly Dad lightens up. "No kidding? That was the same problem we had when I was your age!"

Bursting into laughter, the daughter adds, "Really, Dad? You mean you were actually a teenager once? Are you starting to understand me? Maybe you're not such an old-fashioned, bull-headed, guy after all. Who would have thought you knew so much? And to think you learned it all in just one night!"

COMMUNICATION RECIPROCITY

This curfew model now continues with the "psychological reciprocity, what-goes-around-comes-around" part. The child is now feeling respect and support. She puts her arms around her dad, opens her heart and mind, and accepts his invitation to gently come over to her dad's side of the paper, where she now must admit its color is blue. The admission comes when she asks and honestly answers, "If I had me for a child, would I be nervous? Would I want to know whom I was with, where I was going, and what reasonable time I would be returning home? Would I have a right and desire to know if there would be alcohol, drugs, gangs, or drunk driving involved in the evening?"

Let's face it. Our parents, employers, teachers, and coaches know a lot more than we think they know. When I was growing up, my dad told my sister she could not go out with any guy who drove a van. When this guy drove up in a van a short while later, my dad looked out the window, saw the van, and yelled, "Debbie, you can't go out with him. He's driving a van!"

"Why?" my mother responded, "You used to drive a van."

My dad blurted, "That's what I mean. You cannot go out with a guy who drives a van!"

CONNECTIVE COMMUNICATION FACILITATES CHANGE

To deal with change, all we need to do is seek out those whom we respect to lead us and guide us. Why face change alone when you can have someone you can deeply, honestly, and effectively communicate with; when you can have twice the eyesight, double the heart and mind, and double the insight, wisdom, experience, knowledge, and confidence? We need each other to succeed, and if we will communicate passionately, honestly, empathetically, and positively, we can share our internal and external expectations and become everything we desire to be. When it comes to communication, there is absolutely no reason to be negative. Discipline is not to punish; it is to teach. Constructive criticism is never constructive. Inspiring someone to improve by catching them doing something right and rewarding the behavior and attitude you desire increases performance. Attacking and putting someone down does not make us better, smarter, or more astute.

FREEDOM OF THE PRESS—FREEDOM OF SPEECH

A chapter on communication could not be complete without discussing freedom of speech and freedom of the press. As we have pointed out in previous chapters, there are always two sides to every story, and oftentimes the complete story is not the speech we hear or the account we read. For example, the press and public opinion expressed during and since the Vietnam War was and still is negative and anti-biased. History, however, has proven this lopsided story not to be the case. Because we stood up to communist expansionism in Vietnam in the 1960s and 1970s, we changed the world as it is in 2007. In retrospect, we now know that the Vietnam War is the reason both the Cold War stopped and the Berlin Wall came down in 1989–90. Because we stood up to Russian and Chinese aggression in Southeast Asia and sent the message we would never back down, Russia suffered financially through the arms race and eventually lost its resolve.

Can you imagine all the healing that would occur in America if the press decided to now make it known on TV, radio, and print media that Vietnam vets need to be proud of what they did and when and where they served? They made history and changed the world forever and we as a country are proud of them and thank them for their service. In this more positive light, Vietnam was more of a long, bloody battle than a war, and not one of our men and women who served and died there, served or died in vain. Remember, he who asks the questions is in control of the conversation, and he who controls the hearts and minds of the people controls the people. Communication caused us to weaken our will and pull out of Vietnam as perceived losers, and it is also the way we can strengthen our will to never let it happen again. The power of communication, both negative and positive, is the most significant power of all.

SHOULD COMMUNICATION BE RESTRICTED?

Under what circumstances, if any, should freedom of speech or the press be limited? I'll answer with a few questions. When a college professor tapes a newspaper cartoon to his office door showing two US soldiers talking, one asking the other, "How many Iraqi children have you killed today?" and the college is a state-run institution with many war veterans attending, is this cartoon free speech or hate speech? Is this artwork creating ill feelings, violating the rights of veterans, and inciting animosity from the student body? Is this any different than someone stating that we should resume the Holocaust and kill more Jews?

This is an outrage! In a nutshell, freedom of speech and freedom of the press should be limited when they insight a riot, cause harm to someone else, or infringe on the protected rights or another individual to pursue life, liberty, and happiness. We must always remember that with freedom comes responsibility! For example, people have the right to smoke but not to blow smoke into my space and fresh air. Likewise, it is my right not to smoke. But my not smoking does not affect smokers or infringe on their rights. However, smokers *do* infringe on my space and right to clean air. We are all smart enough to apply this principle to freedom of speech and freedom of the press, and therefore exercise good judgment when our right to express violates another's rights. Without responsibility, it is not our right at all.

MOST IMPORTANT COMMUNICATION

Communication at its best is verbal and nonverbal understanding. However, "right" communication goes beyond understanding into listening for the sounds of silence found in between the lines where we connect through love, service, respect, friendship, support, and the most important communication of all, forgiveness.

Do you know people who apologize for everything? Is apologizing inappropriate? Absolutely not! It is an expression of humility and strength. Those who can admit that they have made a mistake and have done something wrong that offends someone are the strongest among us. Not doing so is a sign of insecurity and weakness. Communicating forgiveness is important, but so is accepting the apology, letting go of the anger, forgetting any grudge, and responding graciously to the apology. No one can ever really know or comprehend the importance of forgiving until they have actually been forgiven.

ETHICAL FORGIVENESS

When I was in college, an emotional tale touched my life forever. A hardcore disciplinarian stood in front of our class with a crew-cut hairstyle and piercing eyes. He had been a marine drill sergeant in the Vietnam War, had his master's degree in psychology, and was welcoming us as the Professor of Business Ethics. Rumors had it that this macho man tolerated nothing. He explained as part of the course orientation that he always could tell if someone cheated. Sarcastically, he illustrated, "One time I called a young man on the carpet. I accused him of cheating. He promised, "No, I didn't." I countered, "Yes, you did." "No, I didn't." "Yes, you did." "How did you know?" he finally confessed. I answered him, "The young lady you were sitting next to wrote on her test paper, "Don't know the answer." You wrote, "Me neither!"

We all laughed at his story, but took it to mean that if anyone got caught cheating, he would "rip their lips off" and flunk them out of school.

The weeks passed uneventfully until the day of the mid-term. A guy on the third row was caught cheating. Everyone held their breath as he was asked to leave and turn his exam in early. Surely he would be kicked out of the university. To our surprise, the young man was back in class the next Monday. One indignant student finally raised his hand to interrupt the lecture. "Mr. Jacobsen, Professor sir. I think this is totally absurd. Here you are teaching a class on ethics. You catch a student red handed, cheating, and you don't suspend him. What kind of a lesson are you teaching us?"

The professor smiled and replied, "Great question, and I'll answer it with a story."

Years ago there was a certain little one-room schoolhouse in the mountains of California, which no teacher could handle. It was a school just for boys with an enrollment so rough that the teachers would resign after only a few short days. A young, inexperienced teacher applied, and the old director warned him about the out-of-control, disrespectful students. The teacher took the job anyway.

On the first day of school the new teacher greeted them, "Good morning, boys, I'm here because I care about you." They yelled, "Yeah, right. You don't even know us," and they laughed and made fun at the top of their voices. The teacher continued, "Now I want a good school, but I confess that I do not know how unless you help me. The things we help create we support. Suppose we have a few rules. You tell me and I'll write them on the chalkboard."

One fellow yelled, "No stealing." Another yelled, "On time." Finally, ten rules appeared.

"Now," said the teacher, "a law is not good unless there is a consequence attached. What shall we do with one who breaks them?"

Big Jake yelled out, "Beat him across the back ten times without his coat on."

"That is pretty severe, boys. Are you sure that you are ready to stand by it?" They all yelled, "Yeah, yeah, beat them to death," and the teacher said, "Alright, we will live by them. Class, come to order."

In two weeks, Big Jake, the toughest of the tough, found that his lunch had been stolen. Upon inquiry the thief was located—a little hungry fellow ten years old. "We have found the thief and he must be punished according to your rule—ten stripes across the back. Vincent, come up here," the teacher ordered.

The frail little boy, trembling, came up slowly with a big coat fastened up to his neck and pleaded, "Teacher, you can lick me as hard as you like, but please, don't take my coat off."

"Take the coat off," the teacher reminded. "You helped make the rules." As he began to unbutton, the little guy had no shirt on and revealed his bony little crippled body. *How can I whip this child?* the teacher thought. *But he must do what he says he will do if he is going to keep control and respect of the others.* "How come you are not wearing a shirt, Vincent?" the teacher asked. "My father died and my mother is very poor," he replied. I have only one shirt to my name, and she is washing it today, and I wore my brother's big coat to keep me warm."

The teacher, with rod in hand, hesitated, and then reluctantly asked Vincent to turn around. Just then Big Jake jumped to his feet and interrupted, "Teacher, if you don't object, I will take Vincent's whipping for him." Hiding his disbelief, the teacher thought quickly on his feet, "Very well, there is a certain law that one can become a substitute for another."

Off came Big Jake's coat, and after five hard strokes the rod broke. The teacher bowed his head in his hands and thought, *How can I finish this awful task?* Then he heard the class of macho men sniffling, sobbing. And what did he see? Little Vincent had reached up and caught Big Jake with both arms around his neck. "Jake, I'm sorry I stole your lunch, but it had been two days since I had anything to eat. I was extra hungrier than usual. It was just sitting there with no one around and I didn't think. Jake, I will love you until I die for taking my beating for me. I will never steal again. Yes, you are my hero!"

The college professor stopped talking. There wasn't a dry eye in the room. With tears streaming down his cheeks, he said to our class, "My name is Vincent Jacobsen. I was that frail, crippled, hungry lad. We all will make mistakes at some point in our lives, and sometimes all we need is just one break to get our lives back on track. This course is on ethics, and if you remember nothing else, remember that forgiveness is a powerful part of ethical behavior. God bless Big Jake wherever you are."

The professor then said, "There is another upper division class I teach called 'Situational Ethics' where we will discuss if Best is always Right—if Fair is always right—if sticking up for Right takes precedence over sticking up for friendship—if being the Right person is more important than selling out, compromising your values, and trying to be the Right person for this specific job. In other words, ethics is an ongoing question and answer session that should always be at the seed cause level of everything we think and do personally and professionally."

Several times in my life I have put my pride in my pocket and basically begged for forgiveness, willing to do whatever it took to patch up the wounds, heal, and carry on. And yet the friend or associate refused to accept the apology. I am still devastated because some friendships died as a consequence.

As leaders, managers, coaches, educators, and parents, we must teach that good character entails not only doing the right thing simply because it's the right thing to do up front, but because it's also doing the right thing in the aftermath of doing the wrong thing. Let us all communicate that life is too short to hold a grudge. And it's horrible if only a few forgive. Forgiveness is always a deep, two-way connection that says, "I forgive you. I love you and need you." It's forgiving and being forgiven. It's remembering that in life there are no mistakes, only lessons. Consequently, through empathetic, honest communication, first with ourselves and then with others, we can turn every lemon into lemonade.

THE GRAND CONCLUSION

There you have it: Forgotten Fundamentals that Are Still in the Box. I have discussed many things, and I have yanked your chain and challenged your belief. Some of you have been shaken and stirred with the concepts of citizen versus resident, have resisted my many military references, and have failed to realize that I too am antiwar. I tried only to put it in its proper moral perspective and use our brave men and women in uniform as examples of what happens when we live our lives on a higher level and believe in something larger than ourselves, such as freedom.

I may have offended some of you left-brain, cognitive intellectuals with elementary solutions to perceived complex issues by minimizing the importance of IQ and emphasizing EQ, sarcastically implying that a four-year college degree isn't going to make a person successful.

Yes, we may have gone head to head, but regardless of our differences, I hope you will continue to be a passionate, imaginative, creative songwriter type who makes everyone else around you say, "I like me best when I'm with you; I want to see you again." I hope you will follow the simplicity of the four cornerstone box to stretch you. And as you *stretch*, not because others expect it but because you demand it of yourself, I hope you will stress your way to success, remember communication is key, and proactively change from the inside out to create personal power.

Michelangelo always looked at the raw block of marble as a prison holding someone captive. All he did was chisel away the rough edges, polish it, and allow it to become more of what it already was. The marble was the *best* piece in all of Italy, but until Michelangelo transformed it into the masterpiece it had the potential to become, it was just stone.

Each of us is also raw stone, much more rare and precious than marble, yet not fully sculpted or polished. With some help, we too can transform ourselves from *best* to *right*. It requires only that we focus on purposes instead of just setting goals, seeking less fortune and fame with more emphasis on being whole and becoming complete. Remember, in Tiger Woods' world, we are either becoming better or becoming worse.

May we realize every day of our lives that there are natural laws at work in the universe, and in order to be totally happy, truly successful, and completely fulfilled, we must get in tune with these laws and stay in sync with their power. Things happen for a reason, but with your understanding of "Pro-Destiny," you are now prepared to constantly engage in the art of execution and always be both *best* and *right* so you can determine what that reason is.

In America, the Constitution's only guarantee is opportunity. This was the theme of one of the most powerful speeches in history. In 1963, Dr. Martin Luther King Jr. pled for free human beings in two ways: 1) In his famous speech, he said, "I have a dream that my four little children will one day live in a nation where they will not be judged by the color of their skin but by the content of their character." 2) Dr. King emphasized urgency. His plea and message was for equal rights, equal education, and equal opportunity. He emphasized that the time for action was now, that the only way he and his people could earn equal respect from their fellow Americans was to take advantage of the dream now!

"It would be fatal for the nation to overlook the urgency of the moment and to underestimate our determination," Dr. King said. "We have come to this hallowed spot to remind America of the fierce urgency of now. This is not the time to engage in the luxury of cooling off or to take the tranquilizing drug of gradualism. Now is the time to make real the promises of democracy. Now is the time to rise from the dark and desolate valley of segregation to the sunlit path of racial justice. Now is the time to open the doors of opportunity to all of God's children."

All of us from every race, religion, creed, and socioeconomic situation want and deserve an opportunity. And the time for acting is now, no matter where we are physically, mentally, spiritually, financially, and emotionally.

MORE THAN WE'VE BEEN

A Chinese philosopher wrote, "There are no tops, only higher places." When should we stop and rest on our laurels? When is our personal, professional, and societal development enough? Is there a time limit and date of completion for seeking excellence?

There is no end—only a beginning from where we are now to better our past best performance. Being bigger, faster, stronger, higher, smarter, more efficient, and more effective are more than mere wants. Sports are more than just muscle and bone going through motion. We see heart, focus, intestinal fortitude, inner commitment, discipline—the very embodiment of the human spirit. Likewise, America was made great by citizens who thought something more and did something more about it.

WHAT WILL YOU DO?

Following are stories of some American legends, and although we may disagree with some of their values and personal politics, we cannot disagree with their purpose. Who they are and what they were able to accomplish truly altered the course of history. What could you, should you, will you do to make a difference, not just a living? When is it your turn to do something more?

ANGELINA GRIMKE FOR SLAVES

What if Angelina Grimke had kept quiet and stayed a contented pacifist? Angelina and Sarah Grimke, sisters from South

Carolina who moved to Philadelphia and became Quakers, were active in the abolitionist movement and were frequent lecturers on the evils of slavery and on the right of women to speak and work publicly for social issues.

In 1836, Angelina (1805–1879) caused a furor with her widely distributed pamphlet, "An Appeal to the Christian Women of the South," which was burned in South Carolina. The building in which she addressed an antislavery convention in May 1838 was surrounded by an angry mob and pelted with stones during her speech and then destroyed by fire a few days later.

BELLA ABZUG FOR WOMEN

What if Bella Abzug had kept quiet and stayed a contented pacifist? The women's movement in the United States was reborn in the 1960s, emerging from the general climate of protests and civil rights agitation. In 1963, Betty Friedan's book *The Feminine Mystique* was published, and the National Organization for Women was formed in 1966. Bella Abzug served as a lawyer for the American Civil Liberties Union, was active in the peace movement, and was an organizer of the National Women's Political Caucus. A US representative from New York in the 1970s, she spoke to a Nashville, Tennessee, conference on "a political strategy for women who have been shut out of power." Although she had some radical ideas and was one of the first to strongly promote aborting babies (which I disagree with), on February 12, 1972, Bella made history and infused a national movement with vision, and she inspired women everywhere to get involved in bettering themselves and their circumstances.

RALPH NADER FOR CONSUMERS

What if Ralph Nader had kept quiet and was content to allow manufacturers to cut corners regarding safety and quality, bamboozle him, and screw over the American consumer? Nader's name has been virtually synonymous with consumer protection since the 1960s. Nader is a lawyer and the university lecturer who wrote a groundbreaking indictment of the auto industry in 1965 titled *Unsafe at Any Speed*. If Nader were a pacifist, he never would have founded numerous public interest organizations, including the Center for Responsive Law, the Center for Auto Safety, Public Citizens, the Disability Rights Center, and The Project for Corporate Responsibility. Nader is only one man, but he is making a difference as a man with passion, imagination, and creativity.

BARBARA JORDAN FOR HONORABLE PUBLIC SERVICE

What if Barbara Jordan had kept quiet and stayed a contented pacifist? As a lawyer and Texas legislator, Barbara Jordan rose to prominence within the Democratic Party with her election as US representative from Texas in 1974 and by virtue of her eloquence as a public speaker. On July 26, 1974, she spoke in favor of the impeachment of President Richard Nixon, whose administration had labored under the cloud of the Watergate scandal since June 1972. She reasoned that "the president has engaged in a series of public statements and actions designed to thwart the lawful investigation by government prosecutors and has made public announcements and assertions which the evidence will show he knew to be false." Clearly Barbara Jordan was responsible for kick-starting the impeachment of Nixon.

Barbara Jordan's action in 1974 had a major influence and impact on the investigation and impeachment of President Bill Clinton. Clinton was impeached and disbarred from practicing law in Arkansas and New York not for his infidelity but for his lying in court and his "public statements designed to thwart the lawful investigation by government prosecutors." I find it interesting and appalling that the media and vocal public minority made Monica Lewinski, special appointed prosecutor Ken Starr, and the Republican-dominated Congress the bad guys.

Whoever would understand in his heart the meaning of America will find it in the life and words of Abraham Lincoln, in

Honest Abe going against the grain because of what was right—striving not to be popular for the moment but to be respected for generations to come. It was in the shadows of the dignified columns of the Lincoln Memorial that we heard and saw another American who was willing to stretch in the right direction and stand up for what is right.

MARTIN LUTHER KING JR. FOR CIVIL RIGHTS

What if Dr. Martin Luther King Jr. had kept quiet and stayed a contented pacifist? I often wonder how the battle for racial equality that still is being fought today would be different and further ahead if Dr. King were alive today. Reverend King came to national attention in 1956 as the leader of the Montgomery, Alabama, bus boycott. As president of the Southern Christian Leadership Conference since its inception in 1957, he initiated a path of nonviolent demonstrations against racial segregation. Dr. King stirred the hearts of more than two hundred thousand civil rights demonstrators assembled on the Washington, DC, mall, when he uttered the evocative phrase that would echo for decades—"I have a dream!"

LINCOLN FOR ONE UNIFIED AMERICA

There would been no dream speech or organized civil rights movement if President Lincoln had sat idly by, kept quiet, stayed contented to let slavery continue, and allowed the United States to divide and separate into a broken nation. The battles of Gettysburg and Vicksburg were turning points for the Union cause in the Civil War. Following great loss of life on both sides, General George Meade halted the Confederate invasion of Pennsylvania at Gettysburg in July 1863. On November 19, 1863, President Lincoln delivered his immortal address at a dedication ceremony for a cemetery at Gettysburg for those who fell in battle. Lincoln's solemn words define what our country is fundamentally about and our responsibility to the rest of the free world to make sure our experiment in self-government works and endures for all others to follow and depend on.

JOHN F. KENNEDY FOR FREEDOM

What if President John F. Kennedy had kept quiet and stayed a contented pacifist and had caved in to the intimidation of the Soviet Union? What if he said, "Oh, no, I don't want to ruffle anyone's feathers, especially the Russians. Let's just have peace at any price and just get along"? Is this what you would have said and done? Is this what has made America great? We must always ask, "Is it peace at any price or freedom at any price?" Remember, prisoners have peace, but no freedom.

Amid the heightened tensions of the Cold War during the early 1960s, the Kennedy administration faced several serious situations involving the Soviet Union during the Cuban Missile Crisis and the Berlin crisis. Kennedy's speech to the nation on July 25, 1961, addressed a potentially serious confrontation in which Soviet Premier Nikita Khrushchev threatened to sign a treaty with East Germany that would unilaterally have ended the West's occupation of its half of Berlin—a city divided between the Western Allies and the Communists since World War II. Because John F. Kennedy stood up to the threat and requested an additional $3.2 billion from Congress for our armed forces and asked for an additional 29,000 Navy sailors, 63,000 Air Force airmen, an increase in our army to a force of one million soldiers, and a call to active readiness of our National Guard and reservists, the Soviets backed down, and West Berlin remained noncommunist.

I don't understand why it is difficult for some people to understand that you fight fire with fire. I have avoided many fights in my life with smaller and bigger individuals because I am six feet, five inches tall, 240 pounds, and in relatively good shape. In high school I was the state amateur Golden Gloves Boxing Champion and have always been able to send a message without throwing a punch. Government and armies interact with respect or disregard for one another in the same way.

ROOSEVELT FOR THE ENVIRONMENT

What if President Theodore Roosevelt had not looked ahead as a pioneer conservationist and had not started the national movement in 1903 to save our forests? His actions inspired and influenced other presidents and politicians to create our National Parks system and to protect federal lands.

FIRST PRESIDENT BUSH FOR WORLD STABILITY

What if the United Nations Security Council and the first President George Bush had kept quiet, sat idly by, and allowed Saddam Hussein and his army to invade Kuwait? Freedom is not political. Human rights are not Republican or Democrat; they're American. Our soldiers do not pledge their lives, sacred honor, and loyalty to a president or political party. They pledge allegiance to the US Constitution and to freedom. Freedom isn't found only in America. Freedom is universal.

We could have helped the Jews at the beginning of World War II, but we didn't, and look what happened. Hitler was trying to expel the Jews, but America turned them away. Had we reached out, millions who died in the gas chambers of the Holocaust could have been saved. History shows that had America been proactive instead of reactive, we could have stopped the fascist Nazis before they gained more momentum, more weapons, more countries, and took more innocent lives. We could have stopped the Japanese when they invaded China in 1928, and we could have reduced the huge cost in human life in the Pacific as they cut off heads and tortured US soldiers beyond imagination during World War II.

GOOD ALWAYS TRIUMPHS OVER EVIL

What if President George W. Bush had kept quiet after terrorists attacked on September 11, 2001, and ended more than three thousand lives? President Franklin D. Roosevelt did not sit idly by and keep quiet when the Japanese attacked Pearl Harbor on December 7, 1941. The next morning he addressed Congress and the nation in a broadcast heard worldwide. More than two thousand American lives and a large number of ships and airplanes were lost in a single morning. President Roosevelt branded December 7 "as a date which will live in infamy." It has, and now September 11 joins it as another day that will live in infamy.

Our US policy then, because of the attack on Hawaii, is the same as our policy is now because of the attacks on New York and Washington, DC. We must always fight the bad guys in their land, on their turf, when we say, not when they say, and only on our terms—never again here in America!

I find it ironic that most religious groups and individuals who oppose war and want peace live in countries where someone had to fight and die so they can oppose war. Then they protest it. History proves and teaches that pacifists are always killed by aggressors until someone steps in and stands up to stop them! Again, I am antiwar. We all should be. But we all should oppose terrorists and chaos.

THE STRONG REMAIN STANDING

In his speech the morning after the Pearl Harbor attack, President Roosevelt gritted his teeth, stared fear in the eye, rallied American support, and boldly announced to the world, "No matter how long it may take us to overcome this premeditated invasion, the American people in their righteous might will win through to absolute victory. Hostilities exist. There is no blinking at the fact that our people, our territory, and our interests are in grave danger. With confidence in our armed forces, with the unbounded determination of our people, we will gain the inevitable triumph, so help us God."

So I ask, will you be one of these courageous individuals (even if you are not an American) who go against popular opinion and follow the convictions of your heart? Will you be part of the solution or part of the problem? To appropriately close this final chapter, I offer you the summary of the thirty truths contained in this book and its companion book, *Best or Right—Why Great Is Not Good Enough.*

Guaranteed these truths will constantly remind you that what we need to succeed is already inside of us, we need only focus on why, how, and when we should stretch and then do that which is necessary to succeed. Although these truths are simple, through this process we become intellectually and emotionally equipped to take ourselves and our organizations from great to *best*, eventually transforming into right—not because it is expected by others but because it is demanded of ourselves. My promise is that if you will abide by these thirty time-tested truths, you will move life's emphasis from *who* is right to *what* is right, and become strong enough to take yourself, your business, and your team to the ultimate level and coach them to consistently win. How? Why? The answers are still in the box!

DAN CLARK'S THIRTY TRUTHS

1. Some things are true whether you believe them or not.
2. Everybody is entitled to their own opinion, but nobody is entitled to the wrong facts.
3. You should not believe everything that you think.
4. No one can ever exceed his potential. We just misjudge it.
5. If you have to tell them that you are, then you aren't.
6. Self is not discovered, self is created.
7. Focus on purposes instead of just setting goals—not on having fame, but on being whole.
8. The value of something is determined by what you are willing to give up to get it.
9. There is no "I" in team, but it's not all about team— teams lose. There are two "I's" in winning.
10. Winning comes not from who is best, but from what is right.
11. No matter what your past has been, you have a spotless future.

12. When your attitude is right, your abilities will always catch up.
13. Where much is given, much is expected. What goes around, comes around.
14. Wealth flows through you, not to you—not through a scarcity mentality, but through an abundance mentality.
15. It's what you do when the coach is not around that makes you a champion.
16. What you've been in the past does not make you who you are today. What you hope to become in the future makes you who you are today.
17. You must stretch before you strengthen, and all strengthening occurs in the area past the point of discomfort.
18. There's a difference between being depressed and being disappointed and discouraged. Failure is an event. Always separate the person from the performance.
19. It's not what happens to you, but what you do with what happens to you that determines failure or success.
20. When you put a hard-to-catch horse in the same field with an easy-to-catch horse, you usually end up with two hard-to-catch horses. When you put a healthy child in the same room with a sick child, you usually end up with two sick children. To be great you must associate with the great ones.
21. Crisis does not make or break you. It just reveals the true character within.
22. Be true to you—you'll make a lousy somebody else.
23. When you identify yourself in terms of what you do instead of who you are, you become a human doing instead of a human being.
24. It's easier to act your way into positive thinking than to think your way into positive action.

25. It's better to shoot for the stars and miss than to aim for a pile of manure and hit.
26. Pressure is not something that is naturally there. It's created when you question your own ability. When you know what you can do, there is never any question.
27. Pain is a signal to grow, not to suffer. Once you learn the lesson the pain is teaching you, the pain goes away.
28. You can't quit—it's a league rule.
29. The old will die, the young may. But not everyone truly lives. Yes, death is a comma, not an exclamation point, but in this life don't die before you're dead!
30. The answers are in the box at www.danclarkspeak.com

THE END
(Which Is Really The Beginning)